AMNESIOPOLIS

Amnesiopolis

Modernity, Space, and Memory in East Germany

ELI RUBIN

OXFORD UNIVERSITY PRESS

OXFORD
UNIVERSITY PRESS

Great Clarendon Street, Oxford, OX2 6DP,
United Kingdom

Oxford University Press is a department of the University of Oxford. It furthers the University's objective of excellence in research, scholarship, and education by publishing worldwide. Oxford is a registered trade mark of Oxford University Press in the UK and in certain other countries

First Edition published in 2016

Published in the United States of America by Oxford University Press
198 Madison Avenue, New York, NY 10016, United States of America

British Library Cataloguing in Publication Data
Data available

Library of Congress Control Number: 2015944460

ISBN 978–0–19–873226–6

To Isaac, Oliver, Eloise, Lucien, Ezra, and Ari

Acknowledgments

I would like to thank the many people and organizations that have contributed to the research and writing of this volume. First and foremost, I would like to thank the residents of Marzahn, who unreservedly and with the greatest warmth let me in to their homes, showed me around their *Stadtviertel*, and shared with me their life stories, their souvenirs, their family photographs, their garden plots, and everything that makes up a history. Many of them are mentioned in this volume, though some have requested their names be changed. I remain in the debt of all those Marzahners who helped me, whether mentioned directly in this volume or not.

I would also like to thank the archives and the archivists who patiently assisted me in my work, including especially Dorothee Ifland of the Bezirksmuseum Marzahn-Hellersdorf, who helped me not only while I was in Marzahn but also long after I left. I must also thank Brigitte Freudenberg and Ute Lipske at the BStU (Stasi) archive. Their help was invaluable in being able to research the fifth chapter.

The overwhelming majority of this work was completed with the support of the Alexander von Humboldt Foundation's Postdoctoral Fellowship, which I held from 2007–09. Mercedes Barbon and Maria-Bernadette Carstens-Behrens were my main contacts during my fellowship, and both were extremely helpful. It was an honor to be a Humboldt Fellow, and to be associated with such an amazing organization.

Other parts of this work were completed with the financial support of the Burnham-Macmillan Fund of the History Department at Western Michigan University. Beyond the research, the Burnham-Macmillan Fund has supported my travel to many conferences and workshops where I have had the chance to discuss this work with colleagues. I remain extremely grateful to the Burnham-Macmillan Fund, the Burnham-Macmillan Committee, and the Chair of the History Department, Jose Brandao, for their support.

While in Berlin as a Humboldt Fellow, I was also a Visiting Fellow at the Zentrum für Zeithistorische Forschung in Potsdam. There, I benefitted from the lively exchange of ideas, and from the support and guidance of colleagues including Martin Sabrow, Konrad Jarausch, Albrecht Wiesener, and Stefan-Ludwig Hoffmann. In addition to the ZZF, I also owe thanks to the Berlin Program for Advanced German and European Studies, through the Freie Universität Berlin, and in particular Konrad Jarausch and Karin Goihl, for allowing me to make my first major presentation of this research as a guest in the Berlin Program's seminar. In 2012 and 2013, I was a Visiting Fellow of the Centre for Metropolitan Studies at the Technische Universität Berlin, with the support of Dorothee Brantz. There, I was able to present my work in more advanced form to the Graduiertenkolleg, and benefitted once again from the exchange of ideas.

There are others along the way in Germany who helped me. These include Günter Peters, who shared several afternoons with me recounting his role in the planning and construction of Marzahn. It also includes many who were not part of the history of Marzahn, but who are just as passionate about it as I am, including Lidia Tirri and Ylva Quiesser, Christian Domnitz, and Tobias Nagel, who is mentioned at the end of this volume. My thanks as well to the Zeitzeugenbörse, who helped me find several of my oral history interviewees.

I must of course thank everyone at Oxford University Press in the United Kingdom who worked on this project with me, beginning with Christopher Wheeler and Robert Faber, the editors who took this project on and supported it, and including also Cathryn Steele, Gayathri Manoharan, Henry Mackeith, and the anonymous readers who contributed so much to helping to shape this volume into its present form. My thanks also go to Charles Cavaliere of Oxford University Press in New York for encouragement and support.

My colleagues in the History Department at Western Michigan University have been an invaluable source of support and encouragement. Marion Gray provided crucial support and feedback along several stages of the writing of this, but as Department Chair, was also incredibly supportive of my research leave. Lynne Heasley helped to introduce me to the fascinating world of spatial thought and critical geography, a journey undertaken with me by Sally Hadden. Many others provided encouragement and feedback at some point along the way. Of course, my students have also read drafts of this project and offered illuminating words of advice.

Other colleagues outside of WMU deserve thanks here, including Lewis Siegelbaum who also gave me an early venue to present my work in conjunction with the Freie Universität Berlin and the German Historical Institute, Moscow, and who has been a good colleague, friend and supporter going back to the beginning of this project. I have benefitted greatly from my conversations with many amazing colleagues, including Sandrine Kott, Alf Lüdtke, Paul Betts, Andreas Ludwig, Justinian Jampol, Anne Berg, Jan Palmowski, Veronica Aplenc, Malgosia Mazurek, Barry Jackisch, Kristin Poling, Jonathan Bach, Kerstin Barndt, Johannes von Moltke, Marc Silberman, April Eisman, Ben Robinson, and many others.

I must devote special words of thanks to Clara Oberle. Clara helped me complete the last leg of research for this project. In addition to being a great friend and colleague, she is also a godsend. And I cannot give enough thanks to Konrad Jarausch, without whose support early on this project would never have come to fruition. The same is true of Geoff Eley, who has supported this project, and supported me as a mentor and a guide in many ways. Geoff and Konrad are a part of this book.

Finally, there are no words that can really describe how grateful I am to my partner, and colleague, Ari Sammartino. Of course, she has been part of this project since the beginning, and her feedback, advice, patience, and sacrifice have been invaluable and humbling. But more than that, her ideas, and her work, have had a profound influence on me and on my work, and she has been an inspiration in every conceivable way. I can never really repay her.

Contents

List of Figures

List of Abbreviations

AWG	*Arbeiterwohnungsbaugenossenschaft* ("worker's housing construction society:" the main form of access to and financing for apartments in East Germany)
CIAM	*Congrès Internationaux d'Architecture Moderne* (International Congress of Modern Architects, the main international organization for modernist planners and architects from the 1920s to the 1960s)
CMEA	Council for Mutual Economic Assistance (the Eastern Bloc economic union)
DBA	*Deutsches Bauakademie* (Central East German architectural association)
DVP	*Deutsche Volkspolizei* (regular East German police force)
FDGB	*Freie Deutsche Gewerkschaftsbund* (state-controlled workers' union)
FDJ	*Freie Deutsche Jugend* (Free German Youth, the SED's main youth organization)
HG	*Hausgemeinschaft* (building communal association)
HGL	*Hausgemeinschaftsleitung* (building committee)
IM	*Informale Mitarbeiter* ("informal cooperators," citizen collaborators with the Stasi)
ISA	*Institut für Städtebau und Architektur* (East German Institute for Urban Planning and Architecture)
KPD	*Kommunistische Partei Deutschlands* (German Communist Party, forerunner to the SED)
KWV	*Kommunale Wohnungsverwaltung* (Communal Apartment building leadership)
NBI	*Neue Berliner Illustrierte* (*New Berlin Illustrated*, popular weekly newsmagazine in East Berlin)
OPK	*Operativer Personenkontrolle* (Stasi investigation of particularly sensitive nature)
OV	*Operative Vorgang* (Stasi surveillance and investigation operation)
P1	First model of prefabricated apartment blocks in East Germany
P2	Second model of prefabricated apartment blocks in East Germany
PDS	Party of Democratic Socialism, the rump party left by the disintegration of the ruling SED
QP 71	Model of prefabricated apartment block ("QP" stands for "*Querwandbau in Plattenbauweise*" and "71" for the date of its first design, 1971)
SED	*Sozialistische Einheitspartei* (Socialist Unity Party, the ruling Communist Party of East Germany)
VMI	*Volkswirtschaftliche Masseninitiative* ("people's economic mass initiative:" volunteer community service for East German citizens)
WBK	*Wohnungsbaukombinat* (apartment construction combine, a conglomerate of state-run companies involved in all aspects of housing)
WBS 70	*Wohnungsbauserie 70* ("apartment building series 70:" the dominant model of prefabricated block housing developed in East Germany in 1970

Introduction

> Has state socialism produced a space of its own? The question is not unimportant. A revolution that does not produce a new space has not realized its full potential; indeed it has failed in that it has not changed life itself, but has merely changed ideological superstructures, institutions or political apparatuses. A social transformation, to be truly revolutionary in character, must manifest a creative capacity in its effects on daily life, on language and on space—though its impact need not occur at the same rate, or with equal force, in each of these areas.
>
> Henri Lefebvre, *The Production of Space*[1]

In November 1980, Barbara Diehl, her husband Ralf, and her eight-year-old son Dieter moved into a three-bedroom apartment in a newly constructed apartment block in Marzahn, just outside East Berlin. The new home was a radical departure from anything she had known in the past. Her childhood was spent in poverty, in a dilapidated house outside Leipzig. For the previous decade, Barbara and Ralf had lived in a tiny one-room apartment in a decaying nineteenth-century apartment building near the center of East Berlin. It received little light, there was no bathroom, and there was no warm water. After Dieter was born in 1975, the apartment became especially cramped, and life became much harder. Although they lived in the German Democratic Republic, supposedly a "workers' and peasants' state," they lived in much the same conditions that the working class had in the early days of industrialization, when Berlin was known as having the worst living conditions of any industrial city in the West.

When Barbara and her family moved to Marzahn, they entered what seemed like an entirely new world. There they encountered a vast construction site, teeming with tens of thousands of workers, fleets of trucks, excavators and bulldozers churning through a sea of mud and earth, and what seemed like a forest of construction cranes. Towering above the mud and the construction crews were row upon row of newly built and almost identical housing blocks, constructed out of prefabricated concrete panels. Entering theirs, a brand new WBS 70 five-story model on Allee der Kosmonauten 183, they took an elevator to their floor. When they entered their apartment they saw a newly finished, spacious flat, with a modern kitchen, a bathroom with a bath and shower, and a beautiful view. Sunlight streamed in from both sides. Most of all, Dieter had his own room. Neither outside nor inside the apartment bore any resemblance to the life that they had once lived;

[1] Lefebvre, *The Production of Space*, trans. Donald Nicholson-Smith (Padstow, UK: Blackwell, 1991), 54.

indeed, it bore no resemblance to the life that had been lived in Germany by the working class since there had been a working class.

Their experience was one of profound rupture, a rupture experienced in both psychological and spatial dimensions. They had not just moved to an apartment or a district that was new to them. Their WBS 70 flat, and Marzahn itself, were defined by newness. Marzahn was a settlement that had been built on a massive scale upon what had previously just been "green fields" on the edge of Berlin. It was more than just a place where apartments were built—it was an entirely new city, one built on a *tabula rasa*. It was an urban space that reflected the modernist concepts popularized by Le Corbusier, the CIAM, and like-minded planners and architects, and one that reflected the economic and ideological structures of the state that built it. In terms of its aesthetics and spatiality, it bore little to no resemblance to any other aspect of Berlin or Germany's past. It was truly a socialist, and modern, space.

And the Diehls were not alone. In fact, they shared this experience of rupture and beginning a new life in a radically new and socialist world with nearly a half million other East Germans who moved to Marzahn and the adjoining housing settlements of Hellersdorf, Ahrensfelde, Lichtenberg, and Hohenschönhausen in the 1970s and 1980s. Technically part of East Berlin, this massive new urban space became a city unto itself, and, taken as such, was the fourth-largest city in the GDR, behind only Berlin, Leipzig, and Dresden. Indeed, the Diehls' experience was shared by millions more throughout the GDR who moved to similar prefabricated housing settlements (*Plattenbausiedlungen*), many of which were built, like Marzahn, in the 1970s and the 1980s on the edges of cities, such as Leipzig–Grünau, Rostock North-west, or Dresden-Gorbitz. Each contained tens of thousands of residents and formed a self-contained world.

The construction of these new, mass-produced housing settlements was the direct result of the GDR's Housing Program (*Wohnungsbauprogramm*), inaugurated in 1973.[2] A central pillar of Erich Honecker's policy of "real existing socialism," the Housing Program aimed to provide every East German with a new or renovated apartment by the year 1990—aiming to build or renovate three million in all. By 1990 the GDR had managed to construct two million dwellings, most of them in mass-produced apartment blocks, and 1.25 million of these were in settlements on the edges of cities, known as *Plattenbausiedlungen*, *Großsiedlungen*, *Satellitenstädte*, *Neubausieldungen*, or other names.[3] By the time the Wall fell, close to 45 percent of East Germans lived in some kind of prefabricated housing, with 28 percent living

[2] *Wohnungsbauprogramm* translates literally as "apartment building program" but I have chosen the term "housing program" because such a phrase is much more commonly used in English, although, as I will show, the context is in certain important ways quite different to that in the West, and therefore the same kinds of cultural connotations associated with the phrase "housing program," in particular the pejorative sense of "housing projects," should not be associated with the East German context.

[3] Emily Pugh, *Architecture, Politics, and Identity in Divided Berlin* (Pittsburgh: University of Pittsburgh Press, 2014), 289.

in a self-contained "settlement" of 1,000 apartments or more; a much higher percentage than in the West.[4]

The move into to a mass-produced apartment, especially in a settlement on the outskirts of a city was a profound and life-altering event for most of those East Germans who experienced it; and it was an experience that became shared by almost half of all East Germans. Clearly, the Housing Program and the way it was experienced by East Germans—the effects it had on their everyday life—was a central event of East German history. Yet oddly enough, beyond handful of scholars, almost none of them historians, there has been little written on the Housing Program;[5] there has been virtually nothing at all written on the impact it had on everyday East Germans.

This lacuna is all the more odd considering the extent to which scholars of East Germany have endeavored to get at the culture and life experience of all East Germans, and to get away from top-down, political histories. Indeed, East German historiography has been framed over the last quarter-century by the search for a way to understand what Thomas Lindenberger, Alf Lüdtke, and others have called *Herrschaft*—domination—in ways more social and cultural than purely political.[6] How did the SED (Socialist Unity Party, the ruling communist party of East Germany) state maintain and build upon its power, beyond the bare and brute show of state violence, as with the Wall and the Stasi? How did it manufacture stability, consent, or even legitimacy?[7] Was it a "welfare dictatorship" as Konrad Jarausch argued,[8] or a "participatory dictatorship" as in Mary Fulbrook's

[4] See chapter 1, p. 29, and Appendices 1 and 2. I am basing this estimate on the total number of newly built apartments between 1961, when the P2 (the first widely used prefabricated building model) went into production, and 1990. According to Hansjörg Buck, this amounts to roughly 2.5 million apartments built in a *Neubau* or *Plattenbau* style. See Buck, *Mit hohem Anspruch gescheitert. Die Wohnungspolitik der DDR* (Münster: Lit, 2004), 409. (There were some built in this fashion before 1961, but only in a few small pockets, such as Hoyerswerda.) In 1989 the population of the GDR was roughly 16.4 million. In most cases where figures are given for specific prefabricated settlements, the ratio of residents to dwellings falls, usually between 2.8 and 3 residents per dwelling, so I am multiplying the number of dwellings by 2.9. This gives an estimate of 7.25 million, or 44% of the population in 1989.

[5] See Jay Rowell, *Le totalitarisme au concret: Les politiques du logement en RDA* (Paris: Economica, 2006); Christine Hannemann, *Die Platte: Industrialisierte Wohnungsbau in der DDR* (Berlin: Schiler, 2005); Emily Pugh, *Architecture, Politics and Identity in Divided Berlin* (Pittsburgh: University of Pittsburgh Press, 2014); Florian Urban, *Neohistorical Berlin: Architecture and Urban Design in the German Democratic Republic 1970–1990* (Burlington, Vermont: Ashgate, 2009) and *Tower and Slab: Histories of Global Mass Housing* (New York: Routledge, 2012). See also Buck, *Mit hohem Anspruch*.

[6] Lindenberger, ed., *Herrschaft und Eigen-Sinn in der Diktatur: Studien zur Gesellschaftsgeschichte der DDR* (Cologne: Böhlau, 1999), especially his introduction to the volume "Diktatur der Grenzen;" and more recently "SED-Herrschaft als soziale Praxis, Herrschaft und 'Eigen-Sinn:' Problemstellung und Begriffe" in Giseke, ed., *Staatssicherheit und Gesellschaft* (23–47); Lüdtke, ed., *Herrschaft als Soziale Praxis: historische und sozial-anthropologische Studien* (Göttingen: Vandenhoeck & Ruprecht, 1991).

[7] Specifically on the question of creating stability, see Andrew Port, *Conflict and Stability in the German Democratic Republic* (New York: Cambridge University Press, 2007).

[8] Jarausch, ed., *Dictatorship as Experience: Towards a Socio-Cultural History of the GDR*, trans. Eve Duffy (New York: Berghahn, 1999).

formulation?[9] Were there "limits to the dictatorship" as Ralph Jessen and Richard Bessel argued,[10] or was it a "dictatorship *of* limits," per Lindenberger? Indeed, did the domestic take its "revenge" on the Party and state, as Donna Harsch argued?[11] Or was the GDR thoroughly permeated—*durchherrschte*—(in Jürgen Kocka and Alf Lüdtke's formulation)[12] by the state, even if it was a "normal" (in Mary Fulbrook's controversial shorthand) culture and society?[13] Or, further, was the GDR truly characterized by a strange combination of private refuges on one hand, but thorough interpenetration of the state and its forces on the other, as Paul Betts describes?[14]

Thomas Lindenberger argued in 2007 that understanding *Herrschaft* in the GDR means understanding it, as Lüdtke described sixteen years earlier, as a "social practice." In particular, Lindenberger rightly reads Lüdtke's notion through Foucauldian ideas of "diffusion" and "fields of power."[15] Doing so, Lindenberger claims, does not mean ignoring the institutions of power and repression in the GDR, but rather realizing that the social dimensions of *Herrschaft* are also an "institution."[16] And to truly understand the interactions of power between East Germans and the SED regime, he writes, "we must reconstruct the bottommost layer" of this dictatorship, including the many sites at which the regime's power directly interacted with ordinary East Germans on a daily basis—including, among others, the living quarters (*Wohngebiet*).[17]

In search of this "bottommost" layer, also often referred to as "everyday life," cultural historians have produced a flood of work recently, on topics including gender, material culture, tourism, nature, education, fashion, consumption, television, film, and even the subculture of East German hip hop.[18] These have largely

[9] Among other places, Fulbrook, *The People's State: East German Society from Hitler to Honecker* (New Haven: Yale University Press, 2005).

[10] Bessel and Jessen, eds., *Die Grenzen der Diktatur: Staat und Gesellschaft in der DDR* (Göttingen: Vandenhoeck & Ruprecht, 1996).

[11] Harsch, *Revenge of the Domestic: Women, the Family, and Communism in the German Democratic Republic.* (Princeton: Princeton University Press, 2006).

[12] Kocka, Hartmut Kaelble and Hartmut Zwahr, eds., *Sozialgeschichte der DDR* (Stuttgart: Klett-Cotta, 1994).

[13] Fulbrook, ed., *Power and Society in the GDR, 1961–1979: The "Normalisation of Rule"?* (New York: Berghahn, 2009), in particular her "The Concept of 'Normalisation' and the GDR in Comparative Perspective," 1–30. On the controversy see Eli Rubin, *Synthetic Socialism: Plastics and Dictatorship in the German Democratic Republic* (Chapel Hill, NC: University of North Carolina Press, 2008), esp. the introduction; and Lindenberger, "Normality, Utopia, Memory, and Beyond: Reassembling East German Society," *German Historical Institute London Bulletin* 33, 1, (2011), 67–91, as well as Fulbrook's rejoinder in the subsequent issue.

[14] Betts, *Within Walls: Private Life in the German Democratic Republic* (New York: Oxford University Press, 2010). This issue will be explored further in chapter 5.

[15] Lindenberger, "SED-Herrschaft," 30.

[16] Lindenberger, "SED-Herrschaft," 30.

[17] Lindenberger, "SED-Herrschaft," 31.

[18] The titles are too numerous to list here, but a sampling would include: Andreas Ludwig, ed., *Fortschritt, Norm und Eigensinn: Erkundungen im Alltag der DDR* (Berlin: Ch. Links, 1999) and with Katja Böhme, eds., *Alles aus Plaste. Versprechen und Gebrauch in der DDR* (Cologne: Böhlau, 2012); Wierling, *Geboren im Jahr Eins: der Jahrgang 1949 in der DDR: Versuch einer Kollektivbiographie* (Berlin: Ch. Links, 2002); Sandrine Kott, *Communism Day-to-Day: State Enterprises in East German Society*, trans. Lisa Godin-Roger (Ann Arbor, MI: University of Michigan Press, 2014) and Kott and Emmanuel Droit, eds., *Die ostdeutsche Gesellschaft: Eine transnationale Perspektive* (Berlin: Ch. Links,

confirmed that, on one hand, East German society and culture differed substantially from the Cold War stereotypes of a drab and deprived existence—it was its own kind of modernity, an "alternative" or "socialist" modernity, as Pence and Betts have written.[19] Yet, on the other hand, most of this cultural history continues to circle back around to the fact that, as Lindenberger has argued, everything in East Germany, from toys to coffee, from sexuality to nature, was in some way altered and shaped by the ruling ideology of socialism.[20] Using Norbert Elias' notion of the "civilizing process" as a comparison, Sandrine Kott argues that East Germans "internalized" socialism, through everyday acts, through everyday and popular culture, in ways so quotidian that it was barely perceptible, or not perceptible at all.[21]

But if the question of "domination" or "permeation" is to be answered in a place that was, at least partially, imperceptible, this presents a real challenge for historians. It is in this framework that studying a socialist *space* becomes important, because for at least three decades critical geographers, among them Henri Lefebvre, Ed Soja, and David Harvey, have been demonstrating that *space*, as a category unto itself, is one of the most powerful modes for inquiring into and understanding structures of power, domination, and the transmission of ideology in precisely the kinds of mechanisms that are so important because they are so diffuse and quotidian.[22]

2006); Josie McClellan, *Love in the Time of Communism: Intimacy and Sexuality in the GDR* (New York: Cambridge University Press, 2011); Heather Gumbert, *Envisioning Socialism: Television and the Cold War in the German Democratic Republic* (Ann Arbor, MI: University of Michigan Press, 2014); Scott Moranda, *The People's Own Landscape: Nature, Tourism and Dictatorship in East Germany* (Ann Arbor, MI: The University of Michigan Press, 2013); Monika Sigmund, *Genuss als Politikum. Kaffeekonsum in beiden deutschen Staaten* (Berlin: De Gruyter Oldenbourg, 2014) Judd Stitziel, *Fashioning Socialism: Clothing, Politics and Consumer Culture in East Germany* (New York: Berg, 2005); Kathy Pence "A World in Miniature: The Leipzig Trade Fairs in the 1950s and East German Consumer Citizenship," in David Crew, ed., *Consuming Germany in the Cold War* (New York: Berg, 2003) 21–50; Ina Merkel's monograph *Utopie und Bedürfnis. Die Geschichte der Konsumkultur in der DDR* (Cologne: Böhlau, 1999), edited volume *Wunderwirtschaft: DDR-Konsumkultur in den 60er Jahren* (Cologne: Böhlau, 1996); Philip Heldmann's *Herrschaft, Wirtschaft, Anoraks: Konsumpolitik in der DDR der Sechzigerjahre* (Göttingen: Vandenhoeck & Ruprecht, 2004); Patrice Poutrus, *Die Erfindung des Goldbroilers: Über den Zusammenhang zwischen Herrschaftssicherung und Konsumentwicklung in der DDR* (Cologne: Böhlau, 2002), and related Alice Weinreb, "Matters of Taste: The Politics of Food and Hunger in Divided Germany" (PhD. dissertation, University of Michigan, 2009); Jan Palmowski, *Inventing a Socialist Nation: Heimat and the Politics of Everyday Life in the GDR, 1945–1990* (New York: Cambridge University Press, 2009); Leo Schmieding, *"Das ist unsere Party:' HipHop in der DDR* (Stuttgart: Franz Steiner, 2014).

[19] Pence and Betts, eds., *Socialist Modern: East German Everyday Culture and Politics* (Ann Arbor, MI: University of Michigan Press, 2008).

[20] Kott, *Communism Day-to-Day*, 8. [21] Kott, *Communism Day-to-Day*, 8.

[22] Lefebvre, *Production of Space*; Soja, *Postmodern Geographies: the Reassertion of Space in Critical Social Theory* (New York: Verso, 2011) and Soja, *Seeking Spatial Justice: The Reassertion of Space in Critical Social Theory* (Minneapolis: University of Minnesota Press, 2010); Harvey, *The Condition of Postmodernity: An Enquiry into the Origins of Cultural Change* (Cambridge, MA: Blackwell, 1990) and *Consciousness and the Urban Experience: Studies in the History and Theory of Capitalist Urbanization* (Baltimore, MD: The Johns Hopkins University Press, 1985). See also Edward Casey, *The Fate of Place: A Philosophical History* (Berkeley: University of California Press, 1997); Doreen Massey, *For Space* (Thousand Oaks, CA: SAGE, 2005) and *Space, Place and Gender* (Minneapolis: University of Minnesota Press, 1994); Yi-Fu Tuan, *Space and Place: The Perspective of Experience* (Minneapolis: The University of Minnesota Press, 1977); Tim Cresswell, *Place: A Short Introduction* (Padstow, UK: Blackwell, 2004) and *In Place/Out of Place: Geography, Ideology and Transgression* (Minneapolis: University of Minnesota Press, 1996). Mike Davis' *City of Quartz: Excavating the Future in Los Angeles*

As a result, scholars across multiple disciplines have engaged in the so-called "spatial turn" (a phrase coined in part by Soja himself), seeking to understand how spaces both absorb and also radiate or reproduce structures of inequality, exploitation, and hegemony, in a circle that Soja describes as the "socio-spatial dialectic."[23]

This volume, then, seeks to understand East Germany as a socialist state through the lens of space and everyday life—through the lens of the socio-spatial dialectic. In doing so, it argues that space is and must be understood not as a text or a symbolic category, but as a radically material one. As such, it transmits ideology not as something to be "read" but by shaping the phenomenological and experiential life-world of everyday subjects. One of the key modes of this transmission, I contend, is the link between memory and place. In particular, communist housing settlements like Marzahn are important to understanding East German socialism because they created—or sought to create—spaces that were radically new, radically modern, and radically socialist, with no traces of the pre-socialist past, and thus no opportunities for East Germans to retain whatever memories they may have had of an older German historical narrative.

Put more plainly: the move from mostly older, nineteenth-century slum apartments to the concrete utopia of Marzahn was experienced by ordinary East Germans as quite a radical change in all the ways that a physical space can shape a subject's inner consciousness and sense of self. Such a radically new space as Marzahn meant new sights, new smells, new everyday routines for people's bodies, new weather patterns, new flora and fauna, and a new sense of space within a vertical and horizontal matrix. Without the familiar street corners, parks, or neighborhoods, there were less opportunities for the old memories associated with those places to be sparked. People do not, of course, necessarily need to pass by or through a physical space to experience such a Proustian recall of lost time. However, the material rupture that East Germans experienced as they moved into prefabricated housing settlements significantly weakened those internal, emotional bonds with earlier phases of their lives, and the lives of their parents and grandparents; lives which were inescapably intertwined with economic catastrophe, fascism, and war. The architecture of the prefabricated housing settlements was brutally utilitarian and modern, intentionally eschewing any extra ornamentation or self-conscious imitation of past styles, which left even fewer "memory cues" which might in some way spark a memory of a personal or familial past, and therefore the larger past associated with those spaces and memories. In Germany, those larger pasts are often the dark ones of fascism, war, and economic disaster, and in the post-war era there was a continual attempt to forget that past, to induce a kind of historical amnesia. This amnesia took many forms, from policy to education to culture. It

(New York: Vintage, 1992) is foundational in the critical understanding of urban space and social injustice.

[23] See Soja, *Postmodern Geographies*, chapter 3. Relatively few historians have engaged seriously with the techniques and frameworks of analysis developed by critical geographers such as Soja. One important exception to this is Jennifer Evans' recent *Life Among the Ruins: Cityscape and Sexuality in Cold War Berlin* (New York: Palgrave Macmillan, 2011).

also took the form of material rupture, where the past was physically erased from space and therefore from time.

Marzahn was one of the key places of this erasure or forgetting. It was, as I have termed it, an *amnesiopolis*. Of course, as the reader will discover, and as theorists such as Jacques Derrida have argued, there is no real "erasure" or "forgetting"—the past always finds a way to express itself in "traces" through that which seeks to erase it or impose a singular meaning upon it. The more the socialist state sought to treat the open spaces of Marzahn as a *tabula rasa* upon which to build a perfect modern utopia from scratch, the more they found that they were part of a *longue dureé* history of that particular region, repeating in fact the same themes of colonizing the margins of the city that had already been tried in past eras, going back to Frederick the Great, to Albrecht the Bear (the tenth-century Askanian Margrave who "colonized" Berlin and its surrounding territory), and to nameless civilizations stretching back to the end of the last Ice Age.

The central argument of this volume is structured in five layers. First, it is argued that building large, prefabricated housing settlements like Marzahn in the GDR was the culmination of a long history, especially in Berlin, of trying to solve the problem of working-class slums by resettling the working class on the edges of the city. Second, we see that Marzahn and similar settlements were a manifestation of a utopian and modernist desire, especially intertwined with twentieth-century socialism, to literally create socialism by physically constructing it on a *tabula rasa,* where the material traces of capitalism could no longer intrude upon and thus thwart the socialist future. Third, it is discussed that, as much as the GDR tried to erase the past, it found itself, in Marzahn, unearthing (literally) the past as well as repeating a kind of eternal return in the attempt to colonize the lands outside Berlin. Fourth, we observe that the material and spatial reality of the built environment of Marzahn was a manifestation and a conduit for the power of the state and the Communist Party over its citizens in the most intimate ways, both because the ways in which the planning and construction took place flowed from the structure of the state bureaucracy and its planned economy, but also because it provided a nearly perfect opportunity for the state to observe and to control its citizens. Fifth, we discover that the lived experience of those who moved to Marzahn was one of profound rupture in their everyday sensory, spatial, and material world which altered their sense of self through time and was truly effective, if not in creating a "socialist personality," then in creating a new socialist community.

The focus here on prefabricated apartment blocks as socialist spaces of primary importance stands in contrast to most previous work on socialist and East German urban space and urban history, which focuses largely on more well-known and "prestige" architectural projects such as the "Palace of the Republic," Alexanderplatz, or the Nikolaiviertel.[24] Marzahn was also in its own way a "prestige" project, as we

[24] See for example Urban, *Neohistorical East Berlin*, and Pugh, *Architecture, Politics and Identity*, both of which focus more on "prestige" projects than housing, especially mass housing, as well as Brian Ladd "Socialist Planning and the Rediscovery of the Old City in the German Democratic Republic" *Journal of Urban History* 275 (2001), 584–603; there is bountiful literature on famous architects and architectural projects in East Germany, most of which leaves out mass-produced

will see, with guests of honor ranging from Mikhail Gorbachev to Sigmund Jähn. But it is more the quotidian nature of Marzahn, as a place where everyday life, and thus the narrative of lives and the structure of personal memories, was created, that is of interest here. Monuments and tourist destinations are interesting from the point of view of symbolism, but people do not sleep in monuments; they do not go to school in them, they do not drink beer with their neighbors and hold birthday parties for their children in them. If we want to really understand space as a category of diffusion and power, then we have to look beyond central, downtown East Berlin, where much of the space was "produced" or "staged" for international audiences, and to the spaces in which everyday life unfolded for a vast number of East Germans.[25] This shift in focus runs counter to the way most historians, including urban and architectural historians, have treated East German mass housing settlements like Marzahn, which is to largely ignore them, and when they are mentioned, to treat them negatively.[26] By looking at everyday life sources, this volume strives for a more nuanced account of these spaces. In some ways, it paints a more positive and upbeat picture of life in communist mass housing settlements, though it does point to the "dark side" of state control built into the structure of the settlements as well.

It is also the case that prefabricated mass housing has largely been seen as an international phenomenon—something all communist countries had in common, and therefore a failure of all communism. It is true that there are important links between the GDR's Housing Program and those throughout the Soviet Bloc, especially in the Soviet Union itself, and that the ideas that such settlements were based on were developed by modernist architects and planners from the West, such as Le Corbusier and the CIAM. It is also true that much of the technology used to

"*Plattenbau*": Joachim Palutzki, *Architektur der DDR* (Berlin: Reimer, 2000); the two volumes by Werner Durth, Jörn Düwel, and Niels Gutschow, *Architektur und Städtebau der DDR:* Band 1: *Ostkreuz: Personen, Pläne, Perspektiven*, and Band 2: *Aufbau: Städte, Themen, Dokumente* (Frankfurt: Campus, 1998); Andreas Butter, *Neues Leben, Neues Bauen. Die Moderne in der Architektur der SBZ/DDR 1945–1951* (Berlin: Schiler, 2006), and Butter and Ulrich Hartung, *Ostmoderne: Architektur in Berlin, 1945–1965* (Munich: Jovis/Deutsche Werkbund, 2005); Wolfgang Thöner and Peter Müller, eds., *Bauhaus Tradition und DDR Moderne: Der Architekt Richard Paulick* (Berlin: Deutscher Kunstverlag, 2006). Also see Thorsten Scheer, Josef Paul Kleihues, and Paul Kahlfeldt, eds., *City of Architecture of the City: Berlin 1900–2000* (Berlin: Nicolai, 2000), which does touch on the issue of housing more, but again only from a planning perspective, not from the perspective of everyday life. Also see Christoph Bernhardt and Thomas Wolfes, eds., *Schönheit und Typenprojektierung: Der DDR-Städtebau im internationalen Kontext* (Erkner: Institut für Regionalentwicklung und Strukturplanung, 2005), and Simone Hain, ed., *Warum zum Beispiel die Stalinallee? Beiträge zu einer Transformationsgeschichte des modernen Planens und Bauens* (Erkner: Institut für Regionalentwicklung und Strukturplanung, 1999).

[25] This line of argument is more fully developed in Rubin, "From the Grünen Wiesen to Urban Space: Berlin, Expansion, and the *longue durée*: Introduction," *Central European History* 47 (2014, special issue), 221–44.

[26] A good example of this is Buck, in *Hohen Anspruch gescheitert*, who frequently uses prejudicial and unscholarly language to describe the look and feel of the housing settlements, comparing their residents to animals kept in mass feedlots, (358) describing playgrounds as "loveless", and that one finds facilities in general "only in extreme exceptions to be satisfactory" (359). Similar language of such settlements as "bleak," or "failures," or "inauthentic" can be found in Urban, *Neohistorical East Berlin* (1), Pugh, *Architecture, Identity and Politics* (284), and Palmowski, *Inventing a Socialist Nation* (191).

mass-produce the WBS 70 apartments in Marzahn was derived from or even directly imported from other countries, both capitalist and socialist. Nonetheless, this is a history of a specific place that is anchored in space and time, which produces a tension between remembering and forgetting. It is tempting to make a sweeping dismissal of mass-produced housing settlements as "undifferentiated space," as Lefebvre once did, or equally to only see it as a "transnational" and therefore somehow ephemeral story. But the spate of recent work on mass-produced housing in other socialist countries, including Hungary, Poland, Czechoslovakia, Yugoslavia, and the USSR has largely shown that in each case the building of mass-produced housing was more a national, rather than a transnational, narrative.[27] In the end this is a narrative about East Germany, about the German working class, and about Berlin and Germany's north-eastern region, often known as the *märkische Oderland* or simply the "Mark."

The sources I have used throughout reflect this emphasis on the local, the personal, and the quotidian within the context of a state-socialist planned economy operating in the unique geopolitical environment of the Cold War, and within the broad historical scope of the working class in Germany and Berlin since the 1800s. I have tried to find a balance between sources that come from the "state" and those that come from the "bottom up" or "everyday life." I have looked in particular at the files and documents of the planning agencies, including especially the German Architectural Academy (*Deutsche Bauakademie*, DBA) and one of its offices, the Institute for City Building and Architecture (*Institut für Städtebau und Architektur*), as well as the reports of other state and Party agencies involved in the planning and construction of Marzahn. I have used records of the Stasi, especially where they were concerned with life within settlements such as Marzahn and Grünau. I have also used a number of sources, such as periodicals, which were not state-generated but which were censored, either by the state or by themselves.

For perspectives on everyday life, I have relied heavily on published memoirs, of which there is a surprisingly lively cottage industry on a local scale. In particular, I have found that many of those who moved to Marzahn in the 1970s and 1980s

[27] On the Soviet Union, see Mark Smith, *Property of Communists: The Urban Housing Program from Stalin to Khruschev* (DeKalb, Il: Northern Illinois University Press, 2010), and Steven Harris, *Communism on Tomorrow Street: Mass Housing and Everyday Life After Stalin* (Washington, DC: Woodrow Wilson Center Press/Baltimore: Johns Hopkins University Press, 2013); also on Nizhni Novgorod and Togliatti, Lewis Siegelbaum, *Cars for Comrades: The Life of the Soviet Automobile* (Ithaca, NY: Cornell University Press, 2008); on Czechoslovakia see Kimberly Elman Zarecor, *Manufacturing a Socialist Modernity: Housing in Czechoslovakia, 1945–1960* (Pittsburgh: University of Pittsburgh Press, 2011); on Poland see Katherine Lebow, *Unfinished Utopia: Nowa Huta, Stalinism and Polish Society, 1949–56* (Ithaca, NY: Cornell University Press, 2013); on Hungary (as well as East Germany) see Virág Molnár, *Building the State: Architecture, Politics and State Formation in Postwar Central Europe* (New York: Routledge, 2013); on Yugoslavia see Brigitte Le Normand, *Designing Tito's Capital: Urban Planning, Modernism and Socialism in Belgrade* (Pittsburgh: University of Pittsburgh Press, 2014). Beyond the communist world, in France, see Kenny Cupers, *The Social Project: Housing Postwar France* (Minneapolis: University of Minnesota Press, 2014); on Britain, Anthony Alexander, *Britain's New Towns: Garden Cities to Sustainable Communities* (New York: Routledge, 2009); in the developing world, Emily Calacci, "Ujamaa Urbanism: History, Urban Culture and the Politics of Authenticity in Socialist Dar-es-Salaam, 1967–1980" (PhD. Dissertation, Northwestern University, 2012).

have an overwhelming need to tell the story of their lives in Marzahn. The same is often true of those who planned and built Marzahn. This is not uncommon among many former East Germans, who feel that the wholesale condemnation of the GDR by those in the West also invalidated their own life experiences. In Marzahn this seems particularly acute because these are people who at one time believed that they were living in the future-made-present—Marzahn was the lived experience of the promise of socialism, and one day they woke up to find that their new world was suddenly, hopelessly, old, strange, and shameful; an eyesore, a ghetto. They were cut adrift. And as a result, they have been forced to re-narrate the story of their lives in this place in order to reclaim their lives—most of the published sources in this regard are almost completely under the radar, as indeed very little of the broader German public wants to read about their lives, or about places like Marzahn. But these memoirs, assembled either as community service projects, by local publishers, or by the local district museum, form a valuable window on a period of German and European history that will not pass away. For this same reason, I have also used a number of interviews, though I do not treat these specifically as an "oral history," but rather group the interviews together with the memoirs.

In the case of both the memoirs and the interviews, a narrative emerges of Marzahners' lives, but it is a choppy, broken narrative, defined by specific points of rupture—usually 1945, followed by whatever year they moved to Marzahn (which often became "year one" of the new era of their lives), and then 1989, in which everything changed all over again. Each rupture stranded some memories, and erased others, leading to a life narrative for most that is a microcosm of Germany's twentieth century, and as Konrad Jarausch and Michael Geyer so eloquently argue in their book *Shattered Past*:

> Because conditions changed so dramatically and repeatedly . . . all these personae of one person or family and, for that matter, of the nation can be found assembled in photo albums or artfully rendered in vignettes of the century. They are the source of quiet puzzlement and, not infrequently, of shocking discovery. . . . This widespread sense of *temps perdus* pervades the German experience of the twentieth century.[28]

Indeed, most of the memoirs I use are told in the form of short vignettes, and in many of my interviews I conducted, I was handed literal, physical scrapbooks and photo albums. As Jarausch and Geyer suggest, I found these to be moving and sometimes shocking in the bittersweet way they tried to recover the *temps perdus* of their erstwhile concrete utopia.

This volume is structured in five chapters. The first, "From the Slums to the *Tabula Rasa*: Germany's working Class, the Housing Program, and the Marzahn Plan," traces the history of Berlin's slums, and the many plans to clear them and

[28] Jarausch and Geyer, *Shattered Past: Reconstructing German Histories* (Princeton and Oxford: Princeton University Press, 2003), 335. They also quote Peter Fritzsche and Charles Stewart in remarking that the German twentieth century is "inescapably autobiographical," from Stewart and Fritzsche, eds., *Imagining the Twentieth Century: Exploring the Odd Passages and Side Doors of Our Collective Memory* (Urbana, IL: University of Illinois Press, 1997).

resettle the working class on the outskirts of Berlin, from the nineteenth century until the creation of the plan for Marzahn in the 1970s, focusing especially on the genesis of the East German Housing Program. The second, "Moonscape on the Mark: Socialism, Modernity, and the Construction of a New World," describes the massive effort that went into the creation of the largest construction project in European history, arguing that the building of Marzahn both represented a radical rupture from the past and thus a brand new, purely socialist space, yet also literally unearthed layers upon layers of the past which undermined the very idea of a socialist break with the past.

The third chapter, "Rainbows and Communism: Material, Sensory, and Mnemonic Ruptures," tells the story of everyday East Germans who moved to Marzahn, often from inner city slums in East Berlin and elsewhere, by paying attention to how their new spatial surroundings altered their sensory world and their internal, psychological world—in particular their sense of connection to their own place-memories and the meaning of their old, pre-Marzahn lives, especially in the context of German history. In chapter 4, "Growing With Marzahn: Childhood, Community, and the Space of Socialism's Future," we see that Marzahn was the most "child-rich" *Stadtsbezirke* (district) in East Germany, and for many children born there or just before moving there in the mid 1970s, their lives developed parallel to the development of this new city. The fifth chapter, "*Plattenbau* Panopticon: The Stasi, *Durchherrschung*, and the New Housing Settlements," narrates the darker side of such all-encompassing housing settlements; namely, that they made surveillance by the East German secret police over East German citizens much easier and further reaching, especially because the Stasi played a vital role in the building and completion of the Housing Program itself. Finally, in the Conclusion, there is a consideration of the paradoxical reversal of fortune that has befallen Marzahn and places like it since the fall of the Wall in 1989, leaving them as places with no past and no future. The work ends with some cautionary reflections on the standard triumphalist, dismissive attitude that the West often takes regarding communist housing settlements like Marzahn.

1

From the Slums to the *Tabula Rasa*

Germany's Working Class, the Housing Program, and the Marzahn Plan

The prefabricated housing settlements built in East Germany during the 1970s, of which Marzahn was the largest, were in many ways radical breaks from the past. Their functional aesthetic referred to no past style, German or otherwise; they were built as entirely new and preplanned cities on the open lands at the edge of cities; they radically changed and re-engineered the natural landscape. In this sense they were "forgetting" the past. However, such breaks from the past are rarely as radical as they are often described. Like many other such settlements, in East Germany and throughout the socialist world, Marzahn was both new and old, part of a dialectic of remembering and forgetting. In particular, the construction of Marzahn was part of a longer narrative of Berlin's history, dating back to the early 1800s, of profound and chronic housing crises and the remarkably miserable conditions for Berlin's working class. It was also part of Berlin's relationship with its margins, including its north-east edge which served as a blank slate for the city to project its utopias.

As the Marzahn plan was at last put into motion, the GDR was finally realizing plans that had lain about on the desks or in the minds of various planners in Berlin for almost a century. It was going to do what the states of the pre-socialist past did not have the means or the willpower (or either) to do: to resettle the working class out of their rental barracks and miserable quarters and into modern, comfortable housing outside the city where they would be surrounded by light, air, and greenery. In doing so, it was, in a way, closing the circle on the history of the very working-class movement that gave it, and its ruling party, the SED, its very life. The SED and the GDR had their origins, in part, in the miserable slums of Berlin. To move the working class out of them was both a fulfillment of a promise, and a way of negating, or forgetting, its own history.

Throughout Europe, industrialization brought with it the creation of crowded urban slums. However, during the nineteenth century the growth in Berlin of such slums, known colloquially as "misery quarters," (*Elendsviertel*) was particularly rapid. A result of its rapid expansion as both an industrial and political center, Berlin became the most overcrowded city in Europe.[1] Throughout the 1800s and

[1] Alexandra Richie, *Faust's Metropolis: A History of Berlin* (New York: Carroll & Graf, 1988), 162–4. Also see Ruth Glatzer, *Berlin wird Kaiserstadt. Panorama einer Metropole 1871–1890* (Berlin: Siedler Verlag, 1993).

early 1900s Berlin was subject to an intense influx of migrants, looking for work but unable to find affordable housing, or any housing at all. Many of the city's homeless built shanty towns outside the city's customs walls.[2] Those able to find and afford housing usually ended up in dark, cramped apartments known as "rental barracks" (*Mietskaserne*).[3] Partially as a result of the "Hobrecht Plan" of 1861,[4] which created the basis for Berlin's expansion outside its customs gates, the rental barracks derived from the creation of very large city blocks that contained several layers of inner courtyards and apartments folded away from the street-facing façade. These buildings contained very small apartments—many of them simply one large room, which came to be known as the "Berlin room."[5] They often had no indoor plumbing and usually had shared toilets in the courtyard; sometimes placed in between floors off the stairwell landing. By 1871, 75 percent of Berlin apartments were considered rental barrack apartments.[6] In the words of urban reformer and critic Werner Hegemann, Berlin had become the "largest rental barrack city in the world."[7]

The spectacle and reality of urban slums were among the most obvious and tangible manifestations of the inequalities and injustices of the capitalist system, and gave tremendous impetus to the growth of radical, left-wing political movements. Indeed, it was Friedrich Engels himself who wrote about the creation of urban slums as a manifestation of capitalism and its relations of production, arguing that "the satisfaction of the need for shelter is a measure of how well all other

[2] Poling, "Shantytowns and Pioneers Beyond the City Wall: Berlin's Urban Frontier in the Nineteenth Century," *Central European History* 47, 245–74, as well as Poling, "On the Inner Frontier: Opening German City Borders in the Long Nineteenth Century" (PhD dissertation, Harvard University, 2011).

[3] There is a voluminous literature on Berlin's infamous rental barracks. See Johann Friedrich Geist and Klaus Kürvers, *Das Berliner Mietshaus* vols 1–3 (Munich: Prestel, 1980); Brian Ladd, *Urban Planning and Civic Order in Germany, 1860–1914* (Cambridge, MA: Harvard University Press, 1990); Christoph Bernhardt, *Bauplatz Groß-Berlin. Wohnungsmärkte, Terraingewebe und Kommunalpolitik im Städtewachstum der Hochindustrialisierung (1871–1918)* (New York: W. de Gruyter, 1998); Lutz Niethammer, ed., *Wohnen im Wandel: Beiträge zur Geschichte des Alltags in der bürgerlichen Gesellschaft* (Wuppertal: Hammer, 1979) and with Franz Brüggemeier, "Wie wohnten Arbeiter im Kaiserreich?" *Archiv für Sozialgeschichte*, 16 (1976) 61–134; Adelheid von Saldern *Häuserleben. Zur Geschichte städtischen Arbeiterwohnens vom Kaiserreich bis heute* (Bonn: Dietz, 1995) and "The Workers' Movement and Cultural Patterns on Urban Housing Estates" *Social History*, 15, 3 (1990), 333–54; Rudolf Eberstadt, "Die Mietskaserne" in Rainer Nitsche, ed., *Häuserkämpfe 1872/1920/1945/1982* (Berlin: TRANSIT, 1981) 29–34; David Frisby and Iain Boyd Whyte, *Metropolis Berlin: 1880–1940* (Berkeley, CA: University of California Press, 2012); Gerhard Ritter and Klaus Tenfelde, *Arbeiter im Deutschen Kaiserreich 1871 bis 1914* (Bonn: Verlag J.H.W. Dietz Nachf., 1992); Hans Jürgen Teuteberg and Clemens Wischermann, *Wohnalltag in Deutschland 1850–1914: Bilder—Daten—Dokumente* (Münster: F. Coppenrath Verlag, 1985); Ingeborg Flagge, ed., *Geschichte des Wohnens, Bd.4: 1918–1945, Reform, Reaktion, Zerstörung* (Stuttgart: Deutsche Verlags-Anstalt, 1996).

[4] On the Hobrecht Plan, see Ladd, *Urban Planning*; also, Claus Bernet, "The 'Hobrecht Plan' (1862) and Berlin's Urban Structure," *Urban History*, 31, 3 (2004).

[5] Geist and Küvers, 404.

[6] Jutta Wietog, "Wohnungsstandard der Unterschichten in Berlin," in Werner Conze and Ulrich Engelhardt, eds., *Arbeiterexistenz im 19. Jahrhundert: Lebensstandard und Lebensgestaltung deutscher Arbeiter und Handwerker* (Stuttgart: Klett-Cota, 1981) 114–37; 132.

[7] Wietog, "Wohnungsstandard," 132.

needs are met."[8] This was something that resonated especially in many of Berlin's working-class neighborhoods, which became hotbeds of SPD and KPD activism. In particular, districts where rental barracks had been built, such as Wedding, Moabit, Prenzlauer Berg, Friedrichshain, Kreuzberg, and Lichtenberg, became known as "Red Berlin" and formed the backbone of the working-class movement in Berlin.[9] At times, the rental barracks served almost as real barracks, lodging the thousands of KPD foot soldiers of the *Rot Frontkämpferbund* (RFB) who were called upon to fight fascists or the police in the streets at such instances as the cataclysmic "Bloody May" riots of 1929.[10]

In some cases the memory of revolution and insurrection literally had roots in the soil of the urban spaces of a neighborhood; for example, the "lone poplar" (*einsame Pappe*) which stood for more than a century near the corner of Topsstrasse and Cantianstrasse in Prenzlauer Berg. This tree was the site of the first demonstration of the 1848 uprising in Berlin, on March 26 of that year, continuing to grow and remaining as a constant *lieu de mémoire* of revolution and working-class spirit across the generations.[11]

Of course, as much as the misery of the Berlin rental barracks testified to the inequalities and injustices of the capitalist system in Germany, these neighborhoods were also spaces that were infused with the memory and the culture of working-class resistance. In Berlin, the term that became (and remains) popular for such neighborhoods was *Kiez*, which denoted, more than a proximity of buildings, a sense of belonging and community.[12] The extreme overcrowding in the rental barracks of Berliner *Kieze* led many to spend time outside, in parks, pubs, and beer gardens, in courtyards and sidewalks, which, as Pamela Swett argues, became "commons" or "public" areas, closed to outsiders but "open for members

[8] Engels, *Zur Wohnungsfrage* (Berlin: Dietz Verlag, 1962), 231. This is taken from Regine Grabowski, "Wohnungspolitik" in Günter Manz, Ekkehard Sachse, and Gunnar Winkler, eds, *Sozialpolitik in der DDR: Ziele und Wirklichkeit* (Berlin: Trafo, 2001), 227–42, 233.

[9] See Eric Weitz *Creating German Communism, 1890–1990: From Popular Protests to Socialist State* (Princeton, NJ: Princeton University Press, 1996).

[10] See Pamela Swett, *Neighbors and Enemies: The Culture of Radicalism in Berlin, 1929–1933* (New York: Cambridge University Press, 2004), for detailed discussion of the "Bloody May" 1929 riots.

[11] This is taken from Manfred Otto, "Tradition und Gegenwart" *Neue Berliner Illustrierte* (no. 3, 1980, 2) = (this article is discussed below). Also Harald Vieth, *Bemerkenswerte Bäume in Berlin und Potsdam* (Hamburg: Selbstverlag Harald Vieth, 2005). Ironically, that tree died in 1960, and barely lived to see the culmination of the working-class movement whose origins were so associated with it. A daughter of that tree was planted in its parent's exact place, and is now a mature tree, just outside the Friedrich-Ludwig-Jahn Sportpark.

[12] Swett, *Neighbors and Enemies*, 26–7. The term "*Kiez*" appears to have come from old Slavic word "*chyza*," meaning "village" or "hut," demonstrating the Slavic origins of Berlin—itself derived from the old slavic word "*Brl*" meaning "swamp." Many place names in and around Berlin are in fact originally Slavic, and were Germanized after the Askanian reconquest of Berlin and Brandenburg (such as Potsdam, Lankwitz, and Marzahn itself); see Günter Peters, *Hütten, Platten, Wohnquartiere, Berlin–Marzahn: Ein junger Stadtbezirk mit altem Namen* (Berlin: MAZZ, 1998), 16. Also see Heinz Seyer, "In ur- und frühgeschichtlicher Zeit," in Bezirksamt Marzahn von Berlin, Arbeitskomitee 20. Jahrestag, ed., *1979–1999. 20 Jahre Marzahn von Berlin; Festschrift* (Berlin: MAZZ Verlag, 1999), 17–19 and Hartmut Rakow, "Zu Hause in Berlin. Wohnen im Grünen—Siedeln in Biesdorf Süd" in Heimatverein Marzahn–Hellersdorf, ed., *Hundert Jahre Siedlungsgebiete. Geschichte und Zukunft. Tag der Regional- und Heimatgeschichte Marzahn–Hellersdorf 2002* (Berlin: Lokal Verlag, 2002), 56–7.

of the neighborhood."[13] Residents became intimately acquainted with each others' lives, with gossip, and developed a close-knit sense of community.[14]

The problem of the Berlin misery quarters vexed social reformers from Bettina von Arnim to Rudolf Virchow, and spurred numerous plans to clear the slums and resettle the working class on the edges of the city.[15] Indeed, as Beatrix Bouvier writes, it was a "dream" of the working-class movement during these years to one day build "socialist settlements with functional, plentiful, and hygienic living space."[16] This "dream" surfaced in several proposals for the future of Berlin, including those of the influential Greater Berlin Association (*Zweckverband Groß-Berlin*), which sought to expand Berlin's margins during the first two decades of the twentieth century. Part of the Greater Berlin Association plan called for settling 340,000 people in Marzahn, and another 300,000 in Hohenschönhausen and Hellersdorf, using the existing "Royal Eastern" train line (*königlich Ostbahn*) dating back to the 1880s[17] to connect the settlement to central Berlin. In the 1920s, City Building Commissioner and Social Democrat Martin Wagner (who had been a prominent member of the Greater Berlin Association)[18] worked with prominent modernist architects including Bruno Taut, Walter Gropius and Hans Scharoun to build modern, mass-produced, affordable working-class housing settlements on the edges of the city, from the Siemensstadt in Reineckendorf to the Horseshoe settlement in Brix.[19] Wagner had some initial success, including the very first prefabricated concrete panel apartment construction (*Plattenbau*) in Lichtenberg.[20] However he foresaw much more—his 1928 master plan for the "New Berlin" envisioned massive, wholesale constructions of entirely new cities on the edges of

[13] Swett, *Neighbors and Enemies*, 32. She is citing the work of Michael Haben here, in "'Die waren so unter sich:' Über Kneipen, Vereine und Politik in Berlin Kreuzberg" in Karl-Heinz Fiebig et al., eds., *Kreuzberger Mischung: Die innerstädtische Verflechtung von Architektur, Kultur und Gewerbe* (Berlin: Äesthetik und Kommunikation, 1984), 242. Also see Weitz, *German Communism*, 160–88.

[14] Swett, *Neighbors and Enemies*, 42.

[15] On Virchow, and in particular his sewage farms (which will resurface later in this text) see Marion Gray, "Urban Sewage and Green Meadows: Berlin's Expansion to the South, 1870–1920" *Central European History* 47 (2014), 275–306.

[16] Beatrix Bouvier, *Die DDR—Ein Sozialstaat? Sozialpolitik in der Ära Honecker* (Bonn: Dietz, 2002), 155. She is in part quoting here from Günter Manz and Gunnar Winkler, eds., *Sozialpolitik* (Berlin: Verlag die Wirtschaft, 1985), 165.

[17] Peters, *Platten, Hütten, Wohnquartiere*, 182. On the Royal Eastern Line, see Harald Kintscher, "Die Königliche Ostbahn und was darauf folgte" in Sabine Kadow and Harald Kintscher, eds., *Links und Rechts der Wuhle: Biesdorf, Hellersdorf, Kaulsdorf, Mahlsdorf, Marzahn. Heimatskalendar 2002* (Berlin: Lokal Verlag, 2002), 43–4.

[18] On Wagner, and his connections to the *Zweckverband* and plans to resettle Berliners in the "green fields" outside the city, see Barry Jackisch, "The Nature of Berlin: Green Space and Visions of a New German Capital, 1900–45," *Central European History* 47 (2014), 307–33.

[19] Swett, *Neighbors and Enemies*, 48–9. On Wagner and Taut, and modernist mass production of housing generally, also see Sabine Hake, *Topographies of Class: Modern Architecture and Mass Society in Weimar Berlin*, (Ann Arbor: University of Michigan Press, 2008) and Jackisch, "The Nature of Berlin," and see Eric Mumford, *The CIAM Discourse on Urbanism, 1928–1960* (Cambridge: MIT Press, 2000) and David Frisby, *Cityscapes of Modernity: Critical Explorations* (Cambridge: Polity Press, 2001), especially chapter 7, "The City Rationalized: Martin Wagner's New Berlin," 264–302.

[20] Günter Peters, *Historische Stadtplanungen für den Berliner Nordosten* (Berlin: Bezirksamt Marzahn von Berlin, Abt. Jugend, Bildung, und Kultur, Kulturamt/Heimatmuseum, 1997), 22. See also Hannemann, *Die Platte*, 42.

Berlin. This included especially the north-eastern edge of Berlin—the districts (*Stadtsbezirke*) of Marzahn, Hohenschönhausen, and Hellersdorf—for a massive construction program of mass-produced apartments that would hold a total of 366,000 newly settled residents.[21]

Wagner was influenced by Taylorism and Fordism,[22] as well as by the Austrian urban planner Camillo Sitte, who emphasized the need for modern dwellings to incorporate large amounts of green space, sunlight, and fresh air.[23] His ideas also clearly coincided with contemporaries such as modernist urban planner Le Corbusier, founding member of the *Congrès Internationaux d'Architecture Moderne* (CIAM) and representative of what James Scott calls "high modernism."[24] Le Corbusier and the CIAM advocated the demolition of the "old city" as a site of material and moral decay, in which the physical and spatial environment of the city perpetuated class oppression and thus resentment while at the same time cutting the lower classes off from the sunlight, fresh air, and greenery that Le Corbusier (drawing inspiration from Ebenezer Howard's "Garden City" movement) believed all people needed to be happy and healthy.[25] Specifically, Le Corbusier and the CIAM wanted to clear away the "detritus of dead epochs"[26] and looked to the edges of cities—suburbs—as a place to build entirely new cities on a *tabula rasa*, thus placating the working classes and preventing revolution; one of his catchphrases was "architecture or revolution."[27] Le Corbusier's ideas culminated in his design for the "Radiant city" using mass-produced identical living blocks or towers, using steel-reinforced concrete, which would be surrounded by green spaces.[28] Moreover, Le Corbusier and the CIAM believed that only the state had the power and the foresight to recreate the city of tomorrow—not private industry.[29] Although Le Corbusier and the CIAM did not specifically submit plans for building a new Berlin on the margins, their ideas about rebuilding cities using

[21] Peters, *Berliner Nordosten*, 20.

[22] Hannemann makes this point directly in *Die Platte*, 42.

[23] Barry Jackisch, "The Nature of Berlin," 312.

[24] See Scott, *Seeing Like a State: How Certain Schemes to Improve the Human Condition Have Failed* (New Haven, Conn: Yale University Press, 1998), chapter 4. Scott is representative of a highly negative and somewhat one-dimensional reading of Le Corbusier.

[25] *Athens Charter*, published by Le Corbusier (New York: Grossman Publishers, 1973), in particular articles 23, 26, 29, 35–6. On Le Corbusier's influences and on his work generally, see Kenneth Frampton, *Le Corbusier* (London: Thames and Hudson, 2001) and on Le Corbusier and the CIAM in general, see Mumford, *The CIAM Discourse on Modernism*.

[26] Le Corbusier, *City of Tomorrow*, 244.

[27] Le Corbusier, *Toward an Architecture* (Los Angeles: Getty Research Institute, 2007). This is from Anatole Kopp, "Foreign architects in the Soviet Union during the first two Five-Year Plans" in William Brumfield, ed., *Reshaping Russian Architecture: Western Technology, Utopian Dreams* (Cambridge: Woodrow Wilson International Center for Scholars and Cambridge University Press, 1990).

[28] *Urbanisme* was Le Corbusier's major work detailing his ideas on urban planning, published in 1924 by Les Éditions G. Crés & Co., Paris. It was translated into English as "The City of Tomorrow." See Le Corbusier, *The City of To-Morrow and Its Planning* (Cambridge, Mass: MIT Press, 1971). Also see his *La Ville Radieuse: Soleil, Espace, Verdure* (Boulogne-sur-Seine: Éditions de l'Architecure d'Aujourd'hui, 1935), translated as *The Radiant City: Elements of a Doctrine of Urbanism to Be Used as the Basis of our Machine-age Civilization* (New York: Orion Press, 1967).

[29] Le Corbusier, *The Athens Charter*, 65.

mass production, prefabricated concrete slabs, amidst the green fields outside cities were the underpinning of the plan for Marzahn and many other satellite cities built in the communist world from the 1930s until the end of the 1980s.

It is possible that some variation of the "Radiant City" could have been built by Wagner in Berlin's north-east, but Wagner was unable to move forward with his plans to build such settlements because of the onset of the Great Depression in 1929–30. Even though he lost his position after the establishment of the Third Reich, there remained a certain continuity in terms of urban planning for Berlin's slums and its margins. National Socialist urban planners were no less adamant about clearing slums, throughout Germany and especially in Berlin. As Jeffrey Dieffendorf notes, Nazis, especially political leaders and urban planners, were hostile towards large cities precisely because of their proletarian slums, which created "decadence" and "asocial elements and enemies of the state;" many cities initiated slum-clearance projects during the 1930s.[30] Josef Goebbels, the *Gauleiter* of Berlin, made publicized visits to some of the worst of rental barracks, and called for a Housing Program (*Wohnungsbauprogramm*) to build 30,000 new units a year each year.[31]

This call was heard by Albert Speer, Hitler's main architect and chief urban planner of Berlin, who, like Wagner before him, sought to relocate the working class from the slums to the open fields on the edges of the city—and, as previously, looked especially to the north-east, near Marzahn. Speer's 1938 General Plan for Berlin, which sought to dramatically remake the city as Germania, the capital of the entire world, called for the construction of 450,000 apartments in the north-east of Berlin, around the village of Biesdorf,[32] which would be the eastern terminus of the "east–west axis" of Germania.[33] Here, Speer was incorporating plans that had already been proposed by the city of Berlin in 1935 to build workers' settlements, especially for "child-rich" (*kinderreich*—a term that will resurface later in the GDR's plans for settling the north-east of Berlin) proletarian families in Marzahn.[34] Simultaneously, his plan depopulated the inner city to the tune of almost 200,000 people through the demolition of apartments to make room for the grandiose plazas and halls of the future world capital.[35]

[30] Jeffrey Dieffendorf, *In the Wake of War: The Reconstruction of German Cities after World War II* (New York: Oxford University Press, 1993), 113–14.

[31] See Landesarchiv Berlin (LA-B), A Rep. 009 Nr. 28891 "Sanierung der Elendswohnungen; Dr. Goebbels Sofortprogramm 1938–39." Goebbels was also instrumental in renaming Friedrichshain—Berlin's most overcrowded district, and reddest (it was known as "little Moscow")—after Horst Wessel, the famous martyred SA member. See Norbert Podewin, *Marx und Engels Grüssen…Aus Friedrichshain* (Berlin: Dietz, 2010), 172–86.

[32] Peters, *Nordosten*, 24.

[33] Another 200,000 would be built in "South City" at the southern end of the north–south axis. See Speer, *Inside the Third Reich: Memoirs*, trans. Richard and Clara Winston, (New York: Macmillan, 1970); for more on Germania, see Hans Reichhardt and Wolfgang Schäche, *Von Berlin nach Germania: Über die Zerstörungen der "Reichshauptstadt" durch Albert Speers Neugestaltungsplanungen* (Berlin: Transit, 1998); Stephen Helmer, *Hitler's Berlin: The Speer Plans for Reshaping the Central City* (Ann Arbor, MI: UMI Research Press, 1985); Lars Larsson, *Die Neugestaltung der Reichshauptstadt: Albert Speers Generalbebauungsplan für Berlin* (Stockholm: Almqvist and Wiksell: 1977).

[34] LA-B A Rep. 009 Nr. 27675 "Entwurf Bebauungsplan für das von der Landsberger Chaussee, dem Marzahner Weg, und der Gemarkungsgrenze gegen Marzahn umschlossene Gelände des Verwaltungsbezirks 18 1935."

[35] Reichhardt and Schäche, *Von Berlin nach Germania*, 156.

However, as was the case in the Weimar Republic, the Third Reich was not able to realize its plans to resettle workers on the edges of the city. Once the war began in 1939, most of Speer's plans for Germania had to be shelved—including the gigantic settlements in the north-east and south. The standstill in construction could not have come at a worse time from the perspective of trying to build new housing—in 1939 there was a housing shortage in Berlin of at least 200,000 apartments, with another 314,000 Berliners living in small or substandard dwellings, such as garden sheds (*Lauben*) or cellar or attic apartments.[36]

The housing crisis became profoundly worse once the war began, especially once the Royal Air Force began indiscriminate night-time area bombings of German cities, relying heavily on incendiary weapons.[37] Indeed, the RAF's Bomber Command was aiming *specifically* at creating or exacerbating housing shortages in German cities, and their particular goal was to "de-house" the working class by firebombing crowded and shoddy working-class tenements.[38] This of course, in a cruel irony, was welcomed by certain planners in the Third Reich, including those in Speer's office; they saw the British strategy of "de-housing" the working class as doing the work of slum clearance for them. They looked forward to rebuilding German cities along decentered, quasi-exurban lines after the war, with workers spread out in the green, open spaces outside what had been the old city.[39]

And the British strategy worked; the damage during the war to Berlin's housing stock was profound.[40] The target of 288 separate bombing raids,[41] Berlin received more bombs than any other city in the world.[42] In addition, the Battle for Berlin,

[36] Laurenz Demps, ed., *Luftangriffe auf Berlin: Die Berichte der Hauptluftschutzstelle 1940–1945* (Berlin: Berlin: Ch. Links, 2013), 17.

[37] There is a very large literature on the air war and in particular the use of incendiary weapons on German cities. See first and foremost the controversial Jörg Friedrich, *The Fire: The Bombing of Germany, 1940–1945*, trans. Alison Brown (New York: Columbia University Press, 2006); also Jörg Arnold, *The Allied Air War and Urban Memory: The Legacy of Strategic Bombing in Germany* (New York: Cambridge University Press, 2011); W.G. Sebald, *On the Natural History of Destruction*, trans. Anthea Bell (New York: Random House, 2003); Uwe Bahnsen and Kerstin von Stürmer, *Die Stadt, die sterben sollte. Hamburg im Bombenkrieg, Juli 1943* (Hamburg: Convent Verlag, 2003); and Keith Lowe, *Inferno: The Devastation of Hamburg, 1943* (New York: Penguin Books, 2007).

[38] See Friedrich, *The Fire*, 9–12; Demps, *Luftangriffe*, 14–15, 38; Dieffendorf, *Wake of War*, 6. Also Stephen Garrett, *Ethics and Airpower in World War II: The British Bombing of German Cities* (New York: St. Martin's Press, 1993), 13, and Charles Messenger, *'Bomber' Harris and the Strategic Bombing Offensive* (London: Arms and Armour Press, 1984), 69–70.

[39] See for example Bundesarchiv-Berlin Lichterfelde (BArch-BL) R 113, especially 2107: "Wiederaufbau bombenzerstörter Städet Grundsätze und Richtlinien (Hannover, Kassel, Stuttgart, Hamburg, Bremen) incl: Hochbau und Flachbau in volksbiologischer hinsicht," which includes "Abschrift 'Gedanken und Berechnungen zur Lösung des Wohnungsproblems in bombenzerstörten städten from Bohnert to Staatssekretär Dr. Muhs in Berlin, Geheime Reichssache, 15. April 1944.'" Also see Dietmar Süß, *Tod aus der Luft: Kriegsgesellschaft und Luftkrieg in Deutschland und England* (Munich: Siedler, 2011), 238–54.

[40] Because Berlin was a newer city, and had more construction out of stone and cement and less out of wood, as well as wider streets, the firebombing destroyed a lower percentage of housing than in older cities such as Hamburg and Würzburg. See Friedrich, *The Fire*, 98–9.

[41] Demps, ed., *Luftangriffe*, 331.

[42] Friedrich, *The Fire*, 316.

in which the Red Army fought its way into the city center from the outskirts, saw brutal block-by-block and building-to-building fighting which further damaged and destroyed Berlin's dwellings. By the end, out of Berlin's 1,562,000 apartments, only 380,000 survived without being damaged or destroyed.[43] In East Berlin, 870,000 apartments were destroyed, about one-third of all domiciles prior to 1939,[44] and in some places where the fighting was the heaviest, such as Friedrichshain and Mitte, 60 percent of all buildings were destroyed.[45] Observers coming or returning to the ruined city struggled to find superlatives to express the scale of material devastation they saw. Among those were FDR aide Harry Hopkins, who pronounced it a "second Carthage," after flying over the city; and playwright Bertholdt Brecht referred to Berlin as the "pile of rubble outside Potsdam." It was this pile of rubble, or at least half of it, that the GDR inherited as it embarked on building a socialist utopia. To make matters worse, millions of homeless refugees streamed into Berlin in the months and years after the war.[46] It seemed to be the least auspicious circumstances imaginable for such a project.

THE HOUSING CRISIS IN POST-WAR EAST BERLIN

The massive housing crisis that confronted the young GDR was made even worse by the utter neglect with which the country treated housing in its first decade of existence. Under the influence of Stalinist socialist realism, the GDR focused on prestige projects such as the Stalinallee and Stalinstadt rather than trying to build as much housing as possible to accommodate every citizen.[47] Under the leadership of Kurt Liebknecht, the East German DBA rejected mass-produced, prefabricated housing (what was called "formalism") using instead traditional materials and methods, which proved to be too expensive and thus yielded far too few new dwellings.[48]

[43] Demps, ed., *Luftangriffe*, 107. [44] Buck, *Mit hohem Anspruch*, 20.

[45] Jörg Echternkamp, *Nach dem Krieg: Alltagsnot, Neuorientierung und die Last der Vergangenheit, 1945–1949* (Zürich: Pendo Verlag, 2003), 19–20. See also Tony LeTissier's highly detailed account of the Battle for Berlin, *The Battle for Berlin* (Jonathan Cape: London, 1988), more generally for the best account of the fight I have found. Also see Peter Gosztony, *Der Kampf um Berlin 1945 in Augenzeugenberichten* (Düsseldorf: Karl Rauch Verlag, 1970), and Peter Slowe and Richard Woods, *Battlefield Berlin: Siege, Surrender and Occupation, 1945* (London: Robert Hale, 1988).

[46] On homelessness and allied housing policy, as well as a remarkable description of the phenomenology of Berlin's ruined urban landscape, see Clara Oberle, "City in Transit: Ruins, Railways, and the Search for Order in Postwar Berlin" (PhD dissertation, Princeton University, 2006).

[47] Joachim Palutzki, *Architektur in der DDR* (Berlin: Reimer, 2000), 60–4.

[48] For more on the "formalism debate" as it was euphemistically termed by the Party, see Wolfgang Thöner, "From an 'Alien, Hostile Phenomenon' to the 'Poetry of the Future': On the Bauhaus Reception in East Germany, 1945–1970" in *Bulletin of the German Historical Institute*, Bulletin Supplement 2 (2005), 115–38; Rubin, *Synthetic Socialism: Plastics and Dictatorship in the German Democratic Republic* (Chapel Hill: University of North Carolina Press, 2008), 46–8, and specifically on architecture and urban planning, 81–5; and Virag Eszter Molnar, *Building the State: Architecture, Politics and State Formation in Postwar Central Europe* (New York: Routledge, 2013), 39–40. Further, Molnar's PhD. dissertation at Princeton, entitled "Modernity and Memory: The Politics of Architecture

As a result, the GDR spent only one-third of one percent of its total budget on housing in 1950, and this actually fell to one-tenth of one percent by 1955.[49] In the SED's 1949–50 two-year plan, only 34,730 dwellings (including both new construction and renovation) were called for.[50] Though this was achieved, it still left a huge gap—the first five-year plan (1951–5) called for 240,000 dwellings to be built, but only 208,495 dwellings were built—a 13 percent shortfall. The second five-year plan (1956–60), which called for 350,000 new dwellings, was interrupted, but the plan's quota for 1957–8 of 189,000 dwellings resulted in only 126,557 apartments built—a shortfall of one-third.[51] By 1959 Walter Ulbricht admitted openly that the GDR had a housing shortage of more than a half-million—570,000—apartments.[52] Nor were the apartments built in the GDR of sufficient quality—they continued to be built with inadequate facilities, as they had been in earlier days, further proof of the low regard in which the GDR's old guard leadership held modern domestic amenities. So, for example, in 1949, of the newly built apartments, 12 percent *still* did not have a toilet, and only 37 percent were built with a bath or a shower.[53] The amount of apartments built with toilet and bath/shower included improved to nearly 100 percent by 1960, but by 1960 still only 9 percent of *new* dwellings were being built with central heating.[54]

As late as 1961, two-thirds of all dwellings were built before 1918, the majority of these from before the twentieth century; these were the old rental barracks from the 1860s, 1870s and 1880s.[55] 10.3 percent of all apartments in East Germany were officially condemned by the authorities, though people continued to live in them out of necessity.[56] By 1960, still, only ten percent of the GDR's housing stock was built after 1945.[57]

One-third of all apartments had no running water at all. And these were not just the East Berlin rental barracks; the situation was often even worse in smaller cities and towns, such as Neubrandenburg, where only one-third of dwellings *had* running water. In many cases, "running water" meant a spigot in the kitchen that poured cold water at a torrent. Neither the volume nor the temperature could be controlled, and there was no filtering of the water either. To take bath meant to fill a basin with the water from the wall spigot, heat it on the stove, and use a sponge. And 35 percent of dwellings did not even have a spigot—they were not connected to any plumbing whatsoever.[58] Only a third of East German apartments had a toilet.[59] The majority, especially in the old rental barracks, continued to share

in Hungary and East Germany After the Second World War" (2005) gives a much more in-depth background to the formalism debate in East Germany. Also see Palutzki, *Architektur*, 117, and *passim* for more specific examples of Ulbricht's personal critique of modernist architecture.

49 Hannemann, *Die Platte*, 65.

50 Buck, *Mit hohem Anspruch*, 172.

51 Buck, *Mit hohem Anspruch*, 172–3.

52 Buck, *Mit hohem Anspruch*, 179—this is from the third Baukonferenz, May 6–7, 1959.

53 *Statistisches Jahrbuch der DDR*, 1990; this is also in Buck, *Mit hohem Anspruch*, 177.

54 Buck, *Mit hohem Anspruch*, 177.

55 Buck, *Mit hohem Anspruch*, 179.

56 Palutzki, *Architektur*, 194.

57 Buck, *Mit hohem Anspruch*, 179.

58 Buck, *Mit hohem Anspruch*, 181.

59 Palutzki, *Architektur*, 194.

toilets that were accessed from the landing in the stairwell halfway between floors. In rural dwellings, the bathroom was usually in an outhouse. Sixty-five percent of dwellings were not connected to the sewage system at all.[60]

The GDR was supposed to be a radical break from a German past defined by oppression, exploitation, fascism, and imperialist war, but, phenomenologically speaking, East Germans still lived surrounded by that very same past. Wandering through Prenzlauer Berg or Friedrichshain, or peering from a broken window onto a dark courtyard in a rental barrack, Berlin still very much *looked* like the nineteenth or early twentieth century. Officials in the GDR even referred to the building stock from before 1945 as the "capitalist legacy" (*kapitalistische Erbe*).[61]

Not only did it look like the nineteenth century, it smelled and felt like it, too. Because only one in forty residences had central heating,[62] most dwellings in East Germany were heated with heating ovens, which meant lugging sacks of lignite briquettes from the coal cellar up as many as five or six stories, on a daily basis. While the coal cellar was also common for a time in West Germany, central heating was a standard feature of the post-war building programs there and private residences were steadily being retrofitted with modern boilers or forced air systems throughout the post-war years; this was not the case in the GDR. In East Germany, at least in the old towns and working-class neighborhoods, the acrid smell of burning brown coal from thousands of apartments permeated the streets and parks and combined with the noxious odors of the Trabant's two-stroke engine and lawn-mower exhaust system to produce a smell that was fundamentally and uniquely "East German." Visitors to the GDR from the West, in particular, commonly referred to the smell of the burning brown coal, especially acute to the senses on cold Berlin winter days when the ovens were in full swing, as one of their most indelible impressions of East Berlin and the GDR in general. The West did not smell like that. It was not to be, however, the smell of Marzahn.

Worse, this persistence of the old ways was beginning to impact on the new generation. During the first five-year plan (1951–5), there were 208,495 dwellings built, and 837,297 marriages.[63] This meant that only a quarter of newlyweds could find a home of their own—leading to the well-documented phenomenon in the GDR of young newlyweds continuing to live either together with the family of one of the partners, or not living together at all, but remaining in their childhood homes. A new generation of East Germans was unable to begin a new life outside the world of their parents, which was a world older than the GDR.

The neglect of housing was part of a larger neglect on behalf of Stalinism of all things domestic, whether housing or consumer goods. The factory, not the home space, was the focus of traditional communism. It was where workers had

[60] Buck, *Mit hohem Anspruch*, 180.

[61] Buck, *Mit hohem Anspruch*, 254. Florian Urban also notes this same language about the nineteenth-century slum neighborhood of Arkonaplatz in Prenzlauer Berg in *Neohistorical Berlin*, 52.

[62] Palutzki, *Architektur*, 194.

[63] Buck, *Mit hohem Anspruch*, 178.

their meals, where they showered, where their friendships were formed, and how they structured their social relationships. The physical space of the factory as a highly gendered male space was fundamental to the solidarity of the working-class movement.[64] The factory, even more than the slum neighborhood and the beer garden, was the ideal place for political mobilization—for it was there, truly that one could address all the members of the proletariat in one place and in the midst of the very means of production over which the entire dialectic of class warfare was being fought.[65] The neglect of the home space was also part of a systematic misogyny on the part of the SED, as Donna Harsch has demonstrated. [66]

And as Harsch argues, the "domestic" had its revenge. The Party was forced to begin taking housing and consumer goods seriously: as a result of the 1953 uprising; by the success in building housing and creating a consumer paradise in West Berlin and West Germany; and most of all, by the ascension of Nikita Khrushchev to power in the USSR. The neglect of housing, and of the domestic sphere in general, was one of the main targets in Khrushchev's attack on Stalinism, and was made clear in a speech Khrushchev gave in December 1954 at the Moscow All-Unions Building Conference. In it, he demanded that the Soviet Union, and all Soviet satellites, stop wasting their money on construction projects that over-used ornamentation and craftsmanship, that they focus more of their political and economic resources on solving the housing crisis in general, and that they pay close attention to what was happening in the West and rest of the world.[67] His motto, which became the title of a pamphlet he published the next year, was "Better, Cheaper, and Faster Construction." In it, Khrushchev demanded serial production of identical four- and five-storey apartment blocks; though, as Mark Smith demonstrates, developments of this kind were already underway in the post-war reconstruction of Soviet cities and even in the creation of "microrayon" districts dating back to the 1920s; Khrushchev consolidated them into a coherent and forceful vision of the future of socialist urban planning and everyday life.[68] His call reverberated throughout the USSR and the Eastern Bloc, as prefabricated mass-produced housing was used to create vast workers' quarters in factory towns

[64] See Kott, *Communism Day-to-Day* and Kott and Droit, eds., *Die ostdeutsche Gesellschaft*; also Lüdtke, "Ouvriers, Eigensinn et politique dans l'Allemagne du XXe siècle" in: *Actes de la recherche en sciences sociales* 113 (1996), 91–101, "La République Démocratique Allemande comme histoire. Réflexions historiographiques" in: *Annales* HSS 53 (1998), 3–39, *Eigen-Sinn: Fabrikalltag, Arbeitererfahrungen und Politik vom Kaiserreich bis in den Faschismus* (Hamburg: Ergebnisse Verlag, 1993), and Lüdtke, ed., *The History of Everyday Life Reconstructing Historical Experiences and Ways of Life*, trans. William Templer (Princeton, NJ: Princeton University Press, 1995).

[65] See Sandrine Kott, *Communism Day-to-Day*, chapter 2.

[66] Harsch, *The Revenge of the Domestic*.

[67] Dorothea Tscheschner, "Sixteen Principles of Urban Design and the Athens Charter" in Thorsten Scheer, Josef Paul Kleihues, and Paul Kahlfeldt, eds., *City of Architecture of the City: Berlin 1900–2000* (Berlin: Nicolai, 2000) 259–70. In fact, in 1950, Khrushchev had overseen a pilot program to mass-produce prefab concrete apartments in Moscow. He knew that there was tremendous need for such housing, and that he could make himself very popular with the citizens of the USSR and Party members by championing this cause. See Hannemann, *Die Platte*, 61.

[68] See Smith, *Property of Communists*.

such as Nizhni Novgorod in the USSR,[69] Nowa Huta in Poland,[70] as well as others in Czechoslovakia[71] and Hungary.[72]

In fact, one of the strongest motivations for Khrushchev was his awareness of the West and its higher standard of living—and for him the contrast between West and East Germany was a significant problem in his propaganda war with the West. In particular, Khrushchev was aware of the extent to which West Germany, under Adenauer, had made solving the post-war housing crisis a top priority through the mass production of housing and housing settlements, often on the edges of cities.[73] Indeed, prefabricated or serially produced housing had become a global trend by the 1950s, as Florian Urban and others have noted.[74] This included in Western Europe, especially the British "New Towns,"[75] and the French *villes nouvelles* such as the *banlieue* Sarcelles.[76] Beyond Western Europe Corbusian or modernist-inspired new cities were being built, from Brasilia to Dar es Salaam.[77]

Because of East Berlin's proximity to West Berlin, it was always necessarily a showpiece of the communist world—the most visited part of the Soviet empire by citizens of the West, as well as by international and non-aligned visitors. It was vital, therefore, for Moscow that East Berlin in particular be able to compete with and match the West in terms of urban planning, construction, and housing. Furthermore, the proximity of East and West Berlin was not just a matter of competing "showrooms" of capitalism and communism. Berlin was also one of the key places for East Germans to "vote with their feet," by leaving the GDR for the Federal Republic—at least until the border was closed in 1961. And it was clear that, among the many complaints the East Germans had about their republic, inadequate housing was *by far* the most common, as evidenced by the enormous number of complaint letters (*Eingaben*) addressing this issue, compared with others.[78]

[69] See Smith, *Property of Communists*, as well as Siegelbaum, *Cars for Comrades*, especially chapter 2, "GAZ, Nizhni Novgorod—Gor'kii—Nizhni Novgorod," and Heather DeHaan, *Stalinist City Planning: Professionals, Performance, and Power* (Toronto, Ontario: University of Toronto Press, 2013), and Lynne Atwood, "Housing in the Khrushchev Era," in Melanie Ilic, Susan E. Reid, and Lynne Atwood, eds., *Women in the Khrushchev Era* (New York: Palgrave Macmillan, 2004), 177–202.

[70] See Lebow, *Unfinished Utopia*.

[71] See Zarecor, *Manufacturing a Socialist Modernity*. Zarecor's work focuses more on the pre-war and immediate post-war era, however, she argues that in Czechosolovakia Stalinist socialist realism never really threatened modernist functionalist housing projects, as it did in East Germany and in the USSR itself.

[72] Molnar, *Building the State*, 69–82.

[73] Günter Peters, "Zur Geschichte des industriellen Bauens von den Anfängen bis MItte des 20. Jahrhunderts" in Peters and Heimatverein Marzahn–Hellersdorf e.V., eds., *Geschichte und Zukunft des industriellen Bauens: Tag der Regional- und Heimatgeschichte Marzahn–Hellersdorf 2001* (Berlin: NORA Verlagsgemeinschaft, 2002) 59.

[74] See Urban, *Tower and Slab*.

[75] See Alexander, *Britain's New Towns*.

[76] See Cupers, *The Social Project*.

[77] See again Urban, *Tower and Slab*; Scott, *Seeing Like a State*; James Holston, *The Modernist City: An Anthropological Critique of Brasilia* (Chicago: University of Chicago Press, 1989); Iwan Baan, *Brasilia–Chandigarh: Living with Modernity* (London: Springer, 2010); Calacci, "Ujamaa Urbanism"; David Phillips and Anthony Yeh, eds., *New Towns in East and South-East Asia* (New York: Oxford University Press, 1987).

[78] Fulbrook, *The People's State*, 51 and 278. Fulbrook also notes that in the 1980s, when housing became less of an issue (though it still remained one until the end of the GDR), it was rivaled by complaints about being denied travel visas to the West.

In East Germany, the pressure from the USSR, the West, and East Germans themselves meant a sea change in the practice of urban planning and architecture—and in the DBA itself. Liebknecht was replaced in 1954 by Gerd Kosel, a former *Bauhäusler* who had spent the 1930s in the USSR working closely with constructivists like Moshe Ginsburg, and who had developed a prefabricated workers' housing system, the "F type" apartment, an early forerunner to the P2 and WBS 70 models of prefabricated apartments in East Germany.[79] Kosel had worked with Ernst May on prefabricated buildings, and specialized in building prefabricated housing settlements with Ernst May in Siberia.[80] Under his leadership, all of the DBA's resources were focused on functionalist, mass-produced architecture.

Kosel's first major project, begun in 1955, was the Hoyerswerda settlement. Hoyerswerda was the first attempt to build an entire city, for 26,000 people, out of prefabricated concrete panels, or *Platten*. Under the direction of Richard Paulick, Hoyerswerda utilized the beta model of prefabricated panel construction (*Plattenbau*), known simply as the "P1."[81] The five-story P1 was followed in 1962 by the more advanced eleven-story P2, unveiled by the DBA and the Institute for Construction (*Institut für Hochbau*) at the "New Living, New Dwelling" exhibit at Berlin-Fennpfuhl.[82] The P2 was meant to be a highly rationalized "machine for living,"[83] also described as the "apartment of the future" in the popular magazine *Kultur im Heim* (*Culture in the Home*) by the DBA architects and designers, such as engineer-architect Eberhard Keiser, who created it.[84] It was, as the magazine *Neue Berliner Illustrierte* claimed, the model of building that would be replicated "by the million" in the future.[85]

[79] Hugh Hudson Jr., *Blueprints and Blood: The Stalinization of Soviet Architecture, 1917–1937* (Princeton: Princeton University Press, 1994), 31; Anatole Kopp, "Foreign architects in the Soviet Union during the first two Five-Year Plans" in William Brumfield, ed., *Reshaping Russian Architecture: Western Technology, Utopian Dreams* (Cambridge: Woodrow Wilson International Center for Scholars and Cambridge University Press, 1990), 182, as well as Kopp, *Constructivist Architecture in the USSR* (New York: St. Martin's Press, 1985) 22–3 and Hannemann, *Die Platte*, 53, specifically on the F Type as a predecessor to the P2 and WBS 70.

[80] Kosel, similar to many other Bauhäusler, Constructivists, and Corbusians managed to keep a low profile during the years of Stalinist terror in the 1930s and continue to work on the kinds of modernist, mass-produced apartment projects that the Stalinist regime had denounced. Hannemann, *Die Platte*, 78–9.

[81] Palutzki, *Architektur*, 155–7. Specifically on Paulick and Hoyerswerda see Julia Reich, "Chefarchitekt des Industriellen Bauens: Richard Paulick in Hoyerswerda" in Thöner and Peter Müller, eds., *Bauhaus Tradition und DDR Moderne: Der Architekt Richard Paulick*, (Munich: Deutscher Kunstverlag, 2006), 127.

[82] See "Neues Leben—Neues Wohnen: Berliner Ausstellung im Experimentalbau P-2" in *Kultur im Heim*, 1962–4 and Rubin, *Synthetic Socialism* 89–90. Also see Betts, *Within Walls*, 130–1; Gruner, "P2 Macht das Rennen."

[83] The term "machine for living" again derives from Le Corbusier, though this was not explicitly mentioned in publications in the GDR.

[84] See "Wie Sieht der Wohnung der Zukünft Aus?" *Kultur im Heim* 1963–3, 2–12. There were other models of *Plattenbau* tried by the DBA and the Ministry for Construction, such as the QP B55, QP64, Q3a, WHH models, but these were not as widely used as the P2. See Manfred Lamm, "Zur Entwicklung des industriellen Bauens in Berlin-Ost" in Peters and Heimatverein Marzahn–Hellersdorf e.V., eds., *Geschichte und Zukunft des industriellen Bauens*, 122–38.

[85] "P-2: Ja oder Nein?" *Neue Berliner Illustrierte*, January 4, 1965, 8.

The buzz generated in the media and by exhibitions such as "New Living, New Dwelling" was amplified by a culture of fascination with projections of a hi-tech socialist future, widespread throughout the USSR and Eastern Europe in the late 1950s and 1960s. There was a joining of faith in socialism as a science, technology as an inherently progressive and liberating force, and utopianism in popular discourse, much of it inspired by the success of the Soviet space and nuclear programs, as well as the East German chemistry and plastics programs. One popular book, *Unsere Welt von Morgen* (*Our World of Tomorrow*), frequently given as a gift during the Socialist coming of age ceremony (*Jugendweihe*) promised a Soviet world of the near future consisting of entire cities built from scratch on completely blank substrates, such as in the arctic, at the bottom of the ocean, or even on the Moon, encased in plastic domes.[86] The popular East German magazine *Jugend und Technik* (*Youth and Technology*) went so far as to explicitly say that by completely rebuilding new socialist cities far away from any previous trace of civilization, the Soviet world would "avoid the mistakes of capitalist city construction." This included potentially going as far away as Mars to find a place untainted by the traces of the capitalist past.[87] Socialism, at least in the realm of urban planning, was being redefined—no longer did it cling to national traditions; instead, projects like the P2 were an embrace of the futuristic modernism of the Bauhaus and the CIAM from the 1920s as an expression of a socialist utopia.[88]

Despite how exciting visions of a new, modern utopia were, the truth was that the GDR did not build nearly enough housing for its population. Although the seven-year plan called for 770,000 apartments to be built between 1959 and 1965; in reality, the GDR managed to build only 560,445, a shortfall of almost 25 percent.[89] In 1969, East Berlin built only 3,211 new apartments, the third-lowest of all the districts in East Germany, ahead of only Schwerin and Suhl. Worse, new-apartment construction in West Berlin peaked in the 1960s, with 20,000, something East Berliners were very much aware of.[90] To the extent that P2s were built in the city itself, many were built to fill "holes" or empty lots in the urban fabric left from the war, as opposed to building entirely new communities on a *tabula rasa*;[91] or they were built again mainly as prestige projects in central promenades, such as the Karl-Marx-Allee and Jannowitzbrücke dwellings.[92]

[86] Karl Böhm and Rolf Dörge, *Unsere Welt von Morgen* (Berlin: Verlag Neues Leben, 1960), 219.

[87] "Städte von Morgen und Übermorgen," *Jugend und Technik*, October 1966, 986. See also Rubin, *Synthetic Socialism*, 108–10.

[88] Petra Gruner makes this point in discussing P2 architects and their self-stated influence from the Bauhaus in "P2 Macht das Rennen: Wohnungsbau als soziokulturelles Programm," in Andreas Ludwig, ed., *Tempolinsen und P2...Alltagskultur der DDR*, (Berlin: BenBra Verlag, 1996), 87–102, 89. Betts also makes this point in *Within Walls*, 130.

[89] Buck, *Mit hohem Anspruch*, 273.

[90] Peters, *Hütten, Platten, Wohnquartiere*, 90.

[91] Andreas Butter and Ulrich Hartung, eds., *Ostmoderne: Architektur in Berlin 1945–1965* (Berlin: Jovis/Deutscher Werkbund Berlin e.V., 2005), 68.

[92] Most of the apartments along Karl-Marx-Allee were built using earlier versions of the P2, the QP 64 and QP 71. See Irma Leinauer, "Das Wohngebiet Karl-Marx-Allee: Industrielles Bauen zwischen Strausberger Platz und Alexanderplatz" in Butter and Hartung, eds., *Ostmoderne*, 114–23.

To add to the problem, in the mid and late 1960s there was dramatic influx of residents into East Berlin from elsewhere in the GDR, a result partially of the dramatic centralization in government ministries in Berlin, as well as the influx of young adults born after the war, the so-called GDR Generation.[93] And once the border was sealed in 1961, and the Berlin Wall built, a large number of East Berliners who might have left for the West no longer did because they were now "pent up" in East Berlin, meaning there were even less available apartments. According to a 1974 study by the East German Institute for Market Research, the population of East Berlin had grown by over 13,000 between 1960 and 1971, and was picking up—in 1971 alone there had been 15,258 immigrants into, as opposed to only 6,372 emigrants from, the city.[94] By the end of the 1960s, an estimated 90,000 people were unsuccessfully looking for an apartment.[95] Even worse, many of the young twentysomethings arriving in Berlin had been trained as *cadres*, meant to be the hope and the future of the GDR.[96] And yet they were forced to live in the same miserable rental barracks that the proletarians of a generation or three before had been obliged to live in. One had to wonder: how far had socialism really come since the bad old days before the war?

The 1960s in East Berlin saw mainly an emphasis on prestige projects, although these were aesthetically modern or space-age, such as the TV tower and Alexanderplatz, or Karl-Marx-Platz. As a result, East Berlin in the late 1960s was a study in contrast—sparkling, space-age buildings towered in the center over a nineteenth- (and in some cases eighteenth-) century city of crumbling façades, stoops, and walkways spread out through the rest of the city like an open wound, a superterranean archeology of the disasters of industrialization, capitalism, fascism, and war. The glint of the sun on the TV tower was often not visible from deep inside the courtyards of the rental barracks, and when East Berliners were able to glimpse the cross-shaped reflection, it seemed too far away to matter.

THE HOUSING PROGRAM

The failure to meet the needs of the citizenry in terms of consumption and especially housing was one of several factors that led to the removal of Walter Ulbricht from power at the Eighth Party Congress of the SED in 1971 and his replacement with Erich Honecker.[97] As André Steiner notes, the unrest in Poland in 1970 made the leadership of Eastern European communist parties nervous about the continued

[93] See Dorothee Wierling, *Geboren im Jahr Eins. Der Jahrgang 1949 in der DDR. Versuch einer Kollektivbiographie* (Berlin, Ch. Links Verlag, 2002).

[94] BArch-L DL102 (Institut für Marktforschung) 800: "Stellungnahme zur Entwicklung des Bedarfs an Konsumgutern im Neubaugebiet Berlin–Biesdorf–Marzahn 1974" (February 13, 1972), 27.

[95] Oleg Peters and Waldemar Seifert, *Von der Platte bis zum Schloss: Die* Spur der Steine *des Günter Peters*, (Berlin: Forschungsstelle Baugeschichte Berlin, 2003), 17.

[96] On cadres in the GDR, see Dolores Augustine, *Red Prometheus: Engineering and Dictatorship in East Germany, 1945–1990* (Cambridge, MA: MIT Press, 2007).

[97] Hannemann, *Die Platte*, 96.

neglect of their own population in terms of consumer goods and housing. Most of the Eastern Bloc subsequently began a new era of essentially bribing their populations with increased attention to domestic needs, in exchange for compliance, or at least political apathy—what was termed "goulash communism."[98]

In East Germany, this took the form of what Honecker came to call the "unity of economic and social policy" (*Einheit von Wirtschafts- und Sozialpolitik*), which was also known as "real existing socialism."[99] "Real existing socialism" meant a massive investment by the state in raising the living standard of the population, in order to give the East German working class an incentive to work harder and be more productive. Previously, the SED had used the slogan "as you work today, so you will live tomorrow;"[100] now, the state was going to give the working class a taste of utopia in the here in now, in the hopes that they would stay loyal to the vision of an ultimate socialist utopia.[101] In practical terms, "real existing socialism" meant programs that were strikingly similar to pro-natalist policies of past German regimes, including the Third Reich, such as interest-free credits of up to 5,000 marks for newlywed couples, which could be partially remitted if they had children, and priority for distributing new apartments to couples with children.[102]

A central pillar of real existing socialism was also the Housing Program, begun in October 1973 with a resolution of the SED Politburo.[103] This was described by Party members, including the author of the official Housing Program policy, as the "centerpiece" (*Kernstück*) of the new regime's policy of real existing socialism.[104] In a sense the Housing Program was, like "real existing socialism", presaged by the 1968 Constitution of the GDR, and in particular Article 37, which guaranteed every East German citizen the right to a dwelling—although it was not until the change of regime from Ulbricht to Honecker that the real-world implementation of this right was given the urgency and ambition it demanded.[105]

The goal of the Housing Program was to provide every East German a modern, comfortable dwelling by 1990, thereby, as the Politburo's announcement claimed, "solving once and for all the apartment problem as a social problem."[106] It was on one hand a symbol of "real existing socialism," and frequently in official propaganda or in the media young couples and families were portrayed in connection with newly built apartment blocks, as depicted on the GDR's 200-mark note. At

[98] André Steiner, *The Plans that Failed: An Economic History of the GDR*, trans. Ewald Osers (New York: Berghahn, 2010), 143–4.

[99] Steiner, *The Plans that Failed*, 144.

[100] Ina Merkel, *Utopie und Bedürfnis: Die Geschichte der Konsumkultur in der DDR* (Cologne: Böhlau, 1999), 121.

[101] See Bouvier, *Sozialstaat* for a more in-depth study of "real existing socialism."

[102] Steiner, *The Plans that Failed*, 146.

[103] For more on the Housing Program see Bouvier, *Sozialstaat*, 152–94; Pugh, *Architecture, Politics, and Identity*; Rowell, *Le totalitarisme*; Steiner, *The Plans that Failed*; and Grabowski, "Wohnungspolitik."

[104] Wolfgang Junker, *Das Wohnungsbauprogramm der Deutschen Demokratischen Republik für die Jahre 1976 bis 1990* (Berlin: Dietz, 1973), 13, cited in Joachim Tesch, *Der Wohnungsbau in der DDR 1971–1990: Ergebnisse und Defizite eines Programms in kontroversen Sichten* (Berlin: Gesellschaftswissenschaftliches Forum e.V. & Helle Panke, 2001), 11.

[105] Tesch, *Wohnungsbau in der DDR*, 8.

[106] Hübner, Nicolaus, and Teresiak, *20 Jahre Marzahn*, 10.

the same time, it was more than just a symbol. Indeed, what distinguished the Housing Program from all the abandoned or unfulfilled promises of previous regimes in Berlin and Germany itself—from the Kaiserreich to the Ulbricht state—was that at last it was backed by a government with the ambition, political will, and means to finally solve a housing crisis that had existed in Germany and Berlin since the beginning of the Industrial Revolution. It was in this, in part, that the broader significance of the Program lay; it was finally "redeeming" the suffering that Germany's working class had endured, in terms of living standards and housing, since the very beginning of modern capitalism.

And the ambition of the Program was indeed immense—it called for the building or modernizing of 800,000 apartments by 1980, and a whopping three million by 1990.[107] Eventually, it managed to build almost two million apartments (although it claimed in 1988 to have met its goal of three million)—at the cost, by one estimate, of almost 390 billion marks, the largest capital investment in the country's history,[108] and renovated another one million.[109] It also ran up massive debt in the process.[110] In particular, the Housing Program focused on Berlin, where it planned the construction or renovation of 200,000–230,000 apartments between 1976 and 1990.[111]

It is significant here that the Housing Program was announced as part of the broader "unity of economic and social policy" because it went beyond simply dictating the number of apartments, or "living units" (*Wohneinheiten*), to be built. Indeed, the goal of the Program was changed from "the solution to the housing problem" (*Lösung der Wohnungsfrage*) to the "solution to the housing problem as a social problem" (*Lösung der Wohnungsfrage als soziale Frage*).[112] Indeed, one of the laws passed in 1976 governing the implementation of the Housing Program also called for the building of ancillary structures, such as schools, Kindergartens, clinics, shopping centers, and transportation networks—all things that would improve the everyday lives of East Germans.[113] East German planners were not just looking for quick and easy solutions to building as many units of housing as possible; they were looking at the solution to the housing crisis holistically.[114]

These planners were influenced by the state and the Party's thinking. By March of 1973, the Politburo and the Berliner Magistrat were clearly focused on the

[107] Buck, *Von hohem Anspruch*, 389. Tesch points out that the plan was to focus more on building new structures until 1980, and then to begin incorporating renovation in as well. See *Wohnungsbau in der DDR*, 10.

[108] Pugh, *Architecture, Politics, and Identity*, 289; also Grabowski, "Wohnungspolitik," 234.

[109] Tesch argues that the renovated apartments should be considered as part of the total achievement of the Housing Program, and therefore that it is incorrect to claim, as Buck does, that the Housing Program fell short of its goals, or to accuse the regime of having lied about its achievements. See *Wohnungsbau der DDR*, 37.

[110] Buck, *Von hohem Anspruch*, 425. Buck claims that by 1989, the amount of the debts caused by spending on the Housing Program consumed fully half of GDR's state budget.

[111] Peters, *Hütten, Platten, Wohnquartiere*, 89.

[112] Tesch, *Wohnungsbau der DDR*, 11.

[113] "Ordnung der Planung der Volkswirtschaft der DDR 1976 bis 1980," *GBl Sonderdruck Nr. 775a*, 195; cited in Tesch, *Wohnungsbau in der DDR*, 21.

[114] See for example BArch-SAPMO, DY 30 2838, "Wohnungsbau in Berlin, Bd. 4: 1972–73"—Material zu Problemen der Erweiterung des Housing Program im Zeitraume 1972 bis 1975," from March 29, 1972, 64.

question of how to fulfill the mandate of making Berlin the center of the now all-important Housing Program. Inside the Politburo, Central Committee member Günter Mittag, who was essentially in charge of the planned economy,[115] and who was in charge of the Central Committee's Department of Construction,[116] was the most forceful voice arguing that the housing crisis in Berlin and elsewhere was a major problem and that modern, prefabricated housing settlements were the answer to this issue.[117] Indeed, many of the nearly two million apartments that would be built in the coming two decades as part of the Housing Program would comprise holistic settlements, often at the edges of cities, which contained 1,000 or more apartments. There were 649 of these in the GDR, seventy of which contained over 5,000 dwellings.[118] There were also several "large settlements" (*Großsiedlungen*), which had over 25,000 residents, becoming essentially new cities entirely. These too were built on the edges of cities, such as Gorbitz on the western edge of Dresden, which had 15,000 apartments and 45,000 residents, along with eleven upper schools (*Oberschule*), and sixteen Kitas (daycare/preschools, or *Kindertagestätten*);[119] or Grünau, on the south-western edge of Leipzig, which contained 34,000 apartments for 100,000 residents in eight subdivisions—the largest besides Marzahn-Hellersdorf.[120] In total, over four and a half million East Germans would become residents of such settlements—over 28 percent of the population of East Germany in 1989. A total of 1.6 million (or 10 percent of the total East German population) came to live in one of the twenty-six settlements in the GDR larger than 25,000 residents.[121] Of course, of all the large settlements, the Berlin North-east was to be by far the largest, with four separate large settlements planned in Marzahn-Biesdorf, Neu-Hohenschönhausen, Lichtenberg, and Hellersdorf, all of which, taken together, would hold close to a half-million residents (see Figure 1).

In contrast, in West Germany only about 3.2 million—around 5 percent of the population—lived in such settlements. And only 288,000 West Germans—around

[115] Mittag was the Secretary of the National Economic Council from 1962 to 1973 and 1976 to 1989, the Secretary of the Economy for the SED Central Committee from 1973 to 1976, and First Deputy Chairman of the Ministers' Council (*Ministerrat*), one of the most powerful bodies in determining economic policy in the GDR. See Steiner, *The Plans that Failed*, 198 and *passim*.

[116] Hannemann describes the Central Committee's Dept. of Construction under Mittag as being one of the key loci of decision-making, along with the DBA-ISA (*Deutsches Bauakademie–Institut für Städtebau und Architektur*), in the area of city planning and architecture in the GDR. Hannemann, *Die Platte*, 94.

[117] See BArch-SAPMO DY 2838 (Büro Günter Mittag), "Wohnungsbau in Berlin Bd 4, 1972–1973" esp. 345–7, "Entwicklung des komplexen Wohnungsbaues in der Hauptstadt der DDR, Berlin für die Jahre 1976–1980."

[118] See Appendices 1 and 3.

[119] Holger Starke, ed., *Geschichte der Stadt Dresden: Band 3: Von der Reichsgründung bis zur Gegenwart* (Stuttgart: Theiss Verlag, 2006), 616–17.

[120] Buck, *Von hohem Anspruch*, 358. Specifically on Leipzig–Grünau, see Alice Kahl, *Erlebnis Plattenbau: Eine Langzeitstudie* (Opladen: Leske & Burich, 2003), chapter 5. Kahl puts the number of residents in Grünau at the beginning of the 1990s at 80,000 on p. 14. On the planning of Grünau a useful source has been, Karl Czok and Horst Thieme et al., *Leipzig: Geschichte der Stadt in Wort und Bild* (Berlin: VEB Deutscher Verlag der Wissenschaften, 1978), 157–60.

[121] See Appendices 1 and 3.

0.5 percent of the FRG's population—lived in housing settlements larger than 25,000, of which there were only eight (as opposed to the GDR's twenty-six).[122] Most of the housing estates in West Germany were not conceived as self-sufficient and self-contained communities unto themselves, as Beatrix Bouvier has pointed out.[123] This was also true of many of the *banlieues* in France, as Kenny Cupers notes.[124] Indeed, it was the building of new housing in the form of separated "settlements" large enough to be cities unto themselves was a characteristic of housing policy that stands out as being particularly East German—and socialist.

So, the Housing Program in East Germany represented an arena in which the GDR could surpass West Germany, and in a visible, tangible, and indelible way. Often, the GDR's official propaganda—in the Party organ *Neues Deutschland*—would tout the superiority of the GDR over the FRG by using the abstract language of data and statistics, such as unemployment percentage or infant mortality. But housing was something that could be seen and experienced directly. And since Berlin was conceived of as the "stage" (*Schauplatz*) or "arena" of the Cold War, it received special attention within the Housing Program itself. So, Mittag tasked political and planning leaders with developing a plan for realizing the Program in Berlin, beginning with 30,000 living units by 1975 and another 55,000 between 1976 and 1980. These leaders included among others Erhard Krack, the Mayor of Berlin; Konrad Naumann, who led the SED's Berlin district party organization (*Bezirksleitung*); and the young cadre Günter Peters, who by 1966 had risen to the position of Director of Construction of Berlin (*Bezirksbaudirektor der Hauptstadt Berlin*). Peters rose to prominence especially with his dissertation, completed in 1972, devoted to studying solutions to the housing shortage in Berlin, in particular focusing on the Arnimplatz in Prenzlauer Berg, a crumbling nineteenth-century neighborhood typical of Berlin, with what were once attractive rococo and neoclassical façades in the front and rental barracks and cramped courtyards in the interiors. His dissertation proposed one of two solutions—one, demolishing the old buildings and building a Corbusian "towers in a park" settlement on green space, and two, renovating the façades and modernizing the interior apartments.[125]

Even as the Berliner Magistrat used Peters' study to authorize the renovation of Arnimplatz, Peters realized from his study, as well as previous renovation projects such as that of the Arkonaplatz in Prenzlauer Berg, that modernizing rental barracks meant both razing certain dwellings that were unlivable, and knocking down walls to combine apartments, especially where the apartments were still the one-room (*Berliner Zimmer* or "Berlin room") apartments. As a result, 8,000 awful apartments became 6,000 renovated and livable spaces.[126] The problem was

[122] See Appendix 3.

[123] Bouvier, *Sozialstaat*, 155–6. It should be noted, though, that here attempts were made to build some infrastructure into western edge settlements, including schools, shopping, and recreation.

[124] Cupers, *The Social Project*, 101.

[125] Urban, *Neohistorical East Berlin*, 49–50.

[126] Interview with Peters on February 20, 2008; this is confirmed in Peters and Seifert, *Von der Platte bis zum Schloss* 17–18. In Peters, "Die Arbeiterklasse zieht sich nicht ins Dorf!" in Katrin Rohnstock, ed., *(Keine) Platten Geschichten* (Berlin: Rohnstock Biografen, 2004), 45–51, on page 45, Peters confirms that the lower yield was a major factor in deciding in favor of the Marzahn project and

that in a state in which decisions were often dictated by the concerns of quantity over quality—what was referred to in the GDR as "the ideology of tons" or *Tonnenideologie*—producing *less* apartments was no way to fulfill the goals of the Housing Program.[127] As Florian Urban and Emily Pugh note, the GDR counted living units, not square meters, which contributed to the Arnimplatz renovation looking like a *reduction* in living space, even if it was in fact an improvement.[128] Urban has also noted that, among planners and journalists, if not also residents, the renovation of Arnimplatz and other similar old neighborhoods, such as Arkonaplatz, were popular, in part because they preserved the old façades of the nineteenth-century buildings.[129] Peters' study showed that the costs of renovation were lower, largely because the utilities were already present.[130] Still, as Urban notes, these renovation projects did not become the norm. The Politburo, and the Magistrat, opted for massive investment in industrialized housing, usually at the outskirts of cities. In Berlin, four apartments were built anew for every one that was renovated. As Pugh and Urban both note, the privileging of industrialized housing construction was not just a political decision; the emphasis on heavy industry and Fordist mass production throughout the GDR's economy over many years had led to a severe shortage of the kind of trained craftsmen capable of restoring antique façades.[131] As Brigitte Reimann had written in her novel *Franszіska Linkerhand*, there were no more architects, only engineers.[132]

Not only was Peters in charge of construction in Berlin, in 1970 he became Deputy Mayor, with a portfolio that gave him political, and budgetary, control over the construction in the capital city, including the apartment building (*Wohnungsbau*), underground (*Tiefbau*) and above ground (*Hochbau*) construction firms, comprising 10,000 workers and another 60,000 employees. He worked in conjunction with the Chief Architect of the city, a position held during the Marzahn era by Roland Korn;

others, though he notes that the GDR did a better job restoring old neighborhoods when and where it chose to than the West, contrasting Arnimplatz and Arkonaplatz with Kreuzberg, and noting that "many useful insights" were gained from those projects. Also on the Arnimplatz project, see Dorothea Krause and Manfred Zache, "Modernisierungsgebiet Arnimplatz im Stadtbezirk Berlin–Prenzlauer Berg, *Architektur der DDR* (vol. 25, July 1976, 395–400).

[127] Emily Pugh makes this same point in *Architecture, Politics and Identity*, 301. See also Steiner, *The Plans that Failed.*

[128] Urban, *Neohistorical Berlin*, 48–9.

[129] Though, as Urban also notes, the work was often shoddily done, and almost every renovation done in the GDR needed to be re-done ten years later with much better-trained and better-equipped experts.

[130] Interview with Peters, Biesdorf, Germany, February 20, 2008; Simone Hain, "Between *Arkonaplatz* and the *Nikolaiviertel.* The City as Social Form Versus the City as Mise-en-Scène. Conflicts Raised by the Return to the City," in Thorsten Scheer, Josef Paul Kleihues, and Paul Kahlfeldt, eds., *City of Architecture of the City: Berlin 1900–2000* (Berlin: Nicolai, 2000), 337–48; and also Grabowski, "Wohnungspolitik," 238.

[131] Urban, *Neohistorical East Berlin*, 49 and Pugh *Architecture, Politics and Identity*, 294. Grabowski claims that prefabricated construction was, or at least the GDR's leadership believed it was, the most cost-effective means of mass producing housing; Grabowski, "Wohnungspolitik," 238.

[132] Reimann, *Franziska Linkerhand* (Berlin: Aufbau Taschenbuch Verlag, 2005). Also see Elizabeth Mittman, "'Ich habe kein Ortsgedächtnis': Ort und Identität bei Brigitte Reimann," in Margrid Bircken and Heide Hampel, eds., *Reisen Hals Über Kopf: Reisen in der Literatur von Frauen*, (Neubrandenburg: Federchen Verlag, 2002) 89–110.

but he was the main contractor, or *Hauptauftraggeber*, meaning he held the power of the purse strings.[133] This was significant, because it reflected the state's overarching power over many different sectors of the economy—and Peters' role as both Director of Construction and Deputy Mayor reflected this conflation. Building an entirely new settlement was a massive undertaking, which involved the coordination of many sectors of the economy and the state. Coordinating so many different large and small concerns and stakeholders was not impossible in a capitalist or quasi-capitalist system, but it was difficult. One of the reasons why the GDR was the state that was finally able to build housing settlements on the scale needed to completely solve the housing crisis was that, as a communist country, the state and the Party had overarching control over the economy and could coordinate and organize highly complex projects like Marzahn.

The only thing that remained was to determine where this settlement would be. Peters, as the Berlin City Director of Construction, was well aware of the history of past holders of his office, in particular, Wagner and Speer, and their unfulfilled plans to colonize the north-eastern edge of the city. The pre-existing infrastructure, including an industrial area, a power plant, and the railroad and streetcar tracks connecting the villages of Marzahn, Biesdorf, Hellersdorf, and Ahrensfelde to Berlin all combined to make Peters' choice easy, though he claimed that he also considered areas directly to the north of Berlin, between Pankow/Hohenschönhausen and Buch.[134]

Based on input from Peters and several other urban planners, the Politburo passed a resolution on March 27, 1973, which set in motion the Marzahn project. It called for the building of 20,000 apartments in what it called the "Biesdorf-Nord" (northern Biesdorf) area, which would two years later be renamed "Marzahn."[135] The Politburo Resolution was confirmed by the Council of Ministers, making it law, on April 11, 1973; and not long after that, the Berlin city government went to work, putting the plan into reality. The Magistrat held a competition for the best design for the new apartment complex, which was won in 1974 by a group led by Roland Korn and including Ewald Henn, head district architect of Erfurt; Rolf Laasch, head municipal architect of Rostock; and Horst Siegel, head municipal architect of Leipzig.[136] The jury recommended that the plan be expanded to 35,000 apartments, and by 1975, Korn, along

[133] Interview with Peters, Biesdorf, Germany, February 20, 2008.

[134] Interview with Hielfried Kreuzer, former Deputy Chairman of Berlin City Planning Office (*Stadtplanungsamt*), May 25, 2008. Kreuzer states that Peters' claims to have made most of the key decisions regarding the choice of Marzahn are inflated, and that in fact the choice was made in Kreuzer's office, by his Chairman, Horst Kümmel, who decided on the north-east rather than the north, around Buch, or the south, around Oberschöneweide. Kreuzer claimed to the author in an interview that Kümmel chose Marzahn, not Peters, and in particular he chose it because there was already a streetcar depot nearby.

[135] Christa Hübner, Herbert Nicolaus, and Manfred Teresiak, eds., *20 Jahre Marzahn. Chronik eines Berliner Bezirkes* (Berlin: Heimatsmuseum Marzahn, 1998), 9. The March 27, 1973 Resolution also authorized the building of the Palace of the Republic on the grounds of the old Royal Palace.

[136] Hübner, Nicolaus, and Teresiak, eds., *20 Jahre Marzahn*, 10.

with urban planner Peter Schweizer, landscape specialist Hubert Matthes, and artistic-aesthetic expert Rolf Walter, had detailed blueprints ready to be implemented.

THE DNA OF UTOPIA: THE PLAN FOR MARZAHN

The plan for Marzahn, like much of the East German Housing Program, was centered around a new kind of building, called the Apartment Construction System 70, or *Wohnungsbausystem 70*, abbreviated to WBS 70.[137] Virtually all of Marzahn was built using the WBS 70, as were most of the massive housing settlements built throughout the GDR—indeed, after 1973, of the fifteen housing construction combines (meta-organizations formed out of multiple state-owned companies—in this case, *Wohnungsbaukombinaten*) fourteen of them exclusively manufactured and constructed WBS 70.[138] Furthermore, Marzahn was built in close cooperation with similar efforts in the USSR and the CMEA.[139] Developed by the DBA in 1970, and tested first in Neubrandenburg in 1973, the WBS 70 was a more advanced version of the previous generation of prefabricated housing models, such as the P2, and was designed by the DBA in conjunction with the Technical University of Dresden and a number of prefabrication cement factories.[140]

The WBS 70 was the most advanced *Plattenbau* system the GDR had developed, and was designed to respond to previous complaints about such East German mass-produced housing as the P1 and P2. [141] The apartments in the WBS 70 were larger than in previous models, and each apartment received sunlight through both ends of the dwelling, because each living unit spanned the width of the building. Indeed, this was in compliance with recently passed laws requiring all dwellings to receive at least two hours of sunlight a day, another way in which the Housing Program was influenced by Corbusian notions—in this case, the supposedly palliative quality of sunlight.[142] To achieve this level of natural lighting, without increasing costs or compromising efficiency of mass production, the WBS 70 used centrally positioned stairwells—four or more—which would open to two (or three, in the

[137] Hannemann, *Die Platte*, 97. As Hannemann notes, the name was changed to "Wohnungsbau*serie* 70" after the 1971 leadership change, when many of the signature ideas and programs associated with Ulbricht became suddenly no longer in fashion—this included the idea of thinking in terms of complete systems. However, Hannemann notes, the fundamental idea of the WBS as a system—a "sociological system" as she calls it—was not changed by the rather cosmetic change in the meaning of one part of its acronym, nor was the overall plan for Marzahn itself.

[138] Buck, *Von hohem Anspruch*, 359.

[139] Achim Felz and Wilfried Stallknecht, "Die Wohnungsbauserie 70" in *Deutsche Architektur* (vol. 23, January 1974, 4–10; 4).

[140] Hannemann, *Die Platte*, 101.

[141] Roland Korn, "Der elfgeschossige Wohnblok der WBS 70," *Der Neunte* (vol. 2, no. 5, March 1978, 4).

[142] Bezirksamt Marzahn von Berlin, ed., *20 Jahre Marzahn: Geschichte—Bauen—Leben* (Berlin: Holga Wende, 1999), 88–9. The efforts to achieve this by planners using toy building blocks on the fields of Marzahn are documented in Jürgen Hinze, "Das grüne Ungeheuer" in Rohnstock, ed., *Keine Plattengeschichten*, 52.

eleven-storey variant),[143] apartments on either side for each floor of the building.[144] In addition, the kitchens could be positioned along one of the exterior walls so they could have a window—responding to one of the complaints about the P2, namely, the windowless kitchens, as well as the supposed need for sunlight wherever possible.[145] Indeed, the kitchens in the WBS 70 were larger than those in the P2, and designed to be able to accommodate large families as well—apartments with more than five people received larger cooking ranges, as well as a second sink basin.[146]

In theory, the WBS 70 was also supposed to buck the trend of monotony in mass-produced apartment blocks, which had been a major complaint of residents of the P1 and P2,[147] and was a problem with which ISA theoreticians grappled.[148] Because they were to be produced as complete units, they could be rotated towards any orientation; the same was true for the bathroom units, which were also manufactured separately.[149] In addition, the WBS 70 could be further modified for certain special needs; for example, the DBA developed a WBS 70 model designed for the handicapped.[150]

On the outside, moreover, the WBS 70/5 and WBS 70/11 models were designed so that a wedge-shaped extension could be added, allowing a second unit to adjoin at an oblique angle. Further subsequent units could be added in a row using the angled extension, creating a zigzagged line of apartments.[151] In contrast, the P2 and P1 could only be placed in right angles. Another major complaint that the DBA-ISA had discovered when it investigated older prefabricated housing settlements, such as Halle-Neustadt and Hoyerswerda, was that the right angles that defined the pattern of the dwelling units created closed-off spaces, like courtyards.[152] The spaces were too tight, however, and deprived residents of sunlight

[143] Roland Korn, "Der elfgeschossige Wohnblok der WBS 70" in *Der Neunte* (vol. 2, no. 5, March 1978, 4).

[144] Felz and Stallknecht, "Wohnungsbauserie 70," 12.

[145] This is highlighted in numerous sources; here, Korn, "elfgeschossige Wohnblok," 4.

[146] Siegmar Schreiber and Erich Kuphal, "Mehrgeschossige Wohnungsbauserie 70/Dresden" in *Architektur der DDR* (vol. 25, August 1976, 492–9).

[147] BA-L DH2 23447 "Neubauwohngebiete im Urteil der Bewohner: Soziologische Analyse einer Umfrage in zwölf Neubauwohngebieten der DDR September–October 1975." DBA-ISA in conjunction with ZK-SED Abt. Bauwesen and the Institut für Meinungsforschung, 66. Though this study was published in 1975, and the WBS 70 was developed between 1971 and 1972, it makes reference to a number of previous studies done on the level of satisfaction in prefabricated housing settlements such as Halle–Neustadt in the mid and late 1960s, the findings from which are incorporated into the 1975 project. The DBA was undoubtedly aware of the issues and complaints involved with places like Halle–Neustadt, as the work of the Theory Department of the DBA-ISA reflected before the WBS 70 was developed (see BArch-BL DH2 21686, cited in the next footnote).

[148] BArch-BL DH2 21686 R. Linke, DBA-ISA Abt. Theorie und Geschichte der Architektur, "Einheit und Vielheit—ein Problem städtebaulicher Gestaltung" December 1969.

[149] BArch-BL DH2 21686 "Einheit und Vielheit." [150] LA-B C Rep 110-05 Nr. 15, 1.

[151] Felz and Stallknecht, "Wohnungsbauserie 70," 8.

[152] For more on Halle–Neustadt, see Albrecht Wiesner, "Gestalten oder Verwalten? Überlegungen zum Herrschaftsanspruch und Selbstverständnis sozialistischer Kommunalpoitik im Letzten Jahrzehnt der DDR," in Christoph Bernhardt and Heinz Reif, eds., *Sozialistische Städte zwischen Herrschaft und Selbstbehauptung: Kommunalpolitik, Stadtplanung und Alltag in der DDR* (Stuttgart: Franz Steiner Verlag, 2009), 69–94 as well as "steinerne Verheißungen einer sozialistischen Zukunft? Der Bau Halle–Neustadts aus gesellschaftsgeschichtlicher Perspektive" in Bernhardt and Wolfes, eds., *Schönheit und Typenprojektierung*, 229–58.

and a view of green space; indeed, even the grass in the enclosed area had trouble growing because of the lack of sunlight.[153] Repeated studies showed that one thing residents valued above all was a view of green space.[154] Perhaps the most concerning complaint about the closed-off spaces lacking light and green space in older prefabricated housing settlements stated that these settlements seemed to be, as one resident of Halle-Neustadt put it, just a "socialist" version of the old rental barracks.[155] Such a comparison between the GDR's Housing Program and the old misery quarters could not be allowed to stand. In contrast, the WBS 70 was clearly intended to be used in wide open spaces far outside the nineteenth- and early twentieth-century core of German cities, and many of the designs and diagrams depicting its use showed it in a wide-open, featureless landscape.[156]

Like the P2, the WBS 70 was a *Komfortwohnung*—it was equipped with modern amenities such as central heating, and individual, complete bathrooms with hot water, which set it apart from most of the pre-war buildings in the country. But it went further. There were garbage chutes and laundry rooms in the cellar, for example. The eleven-storey models had elevators, and the buildings were designed with central television antennae which fed each dwelling unit with a cable outlet, and which were controlled by a switch box in the cellar, which would be accessible by the building manager.[157] The antennae could get only the two main channels of state television, Channels 5 and 27, and no others—for example, they could not receive West German TV.[158] They could also be used for radio reception, with similar restrictions to GDR-only stations.[159]

But most of these improvements were limited to the buildings themselves. What made the WBS 70 a "system" was the fact that it was designed to be integrated into a complete settlement. In this way, it reflected a strong emphasis in the GDR among politicians and planners during the late 1960s and early 1970s on thinking in terms of "systems." Theorists at the DBA's Institute for Urban Development and Architecture (*Institut für Städtebau und Architektur*, ISA), including Bruno Flierl, espoused a philosophy of building all-encompassing, holistic systems that would seamlessly integrate the economy, daily life, space and materiality, technology, and the needs of the people themselves.[160] Mittag was

[153] BArch-BL DH2 23447 "Neubauwohngebiete im Urteil der Bewohner," 60.

[154] BArch-BL DH2 23428 Ule Lammert, BDA-ISA, Abt. Theorie und Geschichte, Themengruppe Städtebausoziologie, "Einige aktuelle städtebausoziologische Probleme der Gestaltung und Umgestaltung von Wohnbereichen" 1978, 77.

[155] BArch-BL DH2 23428, Lammert, "städtebausoziologische Probleme," 59.

[156] See Mercedes Sanchez-Cruz, "Städtebauliche Grundlagen für die Entwicklung der Wohnungsbauserie 70" in *Deutsche Architektur*, 1973.

[157] LA-B C Rep 110–05, Magistrat Berlin, Hauptauftraggeber komplexer Wohnungsbau, Nr. 15 "Grundsatzuntersuchung für Bauten in Stahlleichtbauweise 1974: Funktionsanlagerungen an WBS 70 (5- und 11-geschossig), 5.

[158] See Heather Gumbert's recent work, *Envisioning Socialism* for a detailed history of East German television.

[159] LA-B C Rep 110-05, "Stahlleichtbauweise."

[160] BArch-BL DH2 21729 Bruno Flierl, "Gesellschaft und Architektur in unserer Epoche: Ein Beitrag zur architekturtheoretischen Forschung in der ideologischen Auseinandersetzung zwischen Sozialismus und Kapitalismus" (dissertation approved by the scientific council of the DBA, April 20, 1972), 10–12.

also connected to the DBA-ISA,[161] and also advocated conceiving of building housing in terms of "complexes."[162]

The WBS 70 was intended to be used in the construction not only of housing, but of new cities, new environments, and ultimately entirely new lives. The planners at the DBA-ISA were concerned with making sure that Marzahn, and similar settlements, were not simply "bedroom cities" or, as the derogatory nickname had often been used, "worker silos" or "worker storage lockers" (*Arbeiterschliessfächer*). They wanted to recreate not only the functional elements of living, but also a sense of neighborhood and community, or *Kiez*; only, it would be a modern, rational feeling of *Kiez*, not the *Kiez* of the old working-class neighborhoods. Peters himself was deeply concerned about whether this new settlement could also recreate the feeling of a *Kiez*.[163]

One DBA theorist, ruminating on the meaning of a "socialist hometown feel" (*sozialistischen Heimatgefühls*),[164] postulated that it was the "sum of all the associations a person makes in all their sensory areas of memory or imagination in which their physiological, psychic, aesthetic and social needs are satisfied," and that, moreover, it was a product of familiarity, of layered experiences in which the satisfaction of needs occurs repeatedly within the same sensory environment.[165] Other studies showed that it was indeed the sense-memories associated with the *Kiez* feeling that residents in earlier prefabricated housing settlements missed the most, such as those who had complained about the functionalism of the eating centers in the older settlements, which were essentially large cafeterias.[166]

So as the architects and planners involved in Marzahn approached the challenge of devising a plan, it was clear to them that they were not simply just building housing, but rather an entirely self-contained city; one that would be a new home. As Roland Korn, the Chief Architect of Marzahn, wrote to Edmund Collein, the president of the German Federation of Architects in 1973, in a letter accompanying the first draft of the plans for Marzahn, "the urban planning solution to this new section of the city, a section which goes far beyond the framework of a normal residential area, means essentially the construction of a new, fully functional, city."[167] Heinz Graffunder, who worked on both the Palace of the Republic as well as the Marzahn plan, argued the same thing on the front page of the Party organ

[161] Mittag sat on Flierl's dissertation committee, for example. See BArch-BL DH2 21729, Flierl, "Gesellschaft und Architektur."

[162] BArch-SAPMO DY 2838 "Wohnungsbau," 348.

[163] Interview with Peters, February 20, 2008, Berlin.

[164] See Palmowski, *Inventing a Socialist Nation*, on a much fuller and richer description of how authorities in the GDR conceived of the notion of *Heimat* and how a specifically "socialist" *Heimat* could be constructed. He ultimately argues that "socialist" *Heimat* meant grafting socialist iconography and ideology onto pre-existing structures of local tradition and cultural memory.

[165] BArch-BL DH2 21686 "Zum Begriff sozialistischen Heimatgefühls," (no author) 1969.

[166] BArch-BL DH2 21686, "Heimatsgefühls," 35. The original plan for the 1967 Berlin-Lichtenberg settlement was to have one large and one intimate eating center, but the municipal district government had changed these plans after the construction of Lichtenberg because a club had demanded one of the halls be converted into a club room.

[167] BArch-BL DH2 21389 "Planung des neuen Stadtteiles Biesdorf–Marzahn, 1973–1975;" Letter from Roland Korn to Edmund Collein, December 19, 1973.

Neues Deutschland in 1973: the new settlement would be a proper city unto itself.[168] By 1975, it was clear to the Politburo that this new settlement would indeed be a self-contained world, and thus demand its own municipal administrative structure.[169] They therefore decided to create a new city district (*Stadtbezirk*), the ninth in East Berlin, just for the development, one formed from parts of the districts of Lichtenberg and Weissensee.[170]

What the name of the new ninth district would be was unclear at first; and the same was true of the settlement itself. In some instances, it was referred to as "Settlement Berlin North-east," in others "New Construction Settlement Biesdorf–Marzahn," or "Living Complex Biesdorf-North" because it touched on both the villages of Marzahn and Biesdorf.[171] In the final proposal that came before the Politburo in 1975, the name of the new district was written as "Biesdorf." To this, however, the Politburo objected; the working class would not allow itself to be moved to a "dorf"—a "village." Thus, the name of the new district, and the settlement itself, became *Marzahn*.[172]

The Politburo's decision for building Marzahn from 1973 called for the construction of 35,000 apartments to house 100,000 people. The construction was to begin in 1976, with 20,000 of the apartments being finished by 1980, and the rest by 1982.[173] The plan for Marzahn was created through the Berlin District Planning Commission, which worked in close cooperation with national organs of power, including the State Planning Commission and the Ministers' Council.[174] The carrying out of the entire project would be led by an *Aufbauleitung*, an executive council consisting of 100 members, led by Günter Peters.[175] The executive council consisted of a wide variety of experts—architects, engineers, geologists, hydrologists, sociologists, traffic engineers, etc., which attested to the totalizing and holistic character of the project being attempted.[176]

[168] Simone Hain, "Marzahn, das sozialistische Projekt zwischen rational choice und Diktatur" in Ylva Quiesser and Lidia Tirri, *Alle der Kosmonauten: Einblick und Ausblicke aus der Platte* (Berlin: Verlag Kulturring in Berlin e.V., 2005), 9–15, 11.

[169] Peters, "Arbeiterklasse," 47.

[170] Peters, *Hütten, Platten, Wohnquartiere*, 91. Also see Teresiak, "Der neunte Stadtbezirk wird gebildet" in *Links Rechts der Wuhle*, 2004, 48. This caused a problem in the context of the Cold War, however, because any fundamental changes to the city of Berlin, such as adding new districts, had to be agreed upon by the four occupying allied powers, meaning the Politburo and the Berlin Magistrat needed to seek the approval of the United States, Britain, and France to create this new municipal district, in theory at least. The Western powers did indeed protest against the creation, but were not willing to risk any kind of confrontation about it. See Bundesbeauftrage der Stasi Unterlagen (BStU) RS 496.

[171] Peters, *Hütten, Platten, Wohnquartiere*, 90.

[172] Peters, "Arbeiterklasse," 47.

[173] Taken here from LA-B C Rep 100 Nr. 1527, Berlin Magistrat, "Vorschlag zur Bildung eines Stadtbezirks auf Grundlage der territorial-ökonomischen Entwicklung im Raum Berlin–Lichtenberg," July 18, 1973.

[174] BA-BL DH2 21389 Magistrat der Hauptstadt der DDR, Berlin; Abt. Generalplanung, "Grundlagenmaterial für die Bebauungskonzeption des Stadtteils Biesdorf/Marzahn," October 15, 1973, 1.

[175] Hübner, Nicolaus, and Teresiak, *20 Jahre Marzahn*, 11.

[176] Peters, "Eine Aufbauleitung für Biesdorf–Marzahn," in *Links Rechts der Wuhle,* 2004, 49–50.

These groups were tasked by the Politburo with working ultimately towards "sociopolitical" and "people's economic" (*volkswirtschaftlicher*) goals;[177] this was code language for the incorporation of "real existing socialism" into the project, with calls not only for apartments and commercial spaces, but for ample provisions for senior homes, Kindergartens and schools, health clinics, playgrounds, and everything else needed to make Marzahn attractive and welcoming to families with young children.[178] The majority of the buildings, the District Planning Council decided, would be WBS 70 structures—60 percent of which were to be eleven-story, and 22 percent five-story models. Eighteen percent would be in the WHH GT twenty-two-story models, though this in reality would comprise a much smaller proportion of buildings, with essentially only five being built, mostly in the area of Helene-Weigel-Platz.[179]

To decide on a specific plan, the Berliner Magistrat and the Ministry for Construction held a competition, inviting three teams of architects within the GDR, one from Berlin, one from Rostock, and another from Leipzig, to submit plans to a jury. On March 26, 1974, the jury picked the plan submitted by the Berlin team led by Roland Korn, head architect of the city of Berlin. Korn's plan, described in more detail below, successfully combined the trends of architectural theory that had become dominant in the GDR, as well as the demands of the Politburo, both in achieving the target of 35,000 apartments, and the incorporation of "real existing socialism." Refined in 1975, it became the basis for Marzahn, and would be changed only insofar as it would be expanded later in the decade.

In Korn's plan, Marzahn would be platted as a strip on a north–south axis, 5.5 km long and 1.8 km wide. It was to be bordered on the west by the extension of the S-bahn line, which would follow the old Reichsbahn bed; on the opposite side of the tracks was the industrial infrastructure of the old Hasse and Wrede factory built by Speer, now the VEB Machine Tool Factory (*Werkzeugfabrik*). This factory would be the core of an expanded industrial zone, where many other state-owned factories and workshops would be built.[180] These would be the place of employment for a substantial number of Marzahners—there were over 2,300 employees of the VEB Machine Tool Factory alone, many of whom would get apartments in the new settlement (see chapter 4).[181] The Politburo had also decreed in 1975 that

[177] LA-B C Rep 902, File 3238, SED Bezirksleitung Berlin, "Vorlage für die Sekretär der Bezirksleitung, Beschlußentwurf über die Ordnung über die Aufgaben, Stellung und Arbeitsweise der Aufbauleitung Stadtteil Biesdorf/Marzahn," October 17, 1974, 2.

[178] LA-B C Rep 902, File 3255, SED Bezirksleitung Berlin, "Vorlage für die Politburo des ZK der SED. Betreff: Vorschlag für die Bebauungskonzeption des Stadtbezirks Biesdorf/Marzahn der hauptsatdt der DDR, Berlin," 1974, 3.

[179] LA-B C Rep 902, File 3255, "Bebauungskonzeption Biesdorf/Marzahn," 5. Of course, the decision to use almost exclusively WBS 70 buildings had essentially been made by the Politburo; such large decisions usually were, and the subordinate municipal and national organs had to reinforce and refine the decisions. Later, the Berliner Magistrat would make alterations to this quota, and raise the number of buildings built from the type QP 71, though WBS 70 buildings remained the majority by far.

[180] BArch-BL DH2 21389 "Planung des neuen stadtteiles Biesdorf–Marzahn; Information über die Beratung am 8.1.1974 zur städtebaulichen Lösung des neuen Stadtteiles Biesdorf–Marzahn,'" 1–3.

[181] Verein Kids & Co., ed., *Marzahn-Südspitze: Leben im ersten Wohngebiet der Berliner Großsiedlung* (Berlin: Bezirksamt Marzahn–Hellersdorf Abt. Ökologische Stadtentwicklung, 2002), 14.

approximately 60 percent of the residents in Marzahn should be workers.[182] On the east, Marzahn was bounded by the Wuhle river, a tributary to the Spree, along which a recreational area would be built. To the north, Marzahn was bordered by the village of Ahrensfeld, and the old sewage farms and the Falkenberg treatment facility. On its southern border, the settlement narrowed to a tip, known as the *Südspitze* ("southern point"), centered around a spring-fed pond, known as the *Springpfuhl*. A road, called Springpfuhlstrasse, but later to be renamed "Allee de Kosmonauten" was the southern border—and to the south lay the old village of Biesdorf.[183]

Marzahn was split into three sections, called "residential areas" (*Wohngebiete*, or WG)—similar to other housing settlements in the GDR, such as Leipzig-Grünau.[184] WG 1 was the first to be built, and encompassed the southern third of the settlement, including the Südspitze. WG 2 and WG 3 were to be built subsequently, in order, with the construction moving from south to north, each occupying a third of the total territory. WG 3 was essentially built over the old sewage fields, drenched with a century of filth spewed out from industrial and overcrowded Berlin[185] (see Figure 3).

The plan hewed close to the Corbusian model of "towers in a park." Each WG was to be filled with five-, eleven-, and in some cases twenty-two-story prefabricated apartment buildings, as well as numerous other prefabricated buildings. The predominant building type was the WBS 70—comprising 451 of the roughly 500—although two other types of prefabricated building models, called the QP 71[186] (a ten-story model) and the WHH GT (a nineteen- or twenty-one-story model) were also to be used.[187] The buildings were arranged in varying patterns, to avoid the dangers of "monotony" and to preserve a sense of openness and green space, which was to surround them. To this end, sculptures, murals, fountains and other forms of "art" were to be placed through the interstitial spaces, which were crisscrossed with footpaths and small parks and playgrounds. Also to this end, the buildings were to be color-coded, according to which WG they were in: WG 1 was yellow, WG 2 blue, and for WG 3, variations on the theme of "red."[188]

There were only four major traffic arteries, all named after prominent communists,[189] which described the borders of the settlement and each WG.[190] One of the arteries, Heinrich-Rau-Strasse (today Märkische Allee),[191] paralleled the S-bahn line, forming the western border of the settlement. Allee der Kosmonauten

[182] Hübner, Nicolaus, and Teresiak, *20 Jahre Marzahn*, 10.

[183] Hermann Zech, *Marzahner Strassennahmen. Ortsteil Marzahn.* (Berlin: Bezirksamt Marzahn von Berlin Abteilung Jugend, Familie und Kultur, Kulturamt/Heimatmuseum, 1994), 15–16.

[184] Kahl, *Erlebnis Plattenbau.*

[185] Peters, *Hütten, Platten, Wohnquartiere*, 96.

[186] "QP" stands for "Querwandbau in Plattenbauweise" and "71" for the date of its first design. Peters, *Hütten, Platten, Wohnquartiere*, 136.

[187] These statistics are taken from a permanent display at the Bezirksmuseum Marzahn-Hellersdorf.

[188] Hübner, Nicolaus, and Teresiak, *20 Jahre Marzahn*, 12.

[189] Hübner, Nicolaus, and Teresiak, *20 Jahre Marzahn*, 12. The Magistrat had in fact decided that most of the roads in Marzahn should be named after prominent anti-fascists and communists.

[190] BArch-BL DH2 21389 "Planung des neuen Stadtteiles Biesdorf/Marzahn," 3.

[191] Zech, *Strassennahmen*, 43.

was another major artery, forming the southern border and then turning northwards to form the eastern border of WG 1; on the other side was the old village of Marzahn. Otto-Buchwitz-Strasse (today Blumberger Damm),[192] a third artery, paralleled the Wuhle on the eastern border of WG 2, before turning west and becoming Henneckestrasse (today Wuhletalstrasse), following the Wuhle and becoming the border between WG 2 and WG 3. The most central artery, however, sliced through the middle of the settlement on an east–west heading: Leninallee (today Landsberger Allee) fed directly to downtown Berlin, and the other arteries fed into it. Streetcar and bus lines were planned to follow the main arteries, including 19 km of streetcar tracks;[193] all of these would stop at the S-bahn stations.

In fact, the Marzahn plan followed earlier thinking from the DBA-ISA about reconceiving traffic and living quarters in terms of "systems"—in particular, seeing all movement as a system, or a *Bewegungssystem* (movement system).[194] Cars were only one element of this system, integrating with pedestrians, bicycles, and public transportation.[195] Large, open, green spaces were to surround the residential buildings; sidewalks and bike paths would connect the buildings to each other, and to public transportation. Indeed, a minimum distance of 50 m between residences and any roadway had to be maintained.[196] This, in particular, was a major highlight of the plan—in every area Korn's team looked for the "shortest possible connection for pedestrians to reach public transit stops."[197] In practice, this meant that no residence should be more than 600 m from any public transit link.

According to the plan, *everything* should be within walking distance. No residence could be more than 600 m walking distance from any school or "KiKo" (short for *Kindergarten/Kinderkrippekombination*, a kind of Kindergarten, or preschool), nor from any sports field or recreation center, or health clinic.[198] And there was to be plenty to walk to. Over 200 "social facilities" (*Sozialeeinrichtungen*)—schools, clinics, restaurants, and sports and social institutions—were planned, each with a prefabricated "model" specific to it, aligned with the WBS 70. In addition, there were to be forty-one polytechnic high schools (*Oberschulen*), and forty-three

[192] Zech, *Strassennahmen*, 43.

[193] Peters, *Hütten, Platten, Wohnquartiere*, 102.

[194] BArch-BL DH 2 21686 G. Wessel, "Räumliche Ordnung und Bewegungssystem," DBA-ISA, Abt. Theorie und Geschichte der Architektur, December 1969. See also Rubin "Understanding a Car in the Context of a System: Trabants, Marzahn and East German Socialism" in Lewis Siegelbaum, ed., *The Socialist Car: Automobility in the Eastern Bloc*, (Ithaca, NY: Cornell University Press, 2011), 124–42.

[195] See BArch-BL DH 2 23501 Dipl. Ing. Grotewohl, Dr-Ing. S. Kress and Dr-Ing. W. Rietdorf, "Grundlagen für die Entwicklung neuer Wohnformen" DBA-ISA, Abt. Wohngebiete, Zwischenarbeit zu Thema 6, Arbeitsschnitt 2, August 31, 1970, especially p. 19, "Verkehr im Wohngebieten."

[196] Heiner Pachmann, "So klärt sich das Wasser: Zu einigen Aspekten der Umweltgestaltung im 9. Stadbezirk" *Der Neunte* (vol. 1, no. 7, 28 April 1977, 4).

[197] "Das erste Wohngebiet im neuen Stadtbezirk: Städtebauliche Erläuterungen (III)" *Der Neunte*, (vol. 1, no. 17, 15 September 1977, 4).

[198] BArch-BL DH 2 21389 "Grundlagenmaterial für die Bebauungskonzeption des Stadtteils Biesdorf/Marzahn" Magistrat Berlin, Abt. Generalplanungen 15 October 1973," 31. Again, it is important to note the date here; much of the Marzahn plan was already dictated by the Bezirksbaukommission, which in turn had been given very strict instructions from the Politburo, and so Korn's plan was a realization with detailed specs of these instructions.

KiKos (three of which were to be for developmentally disabled young children), built in three-storey models, each with a capacity of up to 180 children.[199]

Attached to these, within easy walking distance, were to be fourteen large and thirteen small school gymnasiums (*Schulturnhallen*), and eleven school sports facilities, which included tracks, soccer fields, volleyball areas, and smaller athletic fields. Another eleven sports recreation facilities were to be built for adults.[200] One of these was to be a central stadium with 5,000 seats.[201] Other social facilities planned included a home for troubled youths (*Heim für Jugendhilfe*),[202] which also had to be no more than 600 m from a polytechnic high school;[203] three pharmacies; up to nine retirement home/hospices, each of seven stories;[204] a central supply depot for gardeners; a music school with a rehearsal studio; an open-air theater with sufficient capacity to hold large festivals, including proper facilities for providing food and drink; and a youth hostel.[205] Later, the Politburo mandated that four churches (Catholic and Lutheran) be added to the plan, all from prefabricated concrete, with a starkly modern and minimalist design[206] (see chapter 5 for more on the role of these churches).

The plan also called for a 300-hectare natural recreational area (*Erholungsgebiet*) along the Wuhle river, to be patterned on the Volkspark Friedrichshain.[207] On the opposite bank from WG 2, in the jurisdiction of the village of Hellersdorf, there lay a natural elevation, known as the "Kienberg,"[208] rising to about 58 m in elevation,[209] making it the highest point around the flat, glacially planed *märkische* landscape. Here there was to be a kind of dry bobsled run called *Rödelbahn* down the hill which could become a real bobsled run in the winter; a bunny ski slope with a rope tow; hiking, biking, and cross-country ski trails; an adventure playground (*Abenteuerspielplatz*) and a beer garden.[210] In the adjacent lake, there were to be paddle boat rentals. There were also plans to dam the Wuhle to make an artificial lake roughly 60,000 m^2 in size.[211] In addition to the outdoor recreational area by the Wuhle, there were to be over thirty-five hectares of gardening plots,[212] and

[199] Peters, *Hütten, Platten, Wohnquartiere*, 106–7.

[200] BArch-BL DH 2 21389 "Grundlagenmaterial," 30.

[201] BArch-BL DH 2 21389 "Grundlagenmaterial," 30.

[202] BArch-BL DH 2 21389 "Grundlagenmaterial," 30.

[203] BArch-BL DH 2 21389 "Grundlagenmaterial," 32.

[204] Peters, *Hütten, Platten, Wohnquartiere*, 107. Nine is the total number built; it is unclear how many were originally planned, but likely less than nine.

[205] BArch-BL DH 2 21389 "Grundlagenmaterial," 30–3.

[206] Bezirksmuseum Marzahn, ed., *20 Jahre Marzahn*, 126–30.

[207] Graffunder, "Zur Projektierung des 9. Stadtbezirkes," *Der Neunte* (vol. 1, no. 8, 17 May 1977, 4–5).

[208] Graffunder, "Projektierung," 4–5, and Peters, *Hütten, Platten, Wohnquartiere*, 118. The hill was also known as the "Hellersdorfer Kippe," "Hellersdorfer Berg," or "Marzahner Kippe."

[209] Kitzmann, "Kienberg," 12.

[210] "Vorflutkanal wächst im Biesdorfer Grenzgraben" *Der Neunte* (vol. 2, no. 5, 2 March 1978, 2–3); as well as BArch-BL DH 2 21389 "Grundlagenmaterial," 32; Hübner, Nicolaus, and Teresiak, *20 Jahre Marzahn*, 14.

[211] BArch-BL DH 2 21389 "Grundlagenmaterial," 32.

[212] Peters, *Hütten, Platten, Wohnquartiere*, 96.

several wooded areas along the Wuhle and across it, into Hellersdorf, where future residents could enjoy the outdoors.

Each WG was to have its own "center" containing eating, drinking, and entertainment facilities, including a restaurant, a café, a milk bar, a food and dance hall, and a pub; a shopping center, including a grocery store (which had to be of at least 1,000 to 1,500 m^2) and several specialized shops; a collection point for recycling; a branch library and book store (which had to be at least 700 m^2); a service complex and housing repair shops; and a health-care center, including a facility for sports medicine and a public swimming pool.[213] In each center, there needed to be at least one high school and one school for special education.[214] Finally, there was to be a police station and an office for the local (*Kreis*) branch of the ruling SED party.[215]

In addition to the WG centers, there was to be one "municipal district center" (*Stadtbezirkszentrum*) that would serve as the administrative, commercial, and social center of the entire settlement. It was to be the "downtown" of Marzahn, further establishing it as an independent and self-sufficient community. The district center was to be built at the very southern tip—the *Südspitze*—of Marzahn and around a new square, later named Helene-Wiegel-Platz (after the wife of Berthold Brecht). It was to consist of the district municipal administration building (*Rathaus*) where the District Mayor (*Bezirksbürgermeister*) would be located, essentially Marzahn's "city hall," which would have a traditional "Rathskeller;"[216] the district courthouse and prosecutor's office; the main district library; restaurants with both German and international cuisine and a total capacity of 2,000 seats; a pub and a wine bar; a tourist hotel with 500–800 beds; a health-care center with a sports medicine facility; a bowling alley and a billiards hall; a swimming pool with a sauna; and a cinema (with a cloakroom).[217] Connected to the cinema would be a "district culture house" (*Kreiskulturhaus*) which could hold a restaurant, café, dance hall, youth dance hall, and a discotheque; with 700 seats, it could host district council meetings (*Stadtverordnetenversammlungen*), conferences, and major performances, and would have smaller meeting rooms for social clubs, gymnastics events, and other indoor sporting events.[218]

A massive central shopping center catered to every conceivable (at least from the planners' point of view) need that the WG shopping halls did not, including: a 10,000 m^2 department store; a 10,000 m^2 store for industrial wares (similar to a large hardware store); a 2,000 m^2 grocery store with specialized products, including a "rare vegetable" section, similar to a "gourmet" grocery store; a fine bakery with a café; a sports supply store; and a store for "art and cultural" goods, presumably

213 BArch-BL DH 2 21389 "Grundlagenmaterial," 28.

214 BArch-BL DH 2 21389 "Grundlagenmaterial," 29.

215 BArch-BL DH 2 21389 "Grundlagenmaterial," 30.

216 BArch-BL DH 2 21389 "Grundlagenmaterial," 28.

217 BArch-BL DH 2 21389 "Grundlagenmaterial," 25–6.

218 BArch-BL DH 2 21389 "Grundlagenmaterial," 25–6. The "district culture house" was among several elements of the plan directly inserted by the Politburo and the Berliner Magistrat—see Hübner, Nicolaus, and Teresiak, *20 Jahre Marzahn*, 12–16 for other examples.

to decorate the new apartment blocks.[219] A "house of service" would hold the bank, the tourist office, a dry-cleaners, a beauty products store, a tailor, repair services, and other commercial offerings. If at all possible, the planners hoped to put a dual ice/roller skating rink here as well.[220] There would also be a central post office, and a central telephone switchboard here.[221]

In short, Marzahn's planners had thought of everything. Or at least everything that they could reasonably have been expected to; the comprehensive nature of their planning bespoke their modernist ideology, and their extensive emphasis on social facilities revealed the influence of "real existing socialism's" focus on consumption, health care, education, recreation, and other aspects that constituted the "good life" as it was promised to East Germans. However, this "goulash communism" was not the only defining feature of Honecker's term as leader of the GDR. The 1970s and 1980s were the time when the power of the Stasi, and the Party, expanded tremendously. The planners also incorporated the physical structure of oppression and surveillance into the plan.

What this meant was that Helene-Wiegel-Platz also contained ample infrastructure for the organs of the Party and state involved in policing. These included a 2,500 m^2 facility for the district council (*Kreisleitung*) of the SED, and smaller facilities for each of the several "mass organizations"—state-run organizations such as the state-controlled workers' union (*Freie Deutsche Gewerkschaftsbund*, FDGB); the state youth organization (*Freie Deutsche Jugend*, FDJ); the smaller children's youth group, the Young Pioneers; the national gymnastics and sports organization (*Deutsche Turn- und Sportbund*, DTSB), and others. The district culture house also had special meeting and activity rooms designed specifically for the FDJ and the Young Pioneers. The Platz had a central police and civil defense (*Wehrkreiskommando*) post. One of the youth mass organizations, in addition to the FDJ, given official space in the complex in Marzahn's center was the Society for Sports and Technology (*Gesellschaft für Sport und Technik*, GST) which conducted pre-military training, such as shooting competitions, and was connected to the National People's Army. Most importantly of all, however, was the creation of a central District Office for the Stasi[222]—from the beginning the Stasi was present in the creation of Marzahn, reporting back to its headquarters in Normanenstrasse on every detail of the planning and construction of Marzahn, as we will see in Chapter 5.

It was important to provide not merely apartments and communal facilities but also the infrastructure that made these facilities and homes viable. In doing so, planners faced enormous logistical challenges. As mentioned, one of the great costs associated with building settlements like Marzahn was the cost of extending utilities from the old city to the margins. Planners thus had to find a way to supply the new apartments and buildings with water, electricity, heat, sewers, telephone lines,

[219] BArch-BL DH 2 21389 "Grundlagenmaterial," 25–6.
[220] BArch-BL DH 2 21389 "Grundlagenmaterial," 28.
[221] BArch-BL DH 2 21389 "Grundlagenmaterial," 21.
[222] BArch-BL DH 2 21389 "Grundlagenmaterial," 25–6.

gas, storm drainage, etc. In some cases, the earlier development of the Berlin North-east settlement had provided pre-existing infrastructure, as in the case of the building of the Falkenberg sewage treatment plant over the sewage farms in Ahrensfeld, begun in 1969 and already well underway—though it would need to be expanded, and others built as well.[223] For other utilities this was not the case, and eventually the plan was for facilities to be built in or just outside Marzahn, including a power station, a water works, and a brown coal heating plant that would pipe heat into every building unit. Until then, Marzahn would have to remain "tethered" to the utility lines of the inner city; branches from water mains, gas mains, power lines and so on would lead from the main lines out to Marzahn.[224]

These lines were all laid in underground tunnels, including one central tunnel called a *Sammelkanal*, which had several access points throughout Marzahn and was wide enough for workers to walk around inside. This tunnel contained the telephone and electricity lines, and heating and water pipes—supposedly enabling major cost-savings.[225] What is significant about the planning for the utilities in Marzahn was that although it was tremendously expensive—710 million East German marks[226]—to build an entirely new utility infrastructure for Marzahn, it revealed one important advantage of building a city from scratch: the utility lines could be laid down first, before anything else on the surface was built. The electricity, gas, heat, telephone, sewers and water would be easy to place, because every detail had already been planned out in advance; there needed to be only one laying-down of lines and mains, and never again would a street need to be ripped open for new utility work, as was often the case in crowded, older, capitalist-era cities. Indeed, the ability to secure a municipal water supply has been the defining, central event in the founding and development of cities from ancient times to the present, as urban historian Matthew Gandy[227] has recently noted.

As much as Marzahn may have seemed to be a *tabula rasa* in the middle of the Brandenburg plains, it was not, in fact, unpopulated. The development was to sit in the midst of the old villages of Marzahn and Biesdorf. Planners made an effort to build the new settlement around the old villages, using the open fields and forests north and south of old Marzahn. As will be covered in the next chapter, many houses were demolished anyway, but a pocket of older homes remained, which became surrounded on the north, west, and south by WG2. Most significantly, planners were determined to preserve the historical village center of Marzahn, including the old church, the cobblestone streets, and the old buildings lining the old town green (*Anger*), which included the old schoolhouse and the town pub, called the "Marzahner Krug" ("Marzahn Jug"). The old village center was to be preserved as a historic landmark and a living museum, a place where the new

223 BArch-BL DH 2 21389 "Grundlagenmaterial," 21.

224 Peters, *Hütten, Platten, Wohnquartiere*, 100–3.

225 Interview with Günter Peters, February 20, 2008.

226 Peters, *Hütten, Platten, Wohnquartiere*, 100.

227 Gandy, *Concrete and Clay: Reworking Nature in New York City* (Cambridge, MA: MIT Press, 2003), 32.

inhabitants could come and meet for a change of scenery;[228] in fact, ringed by five- and eleven-story WBS 70 units, it was to serve much of the same purpose as the green spaces—predating capitalism entirely, but rather tracing collective memories back to an earlier time of German colonization, the old village was sufficiently removed from any history of the working class and thus did not present a threat to the amnesiopolis of Marzahn.

Finally, the plan for Marzahn was not simply something that existed on paper and in the minds of architects and planners; it was put on display for the East German public to see. A scale model showing the settlement as it would come to exist was put on display in the Old Museum, the preeminent neoclassical museum in Berlin's "museum island" between April and May 1976.[229] Architects involved with the plan, including Heinz Graffunder and Günter Peters, welcomed school groups, visiting dignitaries, tourists from the West, and most importantly members of the Politburo and Central Committee, including Erich Honecker himself (see Figure 2). The exhibition was well attended; over 340,000 visitors came to see the scale model and the surrounding information panels.[230] The report from the executive council to the Berlin SED leadership naturally claimed that most of the opinions left by visitors in feedback forms deposited in boxes were overwhelmingly positive and filled with pride for the future of the capital city. Even many of the Western visitors, the council reported, were impressed and wanted to know more about the affordability of the new apartments—though some were so "intimidated" they chose to make provocative statements.[231] But communist countries had excelled in plans—the previous decade had seen plans for plastic socialist cities on the moon—and several generations of Berlin urban planners had also drawn up plans to embark on such ambitious projects. Now, in late 1976, it was time for the state, with all its control of the working class and heavy industry, to put its assets into motion. That summer, 7,000 workers converged on north-eastern Berlin, to make the plan a reality.

They were doing more than just excavating, laying pipe, and building prefabricated apartments—they were building a whole new city from scratch, one that would be socialist, literally and figuratively, down to its foundations. After a quarter-century in power, socialism was finally making good on its promise to deliver a better life to Germany's working class, by using the tremendous political and economic power that the East German state afforded it. After a half-century of planners looking to the north-east edge of Berlin as green fields on which to solve the "social question," they were finally rescuing Berlin's working class from the slums that had caused such misery for over a century.

In the *tabula rasa* of Marzahn, the East German state found itself able to directly transmit its ideological and economic structures into a material and spatial reality,

[228] BArch-BL DH 2 21389 "Planung des neuen Stadtteiles Biesdorf–Marzahn, 1973–1975," 3, and Peters, *Hütten, Platten, Wohnquartier*, 118–19.

[229] Hübner, Nicolaus, and Teresiak *20 Jahre Marzahn*, 15.

[230] LA-B C Rep 110 File no. 1347, "Einschätzung der Meinungen, Vorschlägen und Eingaben von Besuchern der Berlin-Ausstellung 1976," 1.

[231] LA-B C Rep 110 File no. 1347, "Einschätzung," 2.

unhindered by the "capitalist legacy" of the old urban spaces. As the next chapter details, the way Marzahn was built was the mechanism through which East German socialism became materially manifest, and was "in" every concrete panel, every balcony, and every stairwell, in the same way that capitalism and fascism had inhered in the phenomenological and spatial reality of the old rental barracks. What the construction workers, planners, political leaders, and residents of Marzahn also found, however, was that there never is a truly *tabula rasa*; memory, and history, are always there, even if they are hidden underground, waiting to be found by a hundred excavators.

2

Moonscape on the Mark

Socialism, Modernity, and the Construction of a New World

On April 11, 1977, the workers' brigade "Adolf Dombrowski" from the *Tiefbaukombinat* (underground engineering works) in Berlin began excavating the foundation for the first *Plattenbau* building of the Marzahn, a QP 71 ten-story tower.[1] The workers were the vanguard of an army of workers, numbering in the tens of thousands and drawn from all around the GDR, who would completely transform the idyllic small village and pastoral countryside into a modern socialist utopia in concrete over the ensuing thirteen years. During that entire time, this was also the largest construction site in Europe, a place where the utopian ideals to be manifest in the finished product were also to be expressed in its method of production. This chapter explores the construction of Marzahn, because to understand the nature of a built space, it is necessary to understand the process through which that space was built. The ways in which places are built reflect the political, economic, and ideological structures that surround them in unique ways—those structures absorb the meaning of those ideologies, and in this way they "radiate" them every day and all the time. Thus, political and economic meaning is transformed into a consciousness of everyday life.

The story of how this "concrete utopia" was built is significant for another reason. The overall narrative that enveloped the construction of Marzahn was one of pioneers or colonists terraforming a new city which would be socialist from the dirt up on a *tabula rasa*—the "green fields" outside the city. As such, it was a way of putting a discourse into practice, setting in motion a kind of confrontation not only with nature, but with history—the kind of history that is embedded in the natural environment. Digging into the soil under the "green fields" of Marzahn became, though unintentionally, a process of digging up the past of the *longue durée* history of Berlin, and north-eastern Germany more broadly. As much as Marzahn was meant to be a new start, a socialist city from scratch, its construction awakened a sense of a much deeper past that was a reminder that the GDR was only the latest in a long history of German attempts to colonize these lands.

[1] Hübner, Nicolaus, and Teresiak, *20 Jahre Marzahn*, 17.

"PIONEERS OF THE FIRST HOUR"

On January 1, 1977, the new S-bahn stop at Springpfuhl was opened, extending the line northwards from its previous terminus at Biesdorf. Afterwards, it began bringing an "armada" of workers, excavators, bulldozers, dump trucks, and other equipment to the mostly empty, open fields.[2] Virtually every available construction worker in Berlin was sent to the Marzahn project, but this was not enough to meet the figure of 7,000 or so workers necessary for the site, and so construction brigades had to be sent in from all across the GDR. In some cases, these were groups that had already worked on prefabricated housing construction projects; they were drawn especially from cities that had already completed significant prefabricated building projects, such as Rostock, Leipzig, and Gera.[3] Two-thousand of these were members of the Free German Youth (*Freie Deutsche Jugend*—FDJ, the SED's youth organization),[4] mostly in their late teens, sent to the site in order to gain key ideological and practical experience as part of their preparation to be part of the leadership class in the GDR, as well as to ensure that a cadre of politically motivated workers were part of the construction team. This recruitment program was the invention of the SED's Central Committee, which termed it the "FDJ Initiative Berlin."[5]

Most of the workers were housed in barracks constructed in front of a temporary parking lot, across from the southernmost tip, the *Südspitze* ("Southern Tip"), of the construction project,[6] where the first construction began, though some—mainly those who lived in Berlin—commuted using the newly opened S-bahn line.[7] The fact that they lived in barracks and came to complete this major, ideologically and politically important project in the middle of the "green fields" contributed to a sense among them that they were colonizers or settlers, transforming and domesticating an alien landscape, like medieval monks on a grange. Heinz Graffunder called these workers, as well as the engineers and planners who accompanied them, "pioneers of the first hour" who "prepared the ground." They were both "brave," and, Graffunder claimed, "homesick," in this far-away destination, beyond the pale of modern, socialist civilization.[8]

These settlers were not alone, though—they had the full support of the SED, which took pains to help create a sense of identity and community among the workers. So, for example, in December 1976 the SED's Berlin Secretariat passed a

[2] Verein Kids & Co., *Südspitze*, 2.

[3] Interview with Hielfried Kreuzer, Berlin, May 25, 2008.

[4] Hübner, Nicolaus, and Teresiak, eds., *20 Jahre Marzahn*, 27. On the role of the FDJ in state-owned enterprises (which included construction combines) see Kott, *Communism Day-to-Day*, 166–9.

[5] Bezirksmuseum Marzahn, ed., *20 Jahre Marzahn*, 9.

[6] Interview with Evelyn Marquardt, one of the first residents of the initial towers built on the *Südspitze*, Berlin, May 28, 2008.

[7] Though many from Berlin were forced to move with their families to the temporary housing built on site.

[8] Graffunder, "Zur Planung und Projektierung des 9. Stadtbezirkes," in *Der Neunte* (vol. 1, no. 8, 17 May 1977, 4–5).

resolution to start a newspaper just for the workers in Marzahn, called *Der Neunte* (*The Ninth*, a reference to the fact that a final decision on the name of the new city district, the ninth in East Berlin, had not yet been reached); in 1978, it would be renamed *Berlin-Marzahn Aktuell* (*Berlin-Marzahn Now*).[9] The construction site also had the feel of a rowdy outpost—a "Wild East" pioneer town. Fights and drinking were common,[10] as were high jinks, such as workers running time trials for their Trabants in the concrete-reinforced utility canals constructed to connect Marzahn to Berlin.[11]

ETERNAL RETURN: DIGGING UP THE PAST IN MARZAHN

Even before the first construction teams came to Marzahn, a significant amount of groundwork had been done on the site by excavation and utilities engineering (*Tiefbau*) brigades. This was important because as a total "system" Marzahn was to be built literally from the ground up, and so before any buildings were constructed the entire utility infrastructure, including the central canal, had to be put in the ground, so that the connections for sewer, water, gas, electricity, heat, telephone, etc. would already be in place exactly where the buildings' foundations were to be excavated and built. During the course of 1975 and 1976, over 1,200 engineers and workers laid this groundwork, which ultimately grew to include over 208 km of water mains, 337 km of sewage pipes, 247 km of heating pipes, 3,800 km of electric lines, and 3,750 km of telephone lines,[12] with 500 workers from nineteen factories alone working on the heating pipes.[13] A number of workers distinguished themselves in this initial phase, such as Peter Kaiser and Adolf Dombrowski, and were promoted to brigade leaders,[14] making them prominent players in the next phase of Marzahn's construction.

As the engineering teams began digging canals, they discovered that the blank canvas upon which they were building was not blank at all. On the surface, the area may have appeared to be open fields, but underneath the surface the history of Marzahn lay buried, which was really a record of the meaning of this area of Berlin and Brandenburg. Teams quickly found that there were archeological remains of the area's previous settlers. These included the original (or "Ur-") Germanic tribes of the late Stone to Bronze Ages; settlers who had left in the fifth century during the era of the Great Migration; and also the remains of the Slavic settlers who had in many cases built directly on top of the Ur-Germans. Over a hundred archeological sites were investigated, by a team under archeologist Heinz

[9] Hübner, Nicolaus, Teresiak, *20 Jahre Marzahn*, 16.

[10] The rowdiness and brawling was of great concern to the Stasi. See chapter 5.

[11] Interview with Peters, March 11, 2008, Berlin.

[12] Peters, *Hütten, Platten, Wohnquartiere*, 103.

[13] Manfred Berg, "Wärme für Berlin. Bauplatz Berlin." *Neue Berliner Illustrierte*, (vol. 35, no. 12, 26–9).

[14] Peters, *Hütten, Platten, Wohnquartiere*, 103.

Seyer of the Märkisches Museum, where the artifacts found were kept and put on display.[15] Among the discoveries were Ur-German vases and flint stones from the late Stone Age; the foundations of Ur-German and Slavic homes; jewelry, urns, and knives of both German and Slavic provenance;[16] and the most important was a near-intact Slavic fountain with an irrigation system discovered when an excavator struck it in October 1977.[17] Nor were Ur-German and Slavic remains the only ones found—the foundation of the original Romanesque church that was built for the very first German settlers by the Cistercian monastic order after the Askanian reconquest in the twelfth century was found not far from the nineteenth-century church in the middle of the village green.[18] The soil itself was inscribed with the *longue dureé* history of the Mark as a contested zone between Germans and Slavs.[19] It was, as Marzahn architect Wolfgang Eisentraut put it, "a reminder that this was not the first time that people had settled here."[20]

And the record of that contest did not end with the Cistercian settlement. The most recent episode of conflict in the area between Slavs and Germans was World War Two, specifically, the Battle of Berlin in April 1945. Almost as soon as they began digging, workers began to encounter the massive amounts of unexploded ordnance that had been buried in the sandy *märkische* soil around Marzahn. Workers grew accustomed to hearing the dreaded "dull clank" in the soil while digging.[21] A team of ordnance-removal specialists (*Munitionsbergungsdienst*) from the VP (*Volkspolizei*, the main police force in the GDR), stationed under Captain Heinrich Luthe in Potsdam, was called in to remove a four-ton air mine, twenty-two two-ton bombs, 1,863 incendiary bombs, eighty-eight mines, and nine rockets, as well over *one million* smaller pieces of ordnance, such as bullets, grenades, and artillery rounds, all potentially still live—by far the largest single task ever undertaken by Luthe's squad.[22] The widely read *Neue Berliner Illustrierte* (*NBI*) in the summer of 1978 depicted Captain Luthe as having ice water in his veins, able to

[15] Hübner, Nicolaus, and Teresiak, eds., *20 Jahre Marzahn*, 15.

[16] This information is from a display at the Bezirksmuseum Marzahn–Hellersdorf.

[17] Hübner, Nicolaus, and Teresiak, *20 Jahre Marzahn*, 15. Also see Heinz Seyer, "In Ur- und Frühgeschichtlicher Zeit" in Bezirksamt Marzahn von Berlin, ed., *1979–1999: 20 Jahre Bezirk Marzahn von Berlin* (Berlin: MAZZ Verlag, 1999), 17–19.

[18] LA-B C Rep 110-05 Nr. 20 "Dorfkern Marzahn," 4.

[19] In fact, the finds from Marzahn have contributed significantly to an archeological understanding of the Ur-Germans and Slavs who first settled the area, and subsequently towards a fuller picture of prehistoric Berlin. See Laurenz Demps, et. al., *Geschichte Berlins. Von den Anfängen bis 1945* (Berlin: Dietz Verlag, 1987), 32–45.

[20] Bezirksamt Marzahn von Berlin, Abt. Jugend und Kultur, ed., *20 Jahre Marzahn. Geschichte—Bauen—Leben* (Berlin: Holga Wende, 1999), 82.

[21] Elsewhere in Berlin, the amount of live ordinance buried in the soft and sandy soil became and remains a major problem for excavation and any kind of utility operations that require groundwork. On numerous occasions construction workers or highway teams have been injured and killed by accidentally striking unexploded ordnance, the most recent incident occurring in 2010 causing the death of three specialists trying to defuse a bomb dug up in Göttingen. It is estimated that one in eight bombs dropped on Berlin did not explode—and that almost 8,000 bombs have been defused since the 1980s in Berlin alone. See Eric Westervelt, "World War II Bombs Still Menace Germany," National Public Radio, <http://www.npr.org/templates/story/story.php?storyId=127476757>, accessed November 8, 2011.

[22] Peters, *Hütten, Platten, Wohnquartier*, 102.

"defuse a two-ton bomb on the spot with a screwdriver, magnifying glass, and tweezers...sometimes, a couple good whacks from a hammer is all he needs to take the fuse out of the explosive."[23] When Luthe was unable to disarm the bomb, it was detonated away from the construction site,[24] often on hill overlooking Ahrensfeld at the northern tip of Marzahn.[25]

What was significant about the *NBI* article about Luthe's work was the way in which it tied the work of the construction Marzahn to the task of erasing the legacy of World War Two. The bombs uncovered underneath Marzahn were the final traces of the "fascist war of conquest," and after "30 years have passed over this sandy soil and these fields." The magazine argued that Luthe's service to Marzahn was to finally bring closure to World War Two, so that "the traces of that war claim no more victims."[26] The article went on to repeat the famous quote from Harry Hopkins, flying over the ruins of Berlin with President Harry Truman on May 25, 1945, that Berlin was "the second Carthage." The author rebuked that statement, saying "we all know now that Harry Hopkins was wrong. Berlin is no Carthage. On the contrary, it is growing faster than ever. Out in the former village of Marzahn a modern living center is taking shape...this incredible pace of construction is certainly thanks in part to Captain Luthe and the ordnance removal team."[27] By 1978, the work of the ordnance removal squads was completely intertwined and fundamental to the overall construction of Marzahn. Because Marzahn represented a totalizing project, a completely new start from scratch, it required beginning with the soil, the laying of the utilities and the foundations, and therefore demanded a complete excavation of the inscriptions of violence that had been ingrained into the natural landscape of the area.

Other traces of the war were buried in the sand around Marzahn. Just to the western side of what would become the S-bahn tracks lay one of the largest cemeteries in Berlin, the Parkfriedhof Marzahn. It too was a dumping ground of sorts for the inner city—originally built as a paupers' graveyard, political prisoners executed in the Nazi prison at Plotzensee were buried there. It then became one of the largest depositories of victims of the bombing in Berlin—almost 5,000 are buried there, along with a smaller number of Polish slave laborers killed in bombings.[28] The two artificial mountains in Marzahn—the Ahrensfelder Berg and the Kienberg—were both originally made from rubble hills made of the detritus of Berlin's destroyed buildings in World War Two.[29] The construction teams

[23] Frank Kunold, "Ein Bombenkerl" *Neue Berliner Illustrierte*, (vol. 34, no. 26, 10).

[24] Kunold, "Ein Bombenkerl," 9.

[25] Rolf Semmelmann, "Künstliche Berge," *Links Rechts der Wühle 2004*, 6.

[26] Semmelmann, "Künstliche Berge," 10. [27] Semmelmann, "Künstliche Berge," 10.

[28] Fritz Knöfel, "Marzahner Gedanken und Erinnerungen" in Bezirksamt Marzahn, *1979–1999: 20 Jahre Bezirk Marzahn von Berlin*, 204 and Barbara Ludwig, "Der Friedhof am Wiesenburger Weg" in the same volume, 201–2. For more on the fascinating history of cemeteries, burial, and notions of death in twentieth-century Berlin, see Monica Black, *Death in Berlin: From Weimar to Divided Germany* (New York: Cambridge University Press, 2010).

[29] Kitzmann, "Natürlich, reizvoll, unverkäuflich," 12.

deposited most of the nearly two million cubic meters[30] of soil excavated from the digging of 1,293 foundations in Marzahn on the two "mountains," burying the past even further.[31] And yet, even here, the buried past had a way of refusing to be buried, as erosion and desire paths worn by hikers along the sides of the hills would occasionally reveal pieces of rubble.[32]

The past that would not (easily) pass away found form in intact structures as well. Although Marzahn and Biesdorf were small villages, they nonetheless contained well over a thousand residents whose homes stood in the way of the construction plan for Marzahn, which called for the demolition of 575 dwellings, most of them small houses, as well as the removal of 35 ha of small garden plots.[33] In total, about 475 out of 931[34] families that lived in Marzahn before the construction of the new housing settlement were going to have to move,[35] often out of the homes that had been in their families for generations.[36] In the GDR, municipal and national authorities could be granted "eminent domain" (or *Baufreiheit*) to evict property owners for projects such as Marzahn, provided they offered suitable compensation. In this case, most of the residents being evicted were offered apartments in the new QP 71 and WBS 70 high-rise blocks, which many accepted.[37] In some cases, people ended up in high-rise blocks almost directly over the spot where their family home had once been,[38] with preferential treatment given especially for elderly residents.[39] Not all residents were so pliant, however, refusing to move, and writing *Eingaben* to the Party and state, even after personal house calls by Roland Korn and Günter Peters.[40] In the end, Korn and Peters relented, and changed the plan, especially for WG 2—essentially building that section around the houses that were spared, which amounted to eighty-three homes out of the scheduled

[30] Peters, *Hütten, Platten, Wohnquartiere*, 103.

[31] Peters, *Hütten, Platten, Wohnquartiere* 103.

[32] See Jonas Kolenc and Monica Blotevogel, *Fremdenführer Marzahn* (Berlin: Kinderring Berlin and "Aktion Mensch"/Bezirksmuseum Marzahn-Hellersdorf and Marzahner Tor GWG, 2004), 27. One can also find these by exploring the two hills.

[33] Daniela Schnitter, "Der Bezirk Marzahn-Skizzen zur geschichtliche Entwicklung." <http://www.heimatvereinmarzahn.de/downloads/biesdorf.pdf> (accessed November 10, 2011). Schnitter claims that "about" 500 dwellings were to be torn down (see the following note for how this compares with other sources, as this is still a politically sensitive issue).

[34] Hübner, Nicolaus, and Teresiak, eds., *20 Jahre Marzahn*, 14. Günter Peters, in *Hütten, Platten, Wohnquartiere*, 98, claims the scheduled number was 324. It is important to note that Peters' tone tends often towards the apologetic in politically sensitive issues such as the GDR's use of eminent domain to build Marzahn, as he claims that, in relation to the total number of apartments constructed, the number torn down was miniscule, so in this particular case it seems more likely that the figures from Hübner, Nicolaus, and Teresiak, who were working on behalf of the Marzahn Heimatsmuseum and thus not necessarily in a position to defend the *Plattenbau* settlement, are correct.

[35] LA-B C Rep 903-01-03 (Kreisleitung der SED Berlin-Lichtenberg), file 474, "Konzeption sur Durchführung von Versammlungen und Aussprachen mit den im Wohnbezirk 76 in Marzahn wohnenden Bürgern über die Vorbereitung des Komplexen Wohungshaus im Stadtbezirk Nr. 9 (Biesdorf/Marzahn) und die Erhaltung und Räumung von Wohngrundstücken," 7.

[36] Verein Kids & Co., *Südspitze*, 26.

[37] Verein Kids & Co., *Südspitze*, 27.

[38] Verein Kids & Co., *Südspitze*, 27.

[39] LA-B C Rep 903-01-03, file 474, 4.

[40] LA-B C Rep 100 (Berlin Magistrat), file 6919 "Vorschläge zur Reduzierung der Wohnungsbauabrisse im 9. Stadtbezirk (Biesdorf/Marzahn)" 2 October 1975.

575.[41] This was one of the reasons the nature recreation park was never completed.[42]

The original Korn plan envisioned keeping and preserving parts of the old village, which contained the oldest buildings, many of which went back to the 1700s. In 1977, certain buildings, such as the church in the center of the village green, were placed under protection as historic landmarks. A subsequent study by the *Aufbauleitung*, led by its new head, Heinz Graffunder, in 1981, recommended that only certain buildings be preserved and renovated, and others be demolished.[43] All residences were to be torn down or otherwise removed; an area of barns and agricultural buildings just to the north, and the old schoolhouse, were razed.[44]

The parts of the old village to be preserved enjoyed this fate only insofar as they represented a kind of ornamentation to the prefabricated housing blocks. This was illustrated perfectly by the case of the windmill adjoining the village green. For most new Marzahners and visitors, the old village center is decorated by a large wooden windmill adjacent to the north end of the village green, just off the Allee der Kosmonauten, which appears to be from the seventeenth or eighteenth century. This windmill still adds a level of quaintness sufficient to soften the harshness of the surrounding prefabricated concrete high-rises. Indeed, until the 1970s there had been several such quaint wooden windmills, many of them several centuries old. All of them were torn down. However, in 1978, a member of the *Aufbauleitung*, Hans Joachim Müller, set about reassembling the various planks, gears, and blades left from the destroyed windmills, and rebuilt a pastiche version. So it can be seen that, even where it preserved the past, Marzahn did so in such a functionalist way that the past became as artificial and inauthentic as the WBS 70 and the utility canal. This kind of functionalist, artificial reconstruction of the past was in keeping, actually, with the activities of the DBA in the center of Berlin, for example in the Nikolaiviertel or on Wilhelmstrasse. Not that it mattered to new Marzahners: to get a WBS 70 or QP 71 apartment with a balcony view of the windmill was highly desired, and it became a favorite destination of school trips, picnickers, and those enjoying a walk.

RECREATING A GREEN UTOPIA

Like most pre-modern societies, the various settlers who had populated Marzahn and the surrounding villages of Ahrensfeld, Hellersdorf, and Biesdorf had existed in a kind of organic symbiosis with the natural environment, even if they were settlers from other parts of Europe. According to Heidegger, one of the hallmarks of modernity is the upsetting of that symbiosis; the objectification or instrumentalization of nature into pure "being at hand." The prefabricated housing

[41] Hübner Nicolaus, and Teresiak, eds., *20 Jahre Marzahn*, 14.

[42] Hübner, Nicolaus, and Teresiak, eds., *20 Jahre Marzahn*, 14.

[43] Peters, *Hütten, Platten, Wohnquartiere* 119.

[44] LA-B C Rep 110-05 file 20 "Dorfkern Marzahn."

settlement of Marzahn was among the highest expressions of such modernity. If pre-modern Marzahn was an organic symbiosis, then its beating heart may well have been the Wuhle river that ran from its source north of Marzahn and down through Marzahn, Hellersdorf, Biesdorf, Maulsdorf, Kaulsdorf, Kopenick, and eventually into the Spree river near the Muggelsee. It was the river that was the reason for the many settlements over time; along the banks of the Wuhle were discovered archeological remains much older than the Ur-Germanic settlements found in Marzahn. A team building supports for a bridge over the Wuhle stumbled upon a mask made of a deer skull believed to be from the middle Stone Age, about 6000 BC.[45] Other archeological excavations in the area along the river's banks discovered remains from the early Stone Age, around 9000 BC—in other words, only shortly after the glaciers of the last Ice Age had receded, shaping the north German sea plain and creating the hydrogeology of the Spree river valley, including the Wuhle itself.[46] In both cases, the settlers had been of a culture so old they could not even be thought of as Germanic. The Wuhle had been the source of commerce, recreation, and biodiversity—along its banks could be found a plethora of plant, insect, and animal species that were difficult to find elsewhere in the Berlin–Brandenburg area.[47] The Wuhle was central to the ecosystem of the slightly elevated tableau which stretched from north-east Berlin to the Oder river valley, known as the "Barnim High Plain" (and sometimes the "Berliner balcony"), which drains into the Berlin–Warsaw glacial valley (*Urstromtal*), the center of which is the Spree river.[48]

The *Aufbauleitung* completely altered the nature and purpose of the Wuhle. If the Wuhle had been the area's heart, the GDR ripped that heart out, replacing it with an artificial heart made of concrete, metal and PVC piping. Landscape engineers diverted the Wuhle, and built an artificial riverbed and riverbank, not unlike an urban aqueduct, and made of the same prefabricated concrete panels used for the surrounding buildings—widening and deepening the riverbed substantially in the process, to a width of 15 m over a stretch of 18 km.[49] The source was no longer a natural pond near Ahrensfeld; instead, the newly constructed Falkenberg sewage treatment facility became the source of the Wuhle.[50] The underground storm runoff mains which had been laid by the engineering teams in 1975 and '76 led directly to the new concrete riverbed, turning the new, artificial Wuhle into, essentially, a spillway and runoff canal, able to absorb a maximum capacity of 20 m^3 of water per second.[51]

[45] Verein für Technologie, Produktivität und Umweltschutz e.V., *Zwischen Spree und Barnim: Das südliche Wuhletal,* (Berlin: Bezirksamt Marzahn-Hellersdorf von Berlin, Abt. Ökologische Stadtentwicklung Natur- und Umweltamt, 2001), 11.

[46] Verein für Technologie, Produktivität und Umweltschutz e.V., *Zwischen Spree und Barnim*, 12, and *passim.*

[47] Verein für Technologie, Produktivität und Umweltschutz e.V., *Zwischen Spree und Barnim*, 4 and 10.

[48] Verein für Technologie, Produktivität und Umweltschutz e.V., *Zwischen Spree und Barnim, passim.*

[49] Peter Müller, "Die Wuhle erhält ein neues Bett" *Der Neunte* (vol. 1, no. 4n, 17 March 1977, 3).

[50] Pachmann, "So klärt sich das Wasser," 4.

[51] Verein für Technologie, Produktivität und Umweltschütz, ed., *Zwischen Spree und Barnim*, 6.

Near the base, Kienberg, the Wuhle was to be partially dammed, to create an artificial lake that would be the key focus of the "nature recreation park."[52] This would be the lake that was supposed to offer paddle and rowboat rentals, as well as a large recreational swimming area and sunbathing beach.[53] That the water was essentially treated sewage from the Falkenberg plant was apparently of no concern; neither was the fact that the other source of the artificial lake was the enormous storm runoff drains—two main ones in particular of over 600 m in total length, built by the Becker and Wegener Brigades of the VEB Tiefbaukominat Berlin, that would empty out into the lake, to supply it with volume.[54] *Der Neunte* claimed that the re-engineering of the Wuhle was an improvement on nature, which would allow clean, clear, "highly purified" water to flow over the sterile white concrete panels, rather than the "polluted and foul-smelling rivulet (*Flüßchen*)" that it had become due to the drainage of the sewage farms.[55] Whatever the Wuhle had been for the humans, fauna, and flora that lived with and by it stretching back to its creation at the end of last Ice Age, was irreversibly shattered and reconstituted in concrete, steel, and PVC.

This treatment of the Wuhle was not unique within the GDR, which carried out similar projects to straighten and control other rivers, such as the Oder, as David Blackbourn's work explores. Indeed, the socialist planners of the GDR and the USSR saw nature as "there to be beaten into submission," as Blackbourn puts it.[56] They wanted not only to change nature, but to "control it."[57] This said, it should be noted that Blackbourn also locates the desire to "tame" the Oder-Spree water system in a much older tradition stretching back to the Enlightenment, in particular Frederick the Great's schemes for improving the unruly and wild eastern Marches of Brandenburg,[58] or in some cases stretching back to the Cistercians who first drained the swamps in the Oder valley, including in Marzahn, in the thirteenth century.[59]

It was not only nature that was being "conquered" on Berlin's north-eastern edge, however. Or rather, nature was not being conquered for the sake of conquest alone—it was ultimately a way of conquering *human* nature, or at least the "nature" of human society. Specifically, an important part of the reconstruction of Marzahn's nature was the re-creation of its green spaces and its flora in general. Fresh air and abundant green spaces: these were among the most important characteristics of Marzahn (as well as the many other prefabricated housing settlements in the GDR

[52] Heiner Pachmann, "Auch hier soll man singen können: Es grünt so grün . . . : zu einigen Aspekten der Umweltgestaltung im 9. Stadtbezirk (I)" *Der Neunte* (vol. 1, no. 6, 14 April 1977, 4). The term used in this source is "*Staubauwerk*."

[53] Pachmann, "Es grünt so grün," 4.

[54] "Vorflutkanal wächst im Biesdorfer Grenzgraben" *Der Neunte* (vol. 2, no. 5, 2 March 1978, 2–3).

[55] Pachmann, "So klärt sich das Wasser," 4.

[56] Blackbourn, *Conquest of Nature, Water, Landscape and the Making of Modern Germany* (New York: W.W. Norton, 2006), 337.

[57] Blackbourn, *Conquest of Nature*, 336.

[58] See Blackbourn's first chapter, "Conquests from Barbarism," in *Conquest of Nature*, 21–76.

[59] Blackbourn, *Conquest of Nature*, 5.

and beyond). In this, the plan for Marzahn reflected the influence of earlier planners, from Camillo Sitte to Martin Wagner,[60] but especially Le Corbusier. It had been Le Corbusier's maxim that transporting the working classes into verdant surroundings with clean air and sunlight would civilize and placate them, thereby preventing a revolution. Ironically, though the GDR was supposed to be the product of that very revolution, it still sought the same kinds of solutions to the same problems that produced that revolution—and thus implemented the same socio-spatial dialectic that had been advocated by planners who were themselves not communists at all, like Le Corbusier.

The scale of the greenery implemented in Marzahn was as impressive as the work in concrete and earth. The tree, claimed the premier East German architectural journal *Deutsche Architektur*, was a crucial element in constructing urban space.[61] The Barnim High Plain, claimed *Der Neunte*, had been almost "devoid of trees," with just a few "protruding" from the croplands.[62] Of course, as William Cronon has argued, what is assumed to be the original or "first" nature is often the product of earlier transformations by humans.[63] In both the case of the Barnim Plain and the North American prairie, the "original" nature was forest. In this light, the GDR's alterations to the landscape were just the latest in a "deep history" of alterations to the landscape by humans, stretching back to the Stone Age.

Of course, as Blackbourn notes, what is different in the twentieth century is the scale and organization of projects designed to tame and reconstitute nature. This was true especially in the GDR, which, because of its control over its economy, could muster so many cadres of experts, technicians, and resources for its projects. Among the army of construction workers, engineers, geologists, and hydrologists, etc. was a battalion of forestry workers and landscape engineers, mostly from the VEB *Forstwirtschaftsbetrieb* (forestry company) Berlin, as well as the forestry companies in Potsdam, Oranienberg, and Strausberg, and the Berlin city parks office (*Stadtgartenamt*). Their first project was to blanket a stretch of ground including the recreation area and the Kienberg northwards along the Wuhle to the Ahrensfelder Berg with new trees and other plants.[64] Over 38,000 trees were planted in this stretch bordering WG 2 and WG 3. Like everything else in Marzahn, the planting was done serially, according to the techniques of mass production. The ground was torn up, and a boring machine drilled holes in rows into which the trees were inserted by the VEB forestry workers. Hans-George Büchner, the head landscape architect, wanted to achieve a "diversity" of tree types in the "shortest possible time." Broadleafed trees, mainly linden, ash, chestnut, maple, oak, and rowan, made up the bulk of the 38,000 saplings brought in from the VEB's enormous tree

[60] See Jackisch, "Green Space," 312.

[61] Wessel & Zeuchner, "Zur städtebaulich-räumlichen Gestaltung," 218–19.

[62] Pachmann, "Es grünt so grün," 4.

[63] See Cronon, *Nature's Metropolis: Chicago and the Great West* (New York: WW Norton, 1992).

[64] "Linden und Eschen für unsere Neunte," *Der Neunte* (vol. 1, no. 4, 17 March 1977, 4).

nursery.[65] Later, a second round of industrial planting would provide evergreens such as pines and larches.[66] Other machines leveled all surrounding vegetation, to eliminate any harmful "weeds" in the area. Then, in addition to the trees, over 20,000 holes were bored for shrubs, which followed in quick succession. A 1600-meter-long fence surrounded the area to keep out any herbivores tempted to eat the saplings and young bushes.[67]

The mass planting of shrubs and trees was not limited to the area between the Kienberg and WG 3, however. Trees and shrubs were intended to line the entrances to the high-rise buildings, the stores and schools, parks and pathways between buildings, as well as simply populate parts of the open green spaces throughout Marzahn.[68] The landscape architects aimed for "ecological diversity," which meant planting mainly oaks, ashes, trees-of-heaven, and poplars—the latter famous for their fast growth and known to thrive especially in the sandy soil of the Barnim High Plain—as well as evergreens such as Douglas firs and larches.[69] The residents of Marzahn should be able to "unmistakably" see green as the predominant color when they looked outside their window, according to the settlement's planners.[70] Some residential buildings would be given a predominance of one type of tree or another, so that they could be known as the "chestnut house" or the "maple house" (*Kastanienhof* and *Ahornhof* respectively.)

The planting of trees and bushes around the residential buildings and schools, however, was not accomplished solely or even mostly by industrial assembly-line tactics, but rather by the new residents of Marzahn themselves, and in this the flora of the new utopia took on yet another important meaning, which will be explored in the next chapter; more important than the types of trees planted was the process by which this planting took place. For the initial work, the important point here is that even as Marzahn's planners thought of themselves as creating a green utopia, the green was still artificial. The "diversity" of the trees was the diversity of the state-run nursery; little attention was paid to native plant species, and instead the fastest-growing trees, such as poplars, or trees that were not native to the Barnim Plain, such as trees-of-heaven (originally from China), were planted. To the new residents, such distinctions may not have been noticeable, but for those who remembered the old way of life the new trees were as foreign as the high-rise living blocks. Still, it should be pointed out that often the reason for the need to have residents take part in landscaping was because the manpower and material for the landscaping efforts were subordinated to the construction of the buildings themselves.[71]

[65] "Linden und Eschen," 4. Also, Peters, *Hütten, Platten, Wohnquartiere*, 118.

[66] Pachmann, "es grünt so grün," 4.

[67] Pachmann, "es grünt so grün," 4.

[68] Rühle, Leiter Freiflächnprojektierung, "Für jeden etwas!" *Der Neunte* (vol. 2, no. 8, 13 April 1978, 4).

[69] Rühle, "Für jeden etwas!," 4.

[70] Pachmann, "es grünt so grün," 4.

[71] Interview with landscape architect Stephan Strauss, in Quiesser and Tirri, *Allee der Kosmonauten*, 74.

CRANES AND COSMONAUTS: CONSTRUCTION SITES AS PROPAGANDA

All the work to prepare the utilities, reconstruct the Wuhle and the Kienberg recreation area, and to replant Marzahn was really only preparation for the main task: the accelerated mass production of the buildings that would be the core of the new city. The construction of Marzahn began in 1977, and continued all the way until after the fall of the Berlin Wall in 1990. It was, in effect, a gigantic assembly line, involving over 40,000 workers, several factories, construction and engineering teams, and specialists from all around the GDR and even abroad, bound together under one umbrella organization called a Apartment Building Combine (*Wohnungsbaukombinat*, WBK; in this case, the VEB *Wohnungsbaukombinat* Berlin.)

The process was simple—this was the point. It followed a pattern established in the USSR, called the "Slobin method."[72] Cement factories delivered (mostly) Portland cement[73] to a prefabricated panel factory (*Plattenwerk*). The cement was poured into wooden molds with steel rebar lattice already laid inside, and then either hung to dry or placed under hot-air driers.[74] In some cases the panels were sprayed with water to help prevent cracking during the drying process.[75] There were a limited number of panel molds: panels with windows, panels with doorways, and interior wall panels. There were generally panels made only for the WBS 70 and QP 71 models. In some cases, such as the bathrooms, there was enough detail and variation that the entire bathroom unit (not including hardware) could be made in the factory, to be transported later to the construction site.

The GDR already had factories capable of making concrete panels, as did other Eastern Bloc countries. After all, it had already experimented with P1 and P2 prefabricated housing. But the GDR did not have a factory able to handle the volume of output—as much as four million tons of concrete paneling[76]—that was going to be needed to feed a construction assembly line on this scale. Nor did it have the technology necessary to build one.[77] Even if it had, it did not have the economic capacity to ramp up production of cement to the level necessary to feed the panel factory—and neither was there a possibility of importing cement from other CMEA

[72] BA-L DY 30/2838 Wohnungsbau in Berlin Bd. 4 1972–3, 350. The Slobin method was named after Nikolai Slobin, a Soviet construction brigade leader lionized in the wake of Khrushchev's housing program for his Fordist "method," similar to Andrei Stakhanov. See "Was ist die Slobin-Methode?" *Der Neunte* (vol.1 no. 9, 26 May 1977, 3).

[73] In some cases, "slag cement" (*Hüttenzement*), which is stronger and less expensive than Portland, was used, produced by a factory outside Marzahn on the Leninallee. See Ines Lindenthal, "Durch Umbau an der Mischanlage: 10,000 Tonnen Portlandzement durch Hüttenzement ersetzt," *Marzahn Aktuell* (vol. 6, no. 12, 15 July 1982, 3).

[74] Hannelore Dannenberg, "Man muß es wollen: Über den Jugendbrigadier Volker Gneist." *Neue Berliner Illustrierte* (vol. 37, no. 44, 6).

[75] Interview with Klaus Langer, Berlin, August 14, 2012. Langer, a leading engineer at the Hohenschönhausen plant, also noted that not all panels were made with rebar inside.

[76] Franz Marczak, "Wo kamen die Betonfertigteile her?" in Bezirksamt Marzahn von Berlin ed., *1979–1999*, 62.

[77] BA-L DY 30/2838 Wohnungsbau in Berlin Bd. 4 1972–3, 350.

countries.[78] Everyone in the Eastern Bloc was undergoing preparations for a prefabricated apartment building program simultaneously. Cement was the new gold.

The solution for the GDR was to turn to the USSR and non-CMEA countries for help. To expand the ability to mass-produce cement, the GDR had the Institute Giprocement Leningrad build a new, large cement factory in Eichsfelder, known as the Deuna Cement Works, in 1975. The Deuna factory was able to add 2.5 million tons of cement a year to the GDR's yearly output of just under 10 million tons.[79] This factory came at a cost of just under one billion marks.[80]

Then came the need to construct a panel factory. For the WBS 70 and QP 71 series, each apartment consisted of twenty-six discrete prefabricated pieces.[81] The only factory able to supply concrete panels was a small facility in neighboring Hohenschönhausen, which was known for its high quality but could not keep up with the demand. No one—not even the Soviet Union—had the technology to build a factory to the specifications necessary for the WBS 70. Instead, the GDR turned to Finland. Like the Swedes, Finland attempted where possible during the Cold War to position itself firmly between the Soviet Bloc and the capitalist West, able to hold diplomatic and economic relationships with both sides. In particular, the embrace of practical modernism in both furniture and architecture in Scandinavia—which became famous for designers like the Finn Alvar Aalto and brands like Lego and Ikea—carried over into the GDR and other Eastern Bloc countries such as Czechoslovakia.

So too with prefabricated housing: it was a Finnish corporation, Partek, that sold the panel factory to the GDR that became the source for the WBS 70 and QP 71 panels.[82] The factory was superior to anything that the GDR or the USSR could build; for one thing, it could be partially automated, so that not every panel mold had to be filled by hand. This clearly provided the kind of production rate necessary to carry out a project on the scale of Marzahn. Furthermore, the Partek factory could add a level of technical variation to the panels that existing East German technology could not, and variability was a key concept for the WBS 70.[83] Furthermore, it used advanced hydrological technology to maintain consistent moisture levels within the aggregate in the panels, which could prevent future cracking or chipping.[84] Finally, it also provided technology that enabled using different basic colors on the borders of balconies and other panel pieces, which would fulfill the color-coding scheme for each WG, again, to uphold "variability" and prevent "monotony." The Finnish factory could produce over fifteen complete apartments *per day*.[85]

[78] BA-L DY 30/2838 Wohnungsbau in Berlin, 429–30.

[79] BA-L DY 30/2838 Wohnungsbau in Berlin, 429. A new cement factory had just been built in 1973 in Karsdorf, with a yearly capacity of 2.2 million tons, but this was only enough for the needs of the economy pre-Marzahn. Marzahn was to use so much cement it would demand its own new cement factory.

[80] BA-L DY 30/2838 Wohnungsbau in Berlin, 429.

[81] Marczak, "Betonfertigteile," 61.

[82] Peters, *Hütten, Platten, Wohnquartiere*, 94.

[83] Peters, *Hütten, Platten, Wohnquartiere*, 94.

[84] BA-L DY 30/2840 Letter from Ministerium für Bauwesen, September 5, 1977.

[85] BA-L DY 30/2840.

The Finns delivered the entire factory to its location on Gehrenseestrasse (which had previously been Falkenbergerstrasse) in neighboring Hohenschönhausen, constructed it, and then trained the East German workforce, almost 4,000 workers, half of which were part of the "youth initiative" of FDJ members,[86] such as the "Youth Brigade Volker Gneist."[87] The total cost of the factory was 620 million marks,[88] although this had to be paid in hard currency, which was always extremely scarce for the GDR. To underscore the importance of the deal, both in terms of the foreign policy and the export economy of Finland, the president of Finland himself, Urho Kekkonen, was present for the inauguration of the factory in 1977 (along with VIPs from the Politburo, the Berlin Magistrat, and the Berlin branch of the SED).[89] Clearly, when it came to the Housing Program, the GDR was going to spare no expense, and Finland's positioning itself as politically neutral towards the Soviet Bloc, as well as more technologically advanced and more experienced with the kinds of urban planning and housing projects now embraced in Eastern Europe, meant it stood to profit handsomely. As it became clear that Marzahn was going to almost double the 1976 plan, from 180,000 to over 300,000 residents, and expand north and east, the GDR bought another plant from Finland, placing it in the village of Vogelsdorf, just east of the Berlin–Brandenburg border.[90] A further plant south of Marzahn in Koepenick supplied many of the panels for non-residential buildings, such as schools, shopping centers, health clinics, and so on.[91] All together, the prefabricated panel factories of the Berlin WBK, including those in Hohenschönhausen, Vogelsdorf, and Koepenick had a production capacity of twenty dwelling or "communal" units per day.[92] Further factories of the same type were purchased and opened in other East German cities, such as Karl Marx City,[93] as the grand experiment being carried out in Marzahn would be repeated as the Housing Program spread throughout the country. The story of the Finnish concrete panel plant being purchased and installed wholesale was one typical in the GDR, which often found itself needing to spend dearly to important entire production technologies from the West.[94]

Once the prefabricated panels were finished and dried—which took about twenty-eight days—they were removed from their molds and transported to the

86 Marczak, "Betonfertigteile," 61.

87 Dannenberg, "Volker Gneist," 6.

88 Peters, *Hütten, Platten, Wohnquartiere*, 94.

89 Marczak, "Betonfertigteile," 61, and interview with Peters, Berlin, February 26, 2008.

90 Peters, *Hütten, Platten, Wohnquartiere*, 94.

91 Marzcak, "Betonfertigteile," 61. It is unclear whether this factory was also purchased from Finland or from an outside country, but it was constructed anew in connection with the Housing Program.

92 Peters, *Hütten, Platten, Wohnquartiere*, 96. However, other sources claim the capacity should have been higher, as much as thirty-four units a day. See: BStU BV Berlin AKG 1019 "Information über Probleme des Standes der Vorbereitung des komplexen Wohnungsbaues im Gebiet Biesdorf/Marzahn," December 4, 1974. As this was written before the importation of the Finnish factories, it may have been unrealistic.

93 BA-L DY 30/2840 "Umfrageanalysen zur Lebensqualität in Neubaugebieten 1978," 46.

94 Another example of this is the famous Leunawerke plant in Merseburg which had to buy an entire polyethylene facility lock, stock, and barrel from the British Imperial Chemicals International in order to be able to manufacture modern plastic products. See Rainer Karlsch and Ray Stokes, *The Chemistry Must be Right* (Schkopau: Buna Sow Leuna Olefinverbund, 2001), 34, and Rubin, *Synthetic Socialism*.

construction site by specially designed Soviet and Polish trucks over newly built roads, specially designed to withstand their weight.[95] Once the panels were brought to the construction site, they were fed into a building construction assembly line known as a *Taktstrasse*. Here, cranes were mounted on fixed tracks built in straight lines along the foundations that the *Tiefbau* brigades had poured. Workers from what were called montage brigades hooked the cranes to the panels and guided them into place, where welders welded the rebar protruding from the edges of the panels to the rebar from previously placed panels. A strip of synthetic rubber, usually PVC, which was a major product of the Buna-Schkopau plastics factory and in abundant supply in the GDR, was laid along the junction between the two panels to seal and insulate them. Once one floor was complete, the workers repeated the process upwards until the building was finished. Then, the crane moved a couple of hundred meters down its track until it reached the next foundation.

Workers worked around the clock in three shifts on the construction site, as they did at the cement and slab factories. They were able to complete about twenty dwelling units per day, about one story of a WBS 70/5 every forty-eight hours. On average, it took them two weeks to complete the basic shell of a five-storey WBS 70.[96] It took longer for the electricity, plumbing, elevators, hall flooring, etc. to be installed; however, the plumbers, electricians, floor layers, and so on went to work on one floor as soon as it was finished, even as cranes and montage brigades were welding panels in place on the floors above, about which more will be said in the following chapter. In total, then, the average construction time from foundation laying to the top floor being ready to move in was sixty-one days for a WBS 70/5, between eighty-seven and 109 days for a WBS 70/11 and between 194 and 235 days for a QP 71 twenty-two-story tower. In total, each apartment ended up costing about 44,000 East German marks.[97]

The important point here was the nature of the project—it was holistic and serial. The entire process, from the cement factory to the flooring, was under one giant umbrella organization, the WBK. The WBK was guided by a central document, called a "harmonogram."[98] This was a legal document produced by the district council itself, which coordinated all economic and municipal issues into one massive central document. In essence, it was a microcosm of the entire planned economy, which itself was a massive production with tens of thousands of moving parts which all had to be synchronized to a central plan, usually a five- or seven-year plan. Each part depended on the next. This was supposedly one of socialism's greatest advantages over capitalism—rather than leaving the economy in the hands of fate, and allowing the society to be influenced by the unforeseen fluctuations of a "wild" or "untamed" market, socialist economies carried on the

[95] Interview with Klaus Langer, engineer in Marzahn, Berlin, August 14, 2012. Also see Langer, Karl-Heinz Berkenhagen and Rolf Schmidt, "Neuartige Palettenwechselvorrichtung für die 40-Mp-Querpalettentechnologie" in *Kraftverkehr* (no. 11, 1974, 374–5).

[96] Renate Großheim, "In 14 Tagen steht das Haus" *Der Neunte* (vol. 2, no. 2, 19 January 1978, 2).

[97] Peters, *Hütten, Platten, Wohnquartiere*, 106.

[98] See for example LA-B C Rep 110-05 File #4, "Bezirksharmonogramm 1979–80."

great enlightenment task of using reason to conquer irrationality, primitive desires, and accidents of nature. In this way the modernism of a project like Marzahn, and the way in which it dominated and controlled nature, very much flowed from the same source that fed the centrally controlled economic plans.

As much as Marzahn's planners strove to avoid the impression of monotony, the use of the Slobin method to mass-produce the apartments reproduced that monotony anyway. The fact, for example, that cranes had to be mounted on tracks that could only be laid out in straight lines led to a significant degree of linearity and repetition inherent in the spatial structures that defined the settlement. Separate sections and WGs of Marzahn might have had different looks, but within those, repetition of forms was the rule. Therefore, one of the most crucial and modern elements of socialism—its dual needs for holism and serial efficiency—was the a priori meaning of the "text" spelled out by the spatial and physical arrangements that came to define Marzahn.

There was something else fundamental to the nature of the centrally planned economy that was inscribed into the spatiality of Marzahn—the ever-present flaws and quality shortfalls so commonplace in the everyday life of the GDR. Almost as soon as the prefabricated panel factory had gone into operation there were problems—the Finns had not provided enough training, for example, in how to use the measuring instruments designed to monitor the hydration levels of the cement in the panels.[99] Furthermore, serious problems arose as the SED tried to throw the thousands of FDJ members into the factories and worksites of the WBK dealing with Marzahn, because they had minimal technical training, though they had plenty of ideological training.[100] Many were trained on the job by one single senior worker.[101] The factory in Hohenschönhausen was falling behind its quotas, by as much as 60 percent by 1979.[102]

In addition to lacking quantity, the quality of the panels being produced at the panel factory varied widely.[103] The panels were often not produced with exactness and precision, meaning they did not line up flush with other panels at the construction site, leaving either gaps or, if the panel was a couple of centimeters too wide, they had to be pulled out and matched to a panel that was too narrow by the same amount, or discarded entirely. The same was true of panels used to lay the floors/ceilings of the buildings—not all panels were perfectly flat, meaning that often along some of the borders between floor panels, there were small raised ridges which made carpeting or flooring impossible and presented a serious tripping obstacle.[104] The technology used to add color to the panel borders was not done in a uniform way, so that there were different hues of the same color on different panels, meaning the panels would be better off with *no* color than shoddily handled color schemes.[105]

[99] BA-L DY 30/2840, 46.

[100] LA-B C Rep 110-05 File 4, 1.

[101] Hannelore Dannenberg, "Man muß es wollen: Über den Jugendbrigadier Volker Gneist" *Neue Berliner Illustrierte* (no. 44, 1981, 6).

[102] Dannenberg, "Man muß es wollen," 6.

[103] Dannenberg, "Man muß es wollen," 6.

[104] Dannenberg, "Man muß es wollen," 6.

[105] Dannenberg, "Man muß es wollen," 6.

Panels were often damaged while being transported from the factory to the construction site, presumably cracking from the weight of other panels stacked on top of them. Poor welding between the panels was a problem, and panels were often damaged by careless handling while being lowered into place by the crane.[106] Other pieces produced in other factories of the WBK, such as staircases and stairwell railings were also judged to be in poor condition.[107] In some cases the weather was to blame: out in the open fields of the Barnim plateau, away from the windbreaks of the buildings in Berlin, the wind blew harder, especially in the winter. This was a serious problem for the cranes on the *Taktstrassen* (assembly lines); the panels they carried would be literally twisting in the wind.[108] The winters of 1978–9, when the temperatures sank to -22° C (-7° F, very cold for Berlin) and 1979–80 (with heavy snowfall) were unusually bad, impeding progress for construction.[109] Nor were the winters the only problem—a massive storm system that featured "biblical" rains and subsequent flooding in August 1978, along with high winds that damaged cranes and other construction equipment,[110] caused serious problems and delays, according to architect Eisentraut.[111] As *Taktstrasse* leader Ralf Tischendorf recalled, the weather was also a problem when prefabricated sections such as kitchens and heating duct equipment were delivered but the montage brigades were not ready for them. They sat outside, exposed to the elements, bathroom cells lying open in the heavy autumn rains.[112]

More than the weather, Tischendorf remembered, the biggest problem was a general atmosphere of chaos and a lack of materials on the construction site. "We were building with insufficient resources, and we knew it... the plan simply could not be fulfilled when the crane was busted, or no material arrived. The trucks from Romania were useless. Cement was always short. There were too few bulldozers. We had no reserves at the site. You had to organize stuff on your own constantly; trade a box of nails or a double spool for a bulldozer or a front loader." According to Tischendorf, there was a kind of black market of construction materials—the doors for bathroom cells were especially hard to come by, so certain brigades would tear the doors out of the cells delivered to their part of the assembly line and hoard them, using them to procure a wealth of other supplies from other brigades, including cement, cables, and heavy earth-moving equipment. Of course, being hoarded meant they were often exposed for long periods of time to the weather.[113] Here too, the construction site was a microcosm of the GDR's larger economic reality, as it was well known

[106] LA-B C Rep 110-05 File 4, 1. [107] LA-B C Rep 110-05 File 4, 1.

[108] Bezirksamt Marzahn von Berlin, ed., *20 Jahre Marzahn*, 84.

[109] BStU MfS BV Berlin AKG 1419, "Information über bedeutsame und beachtenswerte Probleme und subjektive Faktoren im Zusammenhang mit dem Bezirksharmonogramm des komplexen Wohnungsbaues 1980/81, insbesondere der Sicherung der Vorbereitung und Durchführung der Bauaufgaben 1980 in Berlin–Marzahn," 1.

[110] *Marzahn Aktuell*, (vol. 2, no. 7, 17 August 1978, 1) (picture on the front page of damage to construction equipment).

[111] Bezirksamt Marzahn von Berlin, ed., *20 Jahre Marzahn*, 83.

[112] Bezirksamt Marzahn von Berlin, ed., *20 Jahre Marzahn*, 85.

[113] Bezirksamt Marzahn von Berlin, ed., *20 Jahre Marzahn*, 85.

that the managers of factories and the ministers of entire industrial sectors competed against each other for resources, in a country where the role of money was made ambiguous, to say the least, through price and wage controls—success in the GDR's socialist economy was based on a different, in some ways more primitive form of pre-monetary capitalism.[114]

However, this was all insider information. From the outside, the construction site was an impressive vision—and its propaganda value was almost priceless. The visual impact of the place summed up everything that the Honecker regime had staked its legitimacy on, everything that the GDR and modern state socialism had come to embody.[115] The working class and the technocracy were at work on a vast, massive scale; there were enormous cranes; bulldozers and dump trucks roared and moved through the site as far as the eye could see, a ballet of concrete, dirt, steel, and diesel fuel so complex it could only be a creation of advanced socialist modernity; and all in the service of building a utopian community of dwelling and living. Albert Speer could not have devised a better spectacle of totalitarian aesthetics himself, even if he had been able to carry out his plans for the settlement of the area. This was the future made present.

The ideological importance and the overarching meaning was not lost on the workers on the construction site itself. Looking back on a year of running a construction brigade on *Taktstrasse* no. 12, which built over 1,000 living units in Marzahn in 1980, Herbert Kohlmann remarked "you haven't just built housing blocks, you've also formed and raised modern people."[116] The sight of this beautiful industrial chaos, of a socialist army of workers raising steel and concrete out of the overturned soil, was memorialized in a poem by Rudolf Jenak, a veteran from Berlin, published in the "readers' letters" section of *Marzahn Aktuell* in 1979. Entitled "In Berlin-Marzahn" it read:

> How tirelessly the cranes turn
> As block after block strives daily skyward
> Upon labyrinths, woven under the sand
> In the *märk'schen* field: a beautiful, captivating picture
> My heart quakes from joy, to see it all
> Daily in its transformation. The old falls away
> The new grows. Where once only a bare field
> A new city, with vigor, will come to be.[117]

The regime maximized the propaganda potential of the construction site. Every milestone event, such as the christening of the new concrete slab factory, the mounting of the first concrete panel on the foundation of the first building, and

[114] See Jonathan Zatlin, *The Currency of Socialism: Money and Political Culture in East Germany*, (New York: Cambridge University Press, 2008).

[115] Pugh makes this point in *Architecture, Politics and Identity*, 298.

[116] "Neue Wohnungen—erfüllte Wünsche. Zehnmal Nachdenken zum Jahreswechsel" *Neue Berliner Illustrierte* (vol. 36, no. 1, 1981, 4).

[117] Jenak, "In Berlin–Marzahn," in "aus Leserbriefen notiert," *Marzahn Aktuell* (vol. 3, no. 21, 22 November 1979, 4).

the unveiling of the first finished building,[118] was attended by important figures from the Party and the state, almost always including Konrad Naumann, the head of the Berlin district of the SED (a very important position in the Party); Erhard Krack, the Mayor of Berlin; and Gerd Cyske, the Mayor of the new city and someone very close to the SED and the Stasi. Even the Bishop of Berlin, Joachim Kardinal Meisner, came to Marzahn to oversee the construction and opening of the minimalist, concrete-slab Catholic church.[119] Erich Honecker himself visited the construction site on a number of occasions—the first on June 6, 1978, during which he made sure of having himself photographed, with hard hat on, amidst a brigade of construction workers, with the striking, half-built WBS 70 buildings in the background (see Figure 4).[120]

Honecker returned a month later for an even more significant event. Since late 1977, when the first families had moved into the first finished apartments, the residential population of Marzahn had been growing. Though the bulk of the future residents had yet to arrive, some apartments had been finished. One of these went to the Großkopf family who, the regime announced, had received the one-millionth apartment built in the GDR since 1971, the beginning of Honecker's period in office.[121] Honecker came to Marzahn—as part of a garish ceremony on July 6th involving banners, a stage, cameras, and the unveiling of a plaque on the side of the building on Luise-Zietz-Strasse—to officially hand the keys to the Großkopfs, who were a young family with a small child.[122]

The construction site was a "showpiece" (*Vorziegeobjekt*) for "many foreign delegations," recalled Cyske two decades later—a fact that he claimed had allowed him to pull more strings in the Party and government to ensure deliveries of needed supplies to the construction site.[123] These visitors included Indira Gandhi, Kim Il Sung, Muammar al-Qaddafi,[124] Willy Brandt, the president of Finland (who came on three occasions, including the opening of the concrete panel factory), and the heads of the communist or socialist parties of Italy, Portugal, and Japan.[125] Another notable visitor was the Mayor of Beijing, Chen Xitong, who came to Berlin for its 750-year anniversary in 1987. Chen had never been in buildings so high, and got

[118] See here "Programmablauf für das Richtfest des ersten Wohnblocks im 9. Stadtbezirk der Hauptstadt," in LA-B C Rep 110, file no. 1513, Neubau des Stadtbezirks Marzahn, Maßnahmen des Magistrats, 1976–7.

[119] Hübner, Nicolaus, and Teresiak, eds., *20 Jahre Marzahn*, 57.

[120] Volkhard Kühl, "Um das Wohnen mit freundlichen Farben," *Marzahn Aktuell*, (vol. 2, no. 5, 6 July 1978, 4). This entire issue is dedicated to Honecker's first visit to Marzahn.

[121] See *Marzahn Aktuell* (vol. 2, no. 6, 20 July 1978); most of the issue is dedicated to the one-millionth apartment ceremony.

[122] Peters, *Hütten, Platten, Wohnquartiere*, 108–09, and Hübner, Nicolaus, and Teresiak, eds., *20 Jahre Marzahn*, 22.

[123] Kühling with Cyske, "Weisse Fahnen," 63.

[124] On Qaddafi, "Wir haben die Freundschaft mit Libyens Volk gespürrt," *Neues Deutschland* (June 28, 1978), 3.

[125] Hübner, Nicolaus, and Teresiak, *20 Jahre Marzahn*, 15, and 46, 48, 50, 51, and 57. Gandhi's visit was in late 1976, when only the preparations for the construction site were being made.

vertigo when Cyske took him up to his own apartment on the twenty-fifth (top) floor of the tallest building in Marzahn.[126]

The most important foreign dignitaries to visit were, however, Mikhail and Raisa Gorbachev, who came in 1986.[127] This visit was more important than all the others, of course, because the Soviet Union represented an important element in the propaganda surrounding the Marzahn construction site. The press, both local and national, made certain to highlight the fact that the *Aufbauleitung* was utilizing Soviet construction methods, such as the "Slobin method," or the "Drushba" technique for laying pipeline.[128] The local paper *Der Neunte* trumpeted the accomplishments of the Soviet Housing Program, claiming that the USSR produced "a new city every 18 days, that every year between 10 and 11 million Soviet citizens get a newly constructed apartment," and that the Soviet Union's production of new apartments per year was "more than that of the low countries, the Scandinavian countries and Greece combined."[129]

State propaganda and media coverage of these visits to Marzahn project used the new city as a node through which to connect the GDR of the late 1970s and early 1980s to bigger horizons—across time, to the future and to the past; and across geography, to other countries in the Eastern Bloc and the developing world, and even further, all the way to the Moon and beyond.

So for example, Chief Architect Graffunder organized an event in October 1977 in Marzahn to celebrate the work of the "rubble women" (*Trümmerfrauen*), because there were two former rubble women living at the nursing home in Marzahn, where the event was held. The eldest of these, Gertrude Schade, who was ninety-five at the time, was photographed in *Der Neunte* standing next to Graffunder, and was quoted as saying "It's a good feeling to see all that is growing anew, and to know that we helped create a beginning for it."[130] The article drew a clear progression from the clearing away of the bricks of the old world, many of which were buried under the Kienberg and the Ahrensfelder Berg, to the rebirth of Germany in concrete and rebar. Marzahn was also marked out for a special honor as the place where Red Army units first reached Berlin, subsequently making Marzahn the first part of Berlin to be "liberated," with a memorial erected along Leninallee in 1985, on the fortieth anniversary of the liberation of Marzahn.[131]

The magazine *für dich* described Marzahn as part of a trend sweeping the Eastern Bloc, focusing on similar major projects in other countries such as the Przymorze settlement outside Gdansk or that of Przyjazn outside Szczecin;[132] the New

[126] Cyske, "Mit der Bummibahn in den Kindergarten," in Rohnstock, ed., *Keine Platten Geschichten*, 26.

[127] Hübner, Nicolaus, Teresiak, eds., *20 Jahre Marzahn*, 15 and *passim*.

[128] Berg, "Wärme für Marzahn," 28.

[129] Lothar Görne, "Fakten und Zahlen," *Der Neunte* (vol. 1, no. 15, 18 August 1977, 4).

[130] "Auf das Neue" *Der Neunte* (vol. 1, no. 19, 13 October 1977, 4).

[131] Rat des Stadtbezirks Berlin-Marzahn, ed., *Marzahn Erleben*, 162–3.

[132] "VR Polen: Moderne Wohnsiedlungen" *für dich*, (no. 36, 1977, 4).

Belgrade settlement in Yugoslavia[133] and those of Ujplata in Budapest.[134] These comparisons highlighted the transnational nature of the Marzahn project—the visits by foreign dignitaries were not just meant to impress, but were parts of real exchanges between the GDR and other Eastern Bloc and developing nations about how to duplicate the apparent success of Marzahn. After all, the WBS 70 was based on the "international style" of the CIAM, and was as a result intended to be transportable anywhere.[135]

Indeed, many foreign workers from countries such as Poland, Romania, and Cuba were welcomed to participate in the Marzahn construction site, not necessarily because of a labor shortage, but as a form of diplomacy that the GDR practiced to increase its cachet within the socialist and socialist-aligned world. In the sand pits and construction assembly lines, German workers worked alongside Poles, Cubans, Vietnamese, and even Red Army soldiers who took part in mandatory "subbotnik" labor in Marzahn.[136] This international workers' ethos did not stop there—East German architects and engineers were loaned to other aligned countries to reproduce versions of Marzahn in places such as Vietnam.[137] This was a form of world revolution, of international socialism, and if socialism was to spread from Europe and become applicable throughout the world, it would have to do so in the timeless, cultureless, modern forms of prefabricated concrete homes.

Marzahn, as the representative of the Housing Program, was portrayed in the media as the future of socialism, as it was in an article entitled "Until the Year 2000: A Whole New World" in the magazine *für dich*, which argued that not only in the GDR, but throughout the non-capitalist world, the building of all-encompassing prefabricated housing settlements like Marzahn would be the *only* solution to the coming population explosion around the globe, a solution out of reach for capitalist countries because of their outmoded reliance on real estate markets, profit, and private property—an aspect of capitalism so fundamental to its functioning it could never simply be adjusted as long as capitalism survived.[138] It referenced the recently held housing summit at the United Nations—the "Habitat Conference," held in Vancouver in 1976—which focused on the need to employ the dramatic advances the world had seen in the previous hundred years to produce decent, quality housing for the world's population by the year 2000. The magazine

133 "SFRJ: Moderne Bauten" *für dich* (no. 35, 1977, 5). For more on New Belgrade, see Le Normand, *Designing Tito's Capital*, especially chapter 3, "New Belgrade, Capital of Yugoslav Modernity."

134 Jens Munk, "Ungarische VR: Budapest baut farbenfreundig" (no. 24, 1977, 4). See Molnar, *Building the State*, for more on prefabricated housing in Hungary (though she does not focus on Ujplata specifically.

135 See Urban, *Tower and Slab*. Urban helpfully describes the way in which local cultures from Brazil to India to China have adapted this supposedly universal housing type.

136 Bärbel Felber, ed., *1979–1999, 20 Jahre Marzahn* (Berlin: Pressestelle Bezirksamt Marzahn, 1999), 10. Note: I have only been able to locate this source in the Bezirksmuseum Marzahn–Hellersdorf itself. Also Marte Kühling with Gerd Cyske, "Weisse Fahnen, Hohe Prozente—Anekdoten," in Bezirksamt Marzahn von Berlin, ed., *1979–1999*, 63.

137 "Erstes Plattenwerk Vietnams mit DDR-hilfe fertiggestellt," *Neues Deutschland*, October 3, 1977, 5; Klaus-Dieter Pflaum, "Hauphong und Vinh stehen als Beispiel," *Neues Deutschland* (December 1, 1977, 6).

138 Hannes Zahn, "Bis zum Jahre Zweitausend: Eine gesamte neue Welt" *für dich* (no. 26, 1978, 11).

then made it clear where *Plattenbau* technology fitted in with the march of progress in human history: the various forms of dwelling were shown, from medieval villages to nineteenth-century slums, the piece ending with a WBS 70 building being assembled. It reminded readers of Friedrich Engels' "maxim," which held that providing good dwelling for all people was the single most important task of socialism, and drove the point home perhaps most forcefully with its title photo, spread over two pages, of a nineteenth-century Lichtenberg slum being dynamited in the foreground with a WBS 70 in the background.[139]

The most important single propaganda moment for Marzahn came on September 22, 1978, when East Germany's one and only cosmonaut, Sigmund Jähn, visited the construction site along with his fellow cosmonaut, Valery Bikovsky.[140] Jähn and Bikovsky had returned from a six-day trip to the Soviet space station Soyuz on September 2, and as the first German in space, Jähn had become an authentic national hero, one of the very few in East Germany, and arguably the most popular man in the country at the time (the fact that the first German in space was an East German was a significant event in the two Germanies' competition with each other). The two visited Marzahn first on their way from the USSR to Berlin to receive the Order of Karl Marx from the Central Committee at the futuristic Palace of the Republic—the recently completed other project of Heinz Graffunder.

That Marzahn was one of the main stops on Jähn's triumphal return to East Germany demonstrated the way that Marzahn embodied several important themes in East Germany. (Jähn was also paraded through other prefabricated settlements in the country, including through the Fritz Heckert settlement in Karl Marx City.[141]) One was the centrality of technology and science, especially the Soviet space program, to socialism as a movement. The Soviet space program was in many ways an embodiment of the socialist dream of utopia through technology, and this was true of the WBS 70 as well; for, like Soyuz, the WBS 70 was also a technological artifact of great significance for the Eastern Bloc. While it may not have been quite as technologically sophisticated as the space station, it was better, being here on Earth rather than floating in space. In the 1960s, the East German (and Soviet) media was full of images of the socialist utopia of the near future as one defined by life in outer space—new socialist cities on the Moon or Mars, or in orbit. Socialism became more realistic and pragmatic in the 1970s, literally more down to Earth, but remained linked to technology and utopia, and the visit from Jähn signified this. The *tabula rasa* of the Moon had been traded for that of the Brandenburg Mark—a place accessible to East Germans. This accessibility embodied the essence of "real existing socialism."

It can be said that much of the media's celebration of Jähn's visit sought to connect the Marzahn construction site, and its workers, with the thrill of space travel. While Jähn was still in space, construction workers in Marzahn pledged to raise

[139] Zahn, "Jahre Zweitausend," 11–12.

[140] Hübner, Nicolaus, and Teresiak, *20 Jahre Marzahn*, 22.

[141] Helmut Bräuer, et. al., *Karl-Marx-Stad: Geschichte der Stadt in Wort und Bild* (Berlin: Verlag der Wissenschaft, 1988), 299.

their productivity levels in honor of Jähn's accomplishment; a pledge announced in *Marzahn Aktuell* under the headline "*Our* cosmic deed—fulfilled plans."[142] A special issue of the publication came out in celebration of the visit, containing a poem entitled "Greetings, Cosmonauts." The first stanza read: "It is sung from the scaffolding/ It sounds from every crane/ Praise the Cosmonauts/ Welcome in Marzahn!"[143] On the cover of this issue, a cartoon linked the growing skyline of Marzahn to the Soviet space program, and outer space itself. It depicted Bikovsky and Jähn in the Soyuz, orbiting Earth, looking down at Berlin (depicted by a bear with a crown), and saying "...and what keeps growing each time we orbit the earth, way down there below, is our Berlin-Marzahn."[144]

The Cosmonauts were greeted in Marzahn by two of the construction brigades—the Herbert Kohlmann and Helmut Kohnke brigades —as well as a host of Party and state officials, and Graffunder as well. The two were taken on a tour of the construction site, including the completed WBS 70 units. One of these, unit 60.17, an eleven-story unit, had just had the finishing touches put on by the painters' Reimond Klopp brigade, who greeted them and showed them the work they had completed, including a mural depicting the history of aeronautics and space travel, which Jähn praised as a "brilliant idea."[145] In return, the painters' brigade made Jähn an honorary member.

The climax of the visit came, however, when the Mayor of Marzahn, Erhard Krack, announced that one of the major arteries running through the settlement, Springpfühlstraße, would be renamed the "Allee der Kosmonauten" (Avenue of the Cosmonauts) in their honor.[146] In return for the honor, Jähn remarked that "Here in Berlin-Marzahn one can see how everything conceivable is being done for the well-being of people in socialism." Bikovsky remarked that this was his fourth visit to Berlin over several years, and it was amazing how much the city had changed since his recent visit, meaning in particular Marzahn. Jähn then gave Krack a small pennant (*Wimpel*) that he had taken into space with him, to remain in Marzahn.[147]

Most important of all, Jähn and Bikovksy were invited to plant maple saplings along the now renamed Allee der Kosmonauten. This was important symbolism, because it tied the Cosmonauts to the present reshaping of Marzahn, and its future; trees were being planted in the tens of thousands in Marzahn, and the planting of saplings and shrubs was something that almost every new resident of Marzahn would also take part in. More importantly, the trees they planted grew as Marzahn grew, and so the memory of the two space travelers, and all they symbolized, became inscribed into the physical space of Marzahn. The *Neue Berliner Illustrierte*

[142] "Unsere kosmische Tat sind erfüllte Pläne," *Marzahn Aktuell* (vol. 2, no. 9, 31 August 1978 2–3).

[143] H. Krause, "Grüß den Kosmonauten," *Marzahn Aktuell* (vol. 2, no. 10, 22 September 1978, 1).

[144] Krause, "Grüß den Kosmonauten," 1.

[145] "Kosmoswimpel Ansporn im Wettbewerb," *Marzahn Aktuell* (vol. 2, no. 11, 28 September 1978, 1).

[146] "Kosmoswimpel," 1.

[147] "Kosmoswimpel," 1.

also highlighted the visit and the tree planting by tying it to the history and the future of technological progress and utopia in Germany's twentieth century:

> Bold dreams, often relegated to the realm of the utopian, have all along accompanied the path of humans into the air and into outer space. In the time of [the Berlin aviation pioneer] Otto Lilienthal... it seemed hardly imaginable that in less than a century complex space stations would orbit the Earth, as not even Jules Verne imagined they could. But it goes almost without saying that when Sigmund Jähn and Valery Bikovsky planted the first trees along the Allee der Kosmonauten, they guaranteed that future East German space travelers will be greeted [upon their return] at this very spot.[148]

No other East Germans did go into space, and thus none were greeted again in Marzahn, but the trees the two Cosmonauts planted stand there today, and will for many decades, as specific landmarks within the settlement.

The final process in the construction of Marzahn was the use of artists to add variety, color, and "culture" to the façades, walkways, and public spaces being created as the maze of buildings went up. From the beginning, the *Aufbauleitung* had included a working group of artists formed from the state-run Federation of Visual Artists (*Verband der bildender Künstler*), led by art historian Rolf Walter.[149] These included sculptors Ingeborg Hunzinger and Karl Blümel, painters Horst Göhler, Peter Hoppe, and Heinrich Tessmer, architect/painter Lutz-Werner Brandt, craft artists Gunter Wächtler and Wolfgang Weber, and art historians Walter and Kurt-Heinz Rudolf.[150] The GDR had made several efforts to bring the work of artists and writers under the central control of the state, through organs like the Federation of Visual Artists, and apply them to the work of building the socialist economy. Initially, the SED had tried an initiative called the "Bitterfeld Way" (*Bitterfelder Weg*) in which artists and writers were supposed to use workers and factories as their source of inspiration and focus. This was generally a failure, but, as with many of the GDR's ambitious, utopian projects, a more practical way was found; a more realistic role for artists and sculptors in the service of building a socialist society. They could take part in the actual, physical building of the society itself. Murals, reliefs, and large public sculptures came to define many of the largest and most prominent open urban spaces in East Germany, such as the mural depicting scientists as part of the working class on the façade of the House of Teachers on Alexanderplatz, or the large globe which defined the open vastness of Alexanderplatz.

So it was in Marzahn, where the artists' working group, which came to include around 300 artists, was officially responsible in the planning bureaucracy for the "artistic–aesthetic division of integrated urban planning," adding façades and public art to define and demarcate the monotony and the wide, open spaces between the living units, a desire reflected too in other Eastern Bloc countries, including in Hungary, where, as Virag Molnar has described, the "tulip debate" centered around

148 "Zwischen Orbit und Rautenkranz," *Neue Berliner Illustrierte* (vol. 34, no. 40, 1978, 4–7).

149 Peters, *Hütten, Platten, Wohnquartiere*, 94.

150 Hübner, Nicolaus, and Teresiak, *20 Jahre Marzahn*, 12.

ornamental gestures in prefabricated housing.[151] The theme proposed by the artists' working group was "our life in socialism."[152] They planned to combine their artistic skill with the technology of prefabricated concrete slab production, experimenting with ways of producing façade slabs with images inlaid in the concrete, either with tiles or with a concrete stamping mechanism. In other cases artists painted murals on the outsides of schools, living units, or other buildings, such as the mural along the walls of the school on Bruno-Baum-Strasse by Heinrich Tessmer, which combined elements of abstraction vaguely reminiscent of surrealism and new objectivity with elements of socialist realist murals such as that of the House of Teachers. A cube, with an arrow pointing up, stood in a field with a horse, while the scientific formula for volume was written underneath. A family of workers driving through the field, with smokestacks in the distance, filled out the mural. It may not have been Diego Rivera, but it added variety to the underlying monotony of the concrete slabs.[153]

Not everything the artists' group proposed came to fruition, notably the ambitious scheme of draping the three living sections in distinct and coordinated colors. Individual murals and sculptures could not really be seen when one scanned the vast array of buildings, which, taken from panoramic viewpoints such as the Kienberg or the TV tower at Alexanderplatz, seemed like a labyrinth of concrete cubes. While the WBS 70 had supposedly had flexibility incorporated into its design to allow for varied angles and positions, there was little that could realistically be done within the confines of the assembly-line *Taktstrasse* method of constructing Marzahn. In particular, Eisentraut blamed those responsible, lamenting that in the end, "the monotony of the prefabricated housing block remained."[154]

There was one sculpture that defined Marzahn more than any other. In 1979, at the tip of the *Südspitze*, sculptor Alfred Bernau erected a large concrete *Richtkrone*. A *Richtkrone*, translated as a "topping-out wreath," was a wreath placed on a post, pole, or stele to celebrate the completion of a building; a ritual of ancient origin in central Europe and Germany. This was a brute, concrete version of a wreath, almost two stories high. At its base, a concrete slab, of the same kind used in the WBS 70 buildings, stood upright, with the silhouette of a man with one arm raised cut completely out of the concrete, so that a person could fit themselves inside the concrete panel itself (see Figure 5). The image was a homage to Le Corbusier's "Modulor"—a design similar to da Vinci's Vitruvian Man, intended to create a universal system of measuring space and distance (for, among other things, the mass production of housing), which placed "man as the measure of all things."[155] The panel was more than just a link to the Athens Charter, however—it spoke to

[151] See Molnar, *Building the State*, 175.

[152] From an interview with Wolfgang Eisentraut, in Bezirksmuseum Marzahn, ed., *20 Jahre Marzahn*, 81.

[153] Bezirksmuseum Marzahn, ed., *20 Jahre Marzahn*, 81.

[154] Bezirksmuseum Marzahn, ed., *20 Jahre Marzahn*, 82.

[155] Verein Kids & Co., *Marzahn-Südspitze*, 18–19. Also see Le Corbusier, *The Modulor: A Harmonious Measure to the Human Scale, Universally Applicable to Architecture and Mechanics* (Basel and Boston: Birkhäuser, 2000).

the strange bond formed between the cement panels and people themselves. In a way, the panels *were* people; socialism's people, transfigured into concrete, serialized units for a more efficient and streamlined re-assembly.

Already planned to be the largest housing development in Europe, and one of the largest in the world, by 1980 the plan for Marzahn grew still further. Following a decision of the Berlin Magistrat in February 1980, the original three living sections, WGs, were expanded: smaller zones to the north, west and east, across the Wuhle, were added in the 1980s, called Marzahn-North, Marzahn-West, and Marzahn-East. Another area east of the Wuhle would become the Cecilienstrasse section.[156] By 1990, the construction teams had built 38,332 apartments in the original three living sections, and another 21,314 apartments in the four expanded sections. By 1990, Marzahn had grown from the 35,000 apartments originally foreseen in 1973, and the expanded 1976 vision of 45,500, into 59,646 apartments, into which 167,371 people moved.[157] Then, in 1985, planners began another massive expansion in the small village east of the Wuhle and the Kienberg, called Hellersdorf. Hellersdorf was annexed to Marzahn, officially named the city district Marzahn-Hellersdorf.[158] By 1990, the GDR had built a further 43,319 apartments in Hellersdorf, into which 122,400 people would come to live.[159] As a combined settlement, Marzahn-Hellersdorf would come to hold 102,965 newly constructed prefabricated apartments, into which a total of 289,771 people would move (see Figure 6).

But even this was not the end, for Marzahn-Hellersdorf would become the model for an even greater expansion of housing settlements in Berlin, especially in the north-east of the city, as well as for other similar settlements throughout the country. In the municipal district of Hohenschönhausen, which lay on the other side of the industrial zone and S-bahn tracks to the north-east of Marzhan, 37,830 prefabricated apartments were constructed in the 1980s in a settlement called New Hohenschönhausen. In the municipal district of Lichtenberg, which lay to the south of Hohenschönhausen and west of Marzahn-Hellersdorf, along the Leninallee, another 38,869 new apartments were built.[160] In Friedrichsfelde, south of Marzahn, another 22,500 apartments were constructed in the Friedrichsfelde-Süd settlement just north of the Spree river.[161] Taken as one large complex, the area of Marzahn-Hellersdorf-Hohenschönhausen-Lichtenberg saw 202,164 prefabricated apartments constructed, in which, by 1990, over 400,000 people lived. Taken as a separate urban unit, this meant that the sprawling *Neubausiedlung* in

[156] Peters, *Hütten, Bauten, Wohnquartiere*, 134.

[157] Peters, *Hütten, Bauten, Wohnquartiere*, 154.

[158] For more on Hellersdorf, see Ulrich Domröse and Jack Gelfort, eds., *Peripherie als Ort: Das Hellersdorfer Projekt* (Stuttgart: Arnoldsche, 1999). Also see Wohnungsbaugenossenschaft "Hellersdorfer Kiez," ed., *Wohnungsbaugenossenschaft "Hellersdorfer Kiez:" Festschrift zur 50-Jahrfeier.* (Berlin: MAZZ Verlag, 2004). For a more creative and artistic take on Hellersdorf, see Kurt Buchwald, *Firmament der Dinge: Hellersdorfer Himmelsscheibe. Großsiedlung Hellersdorf, Quartier Mageburger Allee.* (Berlin: S.T.E.R.N/Berliner Senat, 2004).

[159] Domröse and Gelfort, *Peripherie als Ort*, 184. The Bezirksmuseum Marzahn-Hellersdorf itself has a slightly lower figure of 42,200 newly constructed apartments in Hellersdorf.

[160] Peters, *Hütten*, 185.

[161] From the Bezirksmuseum Marzahn-Hellersdorf.

Berlin's North-east became the fourth-largest city in the GDR; aside from Berlin, it came after only Leipzig and Dresden, which had 545,307 and 518,057, respectively, by the end of the GDR.

This massive area, anchored by Marzahn, became the model for similar settlements throughout the GDR, mostly built on the same model, using WBS 70/71 or QP 71 buildings, including Rostock's "North-west" settlement, with 39,400 apartments; Leipzig's Grünau settlement, with 38,500 apartments; Karl Marx City's Fritz Heckert settlement, with 31,300 apartments;[162] Halle's Südstadt/Silberhöhe settlement, with 25,900 apartments; and the Großer Dreesch settlement in Schwerin, with 20,100 apartments. Soon, these settlements would become real places, where East Germans would encounter new sights and sounds, leaving the old world behind. It is to that personal experience of transformation and rupture that we turn next.

[162] From Helmut Bräuer and Gert Richter, et. al., *Karl-Marx-Stadt: Geschichte der Stadt in Wort und Bild* (Berlin: VEB Deutscher Verlag der Wissenschaften, 1988), 292–304.

3

Rainbows and Communism

Material, Sensory, and Mnemonic Ruptures

The experience of moving into a new block apartment was one of radical rupture for most East Germans. It meant a material improvement in their living standards, but it meant something more profound—a new spatial and sensory world that bore little resemblance to where and how they had lived previously. The majority of East Germans who moved to Marzahn came from the rental barracks of the inner cities, almost half of them from Berlin itself. Almost every aspect of their new sensory worlds was new; new sounds, new smells, new views, new angles and sight lines, new patterns of shadowfall, new vegetation, and new relationships to distances—distances to the ground level, distances between buildings, distances to work and daycare and school. The weather had different patterns, out on the edge of the city. Even the way they walked, the ground beneath their feet, was different. Though they had moved in some cases less than 10 km from their old dwellings, it might as well have been a thousand.

More importantly, this was not an environment new to only them, but one that was new in general. It was built for them; they were the first to move there. It may have seemed as if the sun shone and the wind blew for the first time when the first Marzahners arrived, luggage and key in hand, at their WBS 70 apartment. The architecture, the interiors of their apartments, even their furniture was functional, and built for the function of that moment—it had no aesthetic reference to any past era of German history. It was a place with no memory, and intentionally so—it was an amnesiopolis.

This chapter explores the depth of the rupture experienced by the new arrivals to Marzahn. It argues that new sensations and new environments were bound to new routines, relationships, thoughts, and praxes—a phenomenological and existential change managed and shaped by the socialist state and its Housing Program, which made the idea of "building socialism" a lived and literal reality for the workers and new residents of Marzahn. As we will see, this change was often experienced and framed by East Germans as positive, a release from the old, the cramped, the stale, the past, and towards the new and the modern, as well as a rise in status—an *Aufstieg*. This was, of course, the narrative the regime had built into its Housing Program, and not everyone shared it—for many it was simply a jarring experience, moving from one form of discomfort to another. In either case, the new arrivals experienced the move as both a topographical–spatial change and as a chronological change, in that their sense of the history embedded in the old neighborhoods was shed for a new beginning.

MOVING OUT OF THE MISERY QUARTER

As mentioned in chapter 1, many East Germans were forced to live in the same miserable tenements—known as "rental barracks" or *Mietskaserne*—that the working class of a century earlier had lived in. The situation grew worse because of the amount of destroyed housing from the War, and it grew especially acute in the 1960s and early 1970s as a new generation, the "GDR generation" born around the end of the War, moved out of their parents' homes and needed space for themselves and their own families. In Berlin it was still more acute, partially because of the division of the city, and partially because the GDR state had trained many of the members of this generation to become cadres, to raise them up out of the working class to become technocrats—many with hastily acquired degrees in engineering or planned economics—to serve the expanded central government in Berlin.[1] For these young people to move to Berlin and re-experience essentially the same shock felt by those migrants who moved to the newly built tenements in the 1860s and 1870s was a major problem for the GDR.

Barbara Diehl and her husband Rolf exemplified the experience of this generation, upon which state socialism was to pin so many of its hopes, and for which places like Marzahn were built. Barbara was born in a small town outside Leipzig—Magdeborn—in 1948. Her childhood was typical of her generation—one of profound rupture born of the War's ripple effects. A war widow, her mother's life had unraveled, leading to seven children with five different men, alcoholism, and emotional neglect of the children. As the oldest, Barbara was in charge of the younger children. There was little that her own mother passed on to her in terms of values, memories, or practices—Barbara figured things out for herself, learning to cook from a state-published cookbook. The village of Magdeborn was not a happy place for Barbara to grow up in—it was no *Heimat*, and in its quaint eaves and lanes where the old Germany lingered there was nothing but emotional pain and loneliness for Barbara.[2]

When she was fourteen, the state, in its pursuit of heavy industry, decided to completely demolish her village to build a lignite mine—resettling its residents in and around Leipzig, and erasing whatever lingering sense of the past remained for Barbara. A wider world opened up to her, and she ended up going to the Technical University in Merseburg, the town adjoining the Leuna chemical factory, at eighteen, and got a degree as an "economic engineer" (*Ingenieur Ökonom*), specializing in data processing. She got a job with the Economic Planning Division at the Leuna factory, where she met her husband, Ralf, also an economic planner. In

[1] See Augustine, *Red Prometheus*, 40.
[2] Interview with Barbara Diehl, Berlin, March 6, 2008.

1972 they married, and he got a job in Berlin with the State Planning Commission, she as an economic planner for the state cosmetics factory in Berlin.[3]

The only place they could find to live in Berlin, however, was a one-room apartment in the old working-class district of Friedrichshain. The eight-by-six-meter room had one window, which looked out onto a dark and dreary courtyard (see Figure 7). Their toilet was shared, halfway up the stairwell to the next floor. There was no hot water, only a spigot in the kitchen direct from the water main. The kitchen was small—two by six meters. Baths had to be taken in a basin with water warmed on the stove, or as with many other people, showers were taken at work. There was a heating oven, which required Ralf to wake at 4:00 a.m. to light in order that, in the winters, the apartment was sufficiently warm upon waking in the mornings. They did laundry by hand, until they saved up enough to buy a washing machine and a spinner, which then took up the remaining room in their kitchen.[4]

In 1975, Ralf and Barbara had a son, Dieter. The child put severe stress on the family in their cramped living quarters because there was only the one large room in which the entire family lived and slept, so after Dieter went to bed, Barbara and Ralf had to consign themselves to the tiny kitchen, reading books, Ralf sitting on the stove and Barbara on a stool on the floor. Giving their young son a bath was challenging, given how long it took to heat up the necessary water. There were few toys, little space in which to play with them, and very few other children for Dieter to meet in Friedrichshain. Barbara's mother, emotionally distant after all the fractures and chaos of the previous decades, wanted little to do with the child, dismissing him as "unruly," deepening Barbara's sense of isolation.[5] Ralf's side provided even less help; his father had died in the War on the Yugoslavian front, and his mother, who hated his father and never wanted Ralf in the first place, was totally disengaged from most things in Ralf's life, including his new family as a young man.

It was true that they lived in a vibrant neighborhood, a *Kiez*, and they enjoyed being able to walk out of their tenement into the bustle of the city—they enjoyed ambling down to the Karl-Marx-Allee, to go window shopping.[6] But, ultimately, there was little to bind them emotionally to their neighborhood.[7] Dieter felt alienated and even ostracized at his Kindergarten, and had trouble making friends. The advent of the Housing Program changed everything for the Diehls; in the late 1970s, Ralf began applying for a new apartment through the State Planning Commission, an effort that would eventually come to fruition in 1980, with a three-bedroom WBS 70 apartment on the Allee der Kosmonauten in Marzahn.[8]

The Diehls' experience was shared with hundreds of thousands of other Berliners, including Jürgen Hinze, a construction safety inspector, who lived with his wife and two children in a tiny apartment in an old rental barracks on Zionskirchstraße

[3] Interview with Barbara Diehl, Berlin, February 20, 2008.
[4] Interview with Barbara Diehl, Berlin, February 20, 2008.
[5] Interview with Barbara Diehl, Berlin, June 3, 2008.
[6] Interview with Barbara Diehl, Berlin, March 6, 2008.
[7] Interview with Barbara Diehl, Berlin, March 6, 2008.
[8] Interview with Barbara Diehl, Berlin, February 20, 2008.

near the border of the East Berlin districts of Mitte and Prenzlauer Berg in 1975. The building, built in 1862, was, as Hinze put it "practically a ruin, dark and drafty, water ran down the walls and we had to share a toilet a half floor up in the stairwell with the neighbors.... The living conditions had become catastrophic. The ceiling was busted (*kaputt*), the toilets no longer functioned. You couldn't touch most of the windows because otherwise they would break."[9] Detlef Habrom, a road construction worker, lived in a one-room apartment with his wife and her two children from a previous relationship, on the outskirts of town (near Karlshorst) on the Baumschulenweg, in 1978. The place was "far too small" for them, with the entire family sleeping in the same room.[10]

Regina Trappe, a doctor, lived on the fifth (top) floor, in a two-room apartment on Arkonaplatz, before it was renovated, with her husband and son. Water poured into the living room whenever it rained, she recalled.[11] Jutta and Rudi Bartsch shared a three-and-a-half-room apartment in Griefswald, near Berlin, with *three* other families—they lived in the living room with their three kids.[12] Lothar and Helena Hepner recalled their old apartment building in Berlin where the "walls were always damp."[13] Werner Zühlke, a construction worker and aspiring welder, lived in a "through-way apartment"—a room that connected another apartment to the exiting corridor, meaning he had virtually no privacy at all.[14] Gerlinde Paulus lived in a tenement on Arnimplatz, before the renovation, and recalled that she had to cross the courtyard to go to the toilet, which was unpleasant in the winter and at night—and when it was cold enough, the toilet would freeze, and the residents would have to use a bucket in the courtyard. In order to bathe, Paulus remembered, most people used public bath houses once a week, purchasing soap there for 1 mark.[15] Only the most resourceful of East Germans could figure ways around the lack of sanitation, such as Karl-Peter Schermann, who scrounged for showerheads and knobs at construction sites where he worked and managed to jury-rig a shower in the kitchen of his rental-barrack apartment on Stargarderstrasse in Prenzlauer Berg.[16] The Diehls, Hinze, Habrom, Trappe, the Bartsches, the Hepners, Zühlke, Paulus, and Schermann all shared the same life arc, which would lead them from the crumbling tenements of old East Berlin to the *Plattenbausiedlung* of Marzahn.

[9] Hinze, "Das grüne Ungeheuer," in Rohnstock, ed., *Keine Plattengeschichten*, 52.

[10] Habrom, "Orangen gegrillt, Cordhose gewässert, Brand erfolgreich bekämpft," in Rohnstock, ed., *Keine Plattengeschichten*, 64.

[11] Manfred Hemprich, "Zu Hause im Hochhaus: Über Marzahner Kinder und ihre Eltern" *Neue Berliner Illustrierte* (no. 14, 1980, 12–17; 16).

[12] Jutta and Rudi Bartsch, "Die Häuser sind eben so konstruiert und dann sollen sie auch so bleiben," in Quiesser and Tirri, eds., *Allee der Kosmonauten*, 57.

[13] Lothar and Helena Hepner, "Im Altbau wurde gar nicht saniert," in Quiesser and Tirri, eds., *Allee der Kosmonauten*, 87.

[14] Hemprich, "Hochhaus," 16.

[15] Intervew with Gerlinde Paulus, July 22, 2008, Berlin. For more in-depth data on the residents of Arnimplatz and their experiences with renovation or being moved to Neubaugebiete like Marzahn, see BA-L DY 30 2840, Institut für Meinungsforschung "Bericht über eine Umfrage bei Einwohnern von modernisierten Wohngebieten," September 6, 1977.

[16] Interview with Karl-Peter Schermann, Berlin, July 22, 2008.

The hauling of coal up the many stairs to heat the old apartments was especially onerous for East Germans, such as Marianne Fränzel, who hated the eighty-eight steps she had to traverse each morning and night to haul coal to her small apartment in Prenzlauer Berg for herself, her husband, and child.[17] Hauling coal became a major problem for those who were elderly, such as Lilo and Erwin Wandrey, who lived in a one-and-a-half-room apartment in the district of Alt-Friedrichsfelde with a shared toilet, and dreamed of a retirement that did not involve coal;[18] or those who were handicapped, such as Waltraud Hofer, who used a wheelchair and who had to wait for assistance to be carried up the stairs—"how was I supposed to schlep coal?" he asked, reminiscing twenty-five years later.[19]

Other East Germans believed that their apartments were literally making them sick, a common complaint about the damp, dark, and stuffy tenements voiced by social reformers since the nineteenth century. Elisabeth Albrecht, a librarian who moved to Berlin in 1967 from a small town, lived in a one-and-a-half-room apartment in Friedrichshain with her small son, Steffen, born in 1971. "The building was still damaged from the War," Albrecht recalled. "The plaster was crumbling and the bricks had cracks in them which were only plugged with foil." To make matters worse, Albrecht recalled, "by the end of the 1970s, my son and I began to experience frequent headaches. We often felt faint and sick." Measurements showed elevated carbon monoxide levels, and the building was eventually condemned.[20] Gerda Marin, who worked at the state fashion institute, suffered from tuberculosis and claimed that the cause was the lack of fresh air, and the damp and cold conditions in her two-room apartment in Prenzlauer Berg; what she called "Berlin conditions." For her, the oldness of the "plaster ornaments" in the apartment seemed to accompany her ill health.[21] Fränzel, the Wandreys, Hofer, Albrecht, and Marin would also end up in Marzahn.

For others, the old inner-city neighborhoods entombed a dark history, standing as everyday traces of the dark times that had shaped the working class in Germany since its origins in the 1840s and 1850s. This was the case with Luise Schmidt, who was profiled in a feature in *Neue Berliner Illustrierte* in 1979. Schmidt, a member of the National Front's Residential Committee (*Wohngebietsausschüss*, an organ of the state on the neighborhood level that answered common complaints and solved issues for local residents), lived on Teutoberger Platz in Prenzlauer Berg, and was a kind of local neighborhood historian, knowing every bit of the development of the area since the 1850s, every building code and district ordinance ever passed, and the stories of countless families who had lived in and around Teutoberger Platz.[22] Indeed, for her much of it was personal memory.

Born in 1904, Schmidt had lived in the same place since 1924, and seen the turbulence of Germany's twentieth century interwoven with her home. Her *Kiez*

[17] Verein Kids & Co., *Südspitze*, 33.

[18] Hemprich, "Hochhaus," 16. [19] Hemprich, "Hochhaus," 17.

[20] Albrecht, "Balkonblick nach zwanzig Jahren," in Rohnstock, ed., *Keine Plattengeschichten*, 33.

[21] Gerda Marin, "Ich habe hier immer gerne gelebt," in Quiesser and Tirri eds., *Allee der Kosmonauten*, 81.

[22] Uschi Bergmann, "Berliner Fenster," *Neue Berliner Illustrierte* (vol. 35, no. 21, 1979, 16–19; 16).

was more than just a home; it was also a space in which the catastrophes of German and Berliner history—inadequate city planning, capitalist excess, fascism, and war—were indelibly recorded, containing an ever-present phenomenology of memory and history, like the striations of geological events in a cliffside. "In 1853, the city fathers passed the first ordinances here, suited more for a village than a city," she was quoted as saying. "Real estate speculators reaped profit from it as the area just outside the city gates was built up over the next decades."[23] Police repression was inscribed in the fabric of the *Kiez*, she noted, citing the fact that the second-story (first-story in German usage) balconies had to have a clearance of at least ten feet so that officers on horseback could patrol the sidewalks in the event of a riot. She also recited the familiar grievance of cramped inner courtyards (*Hinterhöfe*), and one-room apartments (the "Berliner rooms") with tiny, almost lightless and airless windows ("Berliner windows") looking out on the inner courtyards. The Berliner window was a "heritage of the capitalist past," Schmidt claimed, "which cannot be wiped away in a day."[24]

Nor could the fascist past. Here, in the Teutoburger *Kiez*, she had participated in anti-fascist resistance battles in the 1920s. Her husband was hunted by the Nazis, and lived in hiding here; her teenage son was arrested by "Nazis" here, never to be seen again.[25] "This," Schmidt told the magazine, "is how you become a Berliner, because you share the fate of so many families from Prenzlauer Berg, and you share their life and their habits."[26] Indeed, *NBI* stated, Schmidt was the "fulcrum" of the neighborhood, the National Front rep to whom everyone would go with their problems, and who could marshal the resources of the National Front to fix the crumbling *Kiez*.

In fact, fixing the neighborhood was her way of repairing the trauma that had given birth to it in the first place, and which had played out in her life amidst its spaces: "For Louise Schmidt, the constant involvement with each building, each electric line, each burst water main, is also a way of working through the trauma that played out in her life in these very streets and alleyways."[27] *NBI*'s slant, however, was clear: despite the heroic depiction of Louise Schmidt, her story was a Sisyphusian tragedy. Pointing to the faux neoclassical façades of the rental barracks, Schmidt admitted to *NBI* that "things haven't improved here, and in fact have gotten worse, as the buildings continue to fall apart," and that despite the hard work of the National Front and the district representative (*Abgeordneter*), funds for renovation were "extremely limited." The days of spaces like Teutoburger Platz were numbered; they were too ruined, too haunted by the specters of capitalism and fascism to be redeemed, no matter how bravely people like Schmidt tried to hold back the inevitable. Their steady physical decay was merely the outward

[23] Bergman, "Berliner Fenster," 18. [24] Bergman, "Berliner Fenster," 18.

[25] Schmidt does not elaborate on when this happened, nor which agency it happened through (Gestapo, SD, etc.). Nor does she distinguish between the era of street fighting before the Nazi seizure of power in 1933 and the era of persecution which impacted her husband and son later on, though there must presumably be a long time span in between the two events, because if she was born in 1904 it is hard to imagine her having a son in adolescence much earlier than the early 1940s.

[26] Bergman, "Berliner Fenster," 18. [27] Bergman, "Berliner Fenster," 18.

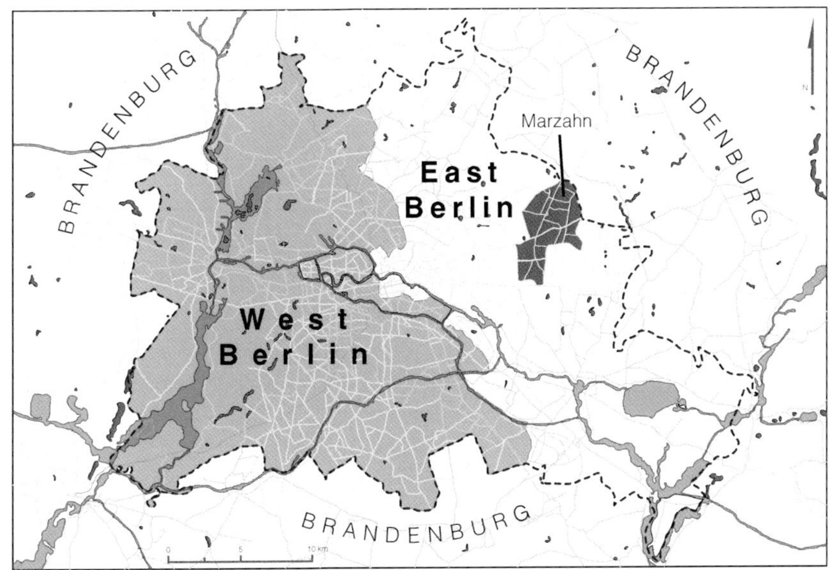

Figure 1. Map of Berlin with Marzahn highlights (courtesy of J. Glatz, Western Michigan University Libraries Mapping Service).

Figure 2. Architect Heinz Graffunder showing Marzahn model to schoolchildren, 1976 (courtesy of the Bezirksmusum, Marzahn–Hellersdorf e.V.).

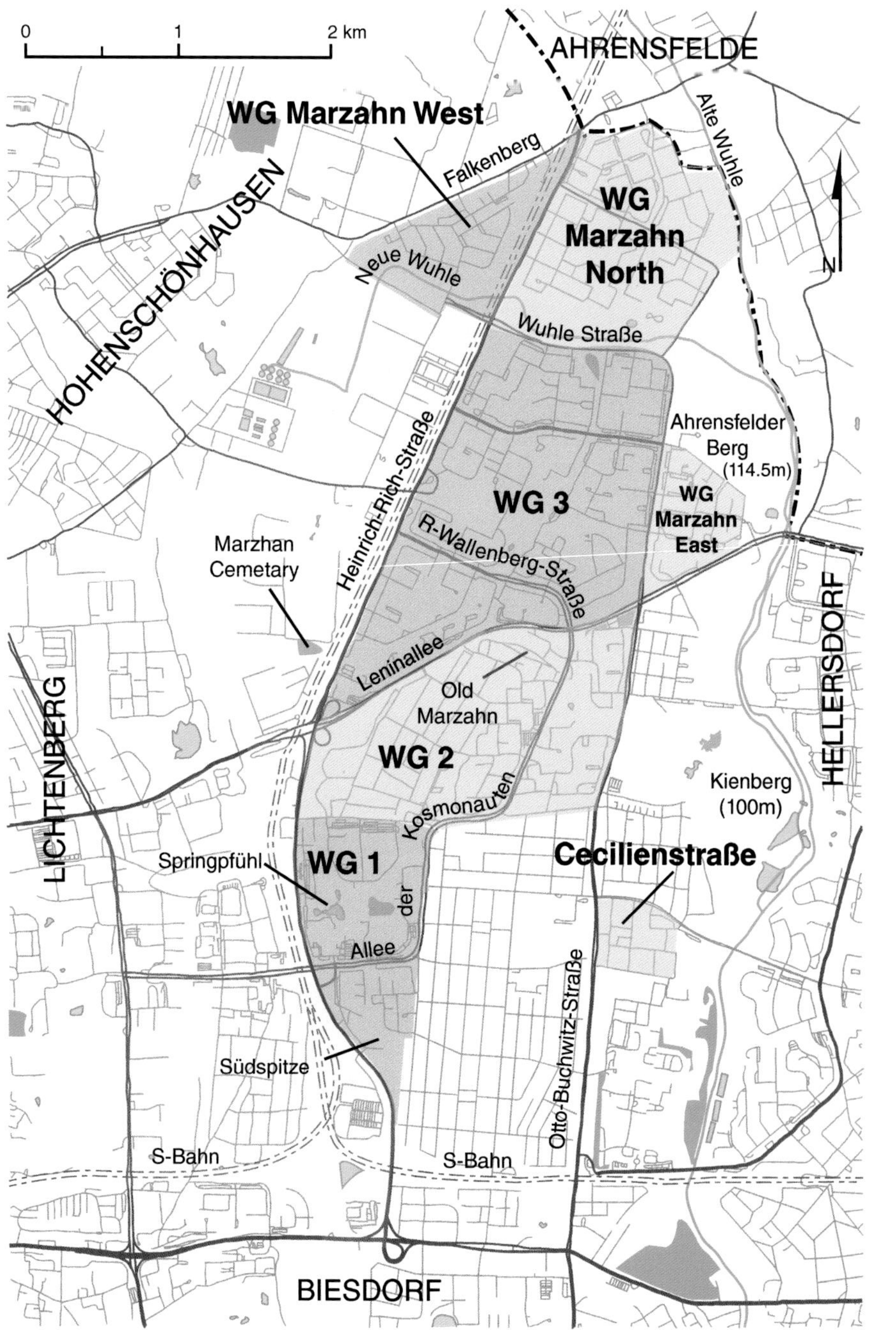

Figure 3. Map of Marzahn settlement (courtesy of J. Glatz, Western Michigan University Libraries Mapping Services).

Figure 4. Erich Honecker posing with construction workers in Marzahn, 1978 (courtesy of the Bezirksmuseum, Marzahn–Hellersdorf, e.V.).

Figure 5. Concrete *Richtkrone* and "Modulor"—homage to Le Corbusier in a concrete panel—at the southern tip (*Südspitze*) in Marzahn (photo by author, 2012).

Figure 6. WBS 70 units in Marzahn, 1984 (courtesy of the Bezirksmuseum, Marzahn–Hellersdorf, e.V.).

Figure 7. View from Barbara Diehl's old rental barrack apartment, Friedrichshain (courtesy of Barbara Diehl).

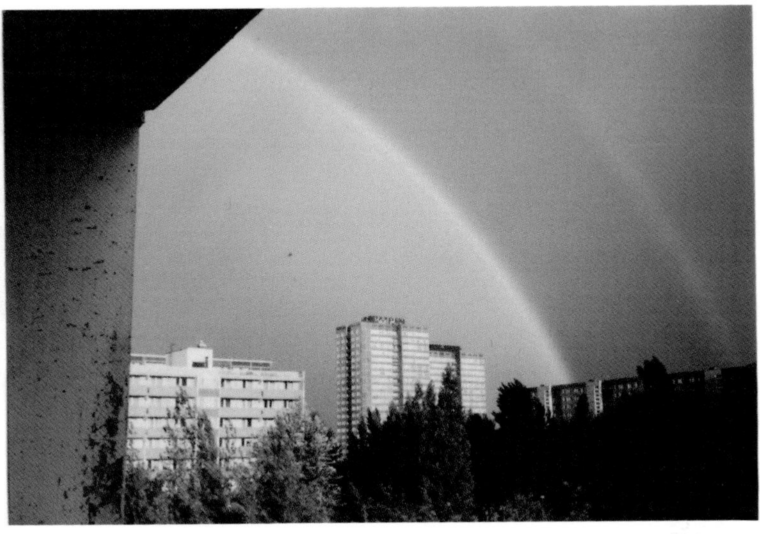

Figure 8. Double rainbow over Marzahn, from Marquardt family apartment (courtesy of Evelyn Marquardt).

Figure 9. The Jütte family, 1978 (courtesy of the Bezirksmuseum, Marzahn–Hellersdorf, e.v./Kühl).

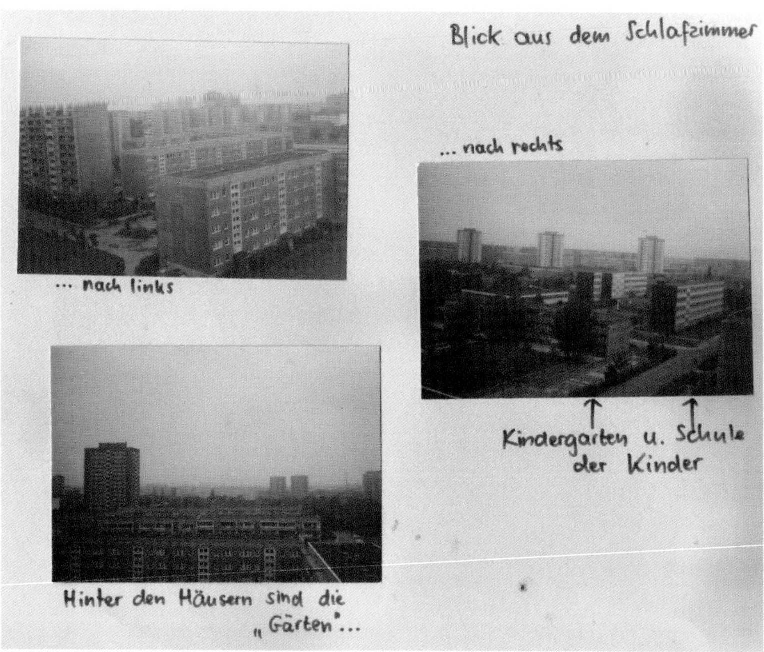

Figure 10. Barbara Diehl's new view in Marzahn, Allee der Kosmonauten, 1985 (courtesy of Barbara Diehl).

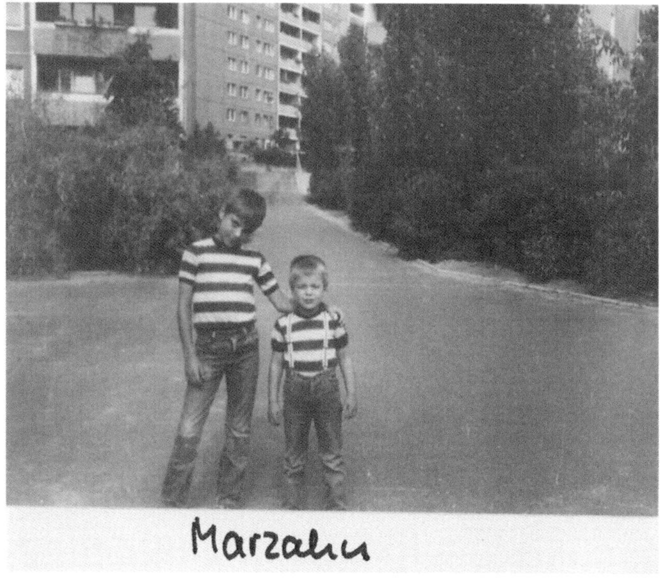

Figure 11. Barbara Diehl's two sons in Marzahn, outside their new home, 1986 (courtesy of Barbara Diehl).

Figure 12. Marquardt family on the first day of school, 1980 (courtesy of Evelyn Marquardt).

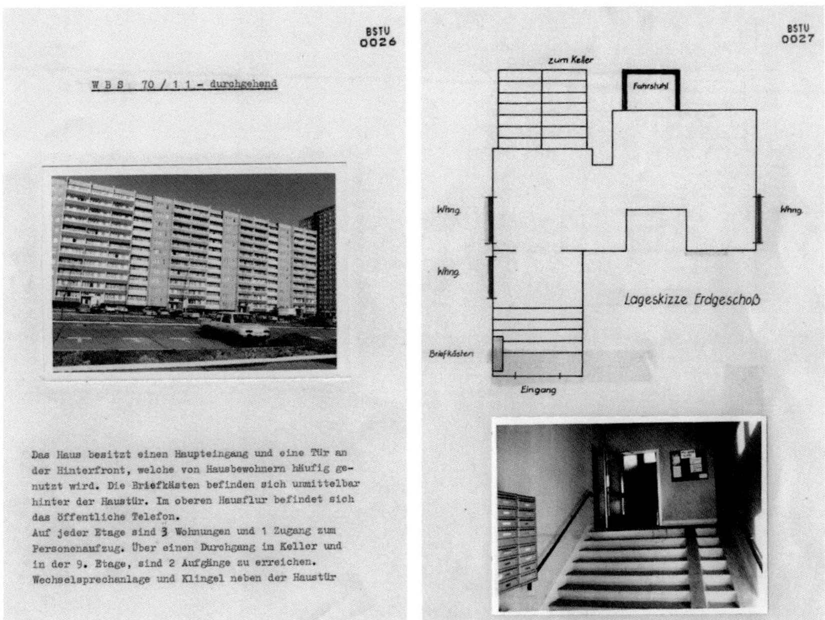

BSTU
0026

W B S 70 / 1 1 - durchgehend

Das Haus besitzt einen Haupteingang und eine Tür an der Hinterfront, welche von Hausbewohnern häufig genutzt wird. Die Briefkästen befinden sich unmittelbar hinter der Haustür. Im oberen Hausflur befindet sich das öffentliche Telefon.
Auf jeder Etage sind 3 Wohnungen und 1 Zugang zum Personenaufzug. Über einen Durchgang im Keller und in der 9. Etage, sind 2 Aufgänge zu erreichen.
Wechselsprechanlage und Klingel neben der Haustür

BSTU
0027

zum Keller
Fahrstuhl
Whng.
Whng.
Whng.
Lageskizze Erdgeschoß
Briefkästen
Eingang

Figure 13. Stasi manual on spying in the WBS 70 buildings of Marzahn (courtesy of BStU).

Figure 14. Seeing like a *Plattenbau*: Stasi photos of suspicious observations of nearby Soviet base, Schönau–Grünau, Leipzig, 1988 (courtesy of BStU).

manifestation of the spiritual decay long at work in the very *Being* of the neighborhood. The only thing holding the *Kiez* together was her, according to *NBI*, "and soon Frau Schmidt will be dead," the newspaper wrote. "And with her, the memories of those bad old times [will die]."[28]

In some cases the erasure of the old *Kiez* could disturb the very ghosts that lay dormant in the neighborhood, as the state carried out demolitions of condemned buildings. This was the case for Anna Elisabeth Heinze, born in 1891, who had lived in Prenzlauer Berg on Fehrbelliner Strasse since the 1920s, and who was profiled in the same *NBI* article. The buildings across the street, 14 and 15 Fehrbelliner Strasse, were being dynamited. Heinze, pictured in the magazine clasping her daughter and granddaughter and gazing grimly out the window, claimed that the demolitions had terrified her, "letting loose memories of experiences and people that she had buried," including "her husband, a mason and a communist." These then reawakened even darker ghosts in yet more intimate spaces—including the kitchen table, a few feet away by the window, where her husband had argued with their young adult son about his decision to join the Nazi party—to no avail. "He fell in the war," she remembered, looking at the table and back out the window.[29] Nor was her son's ghost the only one disturbed by the demolitions—her daughter too died in the war, in this very neighborhood, buried under the rubble of a building that collapsed on top of her when it was struck by an allied bomb.[30]

BABIES AND BUREAUCRATS: THE STRUGGLE TO LAND A NEW APARTMENT

For the millions of East Germans who lived in such untenable conditions, the talk of a new apartment in a settlement outside the city was bound to be highly appealing. They learned of this possibility mainly through articles in the media, from exhibits like the one in the Altes Museum, and by word of mouth—after all, the Marzahn project alone was so enormous that it involved just about every available construction worker and large numbers of workers from other sectors in Berlin and beyond. A similar dynamic existed in Leipzig, Dresden, Rostock, Karl-Marx-Stadt, and the many other East German cities where large housing settlements were underway. However, actually getting an apartment was extremely difficult, and led straight through the apparatus of the state and the party bureaucracy, forcing East Germans to rely on connections, an ability to call upon their own reserves of *Eigen-Sinn* to work the "system," and sometimes pure luck. Above all, the East Germans who made it out of the inner city and into the "socialist suburbs" were those who fit a particular demographic—young families with children, from the working class, firmly within the core institutions of East German life, such as the state bureaucracy, the Party, or a factory.

28 Bergman, "Berliner Fenster," 18.
29 Bergman, "Berliner Fenster," 16.
30 Bergman, "Berliner Fenster," 16.

One of the main ways that people got an apartment in a place like Marzahn was to belong to a "workers' housing construction society" (*Arbeiterwohnungsbaugenossenschaft*, or AWG). The AWG was almost always attached to a place of work—usually a factory or a state organ, most of which had AWGs. It was a vestige of the early days of the German working-class movement, akin to a co-operative market, a late-nineteenth- and early-twentieth-century example of the working class attempting to pool its own resources to solve its own housing woes. In its earlier incarnation, the AWG members would contribute to a central fund, "buying in" to the housing development to be built with the fund. The mechanism was revived in late 1953 by the GDR's Ministers' Council, as part of a series of attempts by the Party and state to respond to the June 1953 uprising through a renewed focus on the needs of East German citizens, including consumer goods and housing. It was given renewed emphasis in the early 1970s as part of the state's plan to help fund the massive Housing Program then in the works.[31] This version of the AWG also required its members to buy in, usually both in terms of money and labor, in order to gain an apartment, but it was also subsidized by the state, and the funds did not necessarily correlate directly with the building projects themselves—instead, the AWGs were "allowed" to buy blocks of apartments in dwellings yet to be built.[32] Though many buildings constructed by the Housing Program were actually owned outright by the state (more than those owned by AWGs),[33] in Marzahn the AWG was the most common path for getting an apartment.

The path was not an easy one, however—even getting membership in an AWG could be difficult.[34] And once in an AWG, an application for an apartment in a new construction settlement like Marzahn could still take a while—Gisela Siedler, whose husband worked for a state-run painting company, applied in 1975 to move out of their old apartment in Weißensee, which had a coal oven and no toilet, and had to wait until 1979 to get a Marzahn apartment;[35] Aribert Bautz, who worked for a factory that built railroad tracks, and his wife Renate, also waited four years from the time they were admitted to his AWG to when they actually got a three-room apartment in Marzahn.[36]

Jürgen Hinze, who was a safety inspector assigned, ironically, to the Marzahn construction site, was fed up with waiting while he and his family themselves lived in squalid conditions on Zionskirchestrasse in Prenzlauer Berg, and used his own connections within the SED, personally hauling an official from the office of Konrad Naumann, the Berlin district Party secretary, to see his apartment. The official agreed that it was not livable, and promised them a Marzahn

[31] Tesch, *Wohnungsbau in der DDR*, 28.

[32] See Larrie Benton Zacharie, ed., *Arbeiterwohnungsbaugenossenschaft* (Saarbrücken: Verpublishing, 2012).

[33] Statistisches Amt, *Statistisches Jahrbuch der DDR*, 200.

[34] Jutta and Wolfgang Wormbs, "Allee der Astronauten," in Quiesser and Tirri, eds., *Allee der Kosmonauten*, 17.

[35] Gisela Siedler, "Wir waren immer darauf aus sie festzunageln," in Quiesser and Tirri eds., *Allee des Kosmonauten*, 71.

[36] Aribert and Renate Bautz, "Wir taten es für uns," in Quiesser and Tirri eds., *Allee der Kosmonauten*, 67.

apartment the next day. Even then, as he and his wife went to collect their key on site, there was a snafu, and he had to march downtown again, into the city council (*Stadtrat*) building, threatening to call the Party authorities on the municipal authorities—a particularly deft move. Only then did the coveted key to a WBS 70 apartment materialize, and he could move himself, his wife, and their two kids to Marzahn.[37]

Of course, as mentioned before, having children was perhaps the most effective way to get a coveted Marzahn apartment. For this reason, starting a new family and moving to a new place were often mixed up in one tangled web of cause and effect. As one resident, Renate Bautz, who moved to the Allee der Kosmonauten with her husband and four-year-old daughter in 1979 recalled, "we were only let into the AWG because we could say that there would soon be three of us. That was the reason that so many young people in the GDR married and quickly had kids; so they could get [a modern] apartment."[38]

Thus, for example, Gabriele Franik applied for an apartment in Marzahn in 1982 upon finding out that she was pregnant with twins. She already lived with her husband, Stefan, and their two-year-old son in a tiny apartment with no bathroom in Lichtenberg. She tried to explain her situation to a woman at the AWG at her work. "I'm expecting twins," Franik told her, to which the woman replied (with typical Berliner *Schnauze*, or brusque attitude) "what do you expect, everyone to just fall over when you want a bigger apartment? Prove to me first that you are having twins." Being pregnant was not good enough, the AWG needed to see real live babies carried to full term. Eventually, a key to a three-room apartment in Marzahn arrived while she was still in the maternity ward, extremely pregnant with the twin girls, presented by a joyous Stefan who declared "We did it! A modern (*Vollkomfort*)[39] apartment in Marzahn! Is this not insane???"[40] For Rainer Niedermann, who moved to Marzahn with his wife and infant son in 1984 from a small apartment in Treptow (which luckily did have warm water), it was a similar experience. Even though his wife was late in her pregnancy, he "would not get into Marzahn if the child was stillborn." This, despite the fact that Nachtmann had distinguished himself enough during his NVA service to be nominated for officer school in 1982. "This was the way it was for many," he recalled.[41]

Even when people did get an apartment, they were still required to provide an early payment. For Siedler, her three-room WHH GT 18 apartment on Allee der Kosmonauten required a deposit of 2,700 marks[42] (the average monthly income

[37] Hinze, "Das grüne Ungeheuer," Rohnstock, ed., *Keine Plattengeschichten*, 55.

[38] Bautz, "Wir taten es für uns," Tirri and Quiesser, eds., *Allee der Kosmonauten*, 67.

[39] The term *Vollkomfort* specifically implied an apartment with modern amenities for the time, especially central heating and air conditioning and a private (as opposed to shared with neighbors) bathroom with bath and hot-water shower. It is translated here as "modern" not to denote any stylistic or aesthetic characteristics per se, but in terms of its comfort and amenities.

[40] Gabriele Franik, "Was heißt Gemini?" in Rohnstock, ed., *Keine Plattengeschichten*, 79–80.

[41] Interview with Rainer Nordmann, Berlin, April 22, 2008.

[42] Siedler, "Festzunageln," 71.

for a factory or office worker at a state-owned enterprise in 1980 was 885 marks).[43] In most cases, this deposit was combined with a certain number of hours of labor—usually at the construction site, and about 500 hours' worth. The Hepners, for example, performed their 500 "AWG hours" on the weekends, building playgrounds, greenways, and paths in Marzahn—"the undertaking of my life," Lothar Hepner recalled, because "doing [those] hours on top of work was not easy."[44] Siedler did her hours along with other mothers who had small children with them, and were given tasks they could do with children in tow, often menial custodial jobs in the workers' quarters, such as emptying ashtrays and washing coffee cups.[45] In some cases "people's economic mass initiative" (*Volkswirtschaftliche Masseninitiative*, VMI) work could also count. So Manuela and Wilfried Klenner, along with their daughter Steffi, were required to pay down 4,000 marks for a three-room apartment in Marzahn Nord in 1987, but they paid half of this amount in the form of 500 hours of VMI labor.[46] The ability to swap labor for money worked the other way as well—Dieter and Irmgard Reimann were fed up with the "insane waste of time" that planting trees or shoveling dirt on weekends and holidays seemed to them, and found friends whom they could pay five marks an hour to take their place.[47] However, if someone did not have the money or the ability to work off the VMI hours, it was also possible that they could turn to yet another official organ governing the building and distribution of apartments, entitled the *Kommunale Wohnungsverwaltung* (Communal Apartment Government), KWV.[48]

Others simply got lucky, such as Bernd and Gabriele Peschke, a young couple with two young children (Franziska and Nicolas) who had applied unsuccessfully for a Marzahn apartment while living on Arkona Platz, when the Arkona project renovation began on their building. Because the modernization of old buildings meant combining the smaller apartments into larger ones, certain residents such as the Peschkes had to be evicted—these people were given the offer of a Marzahn apartment, to which, in 1979, the Peschkes agreed—"from the bottom of their hearts" according to *Neue Berliner Illustrierte*—and were whisked away to the fifth-floor WBS 70 apartment at 99 Allee der Kosmonauten.[49] Gerlinde Paulus managed to get her apartment in Marzahn in a similar way, as part of the Arnimplatz renovation.[50]

If moving to Marzahn meant escaping the "catastrophic" living conditions in the inner city, it also meant an often dramatic increase in rent, on top of the

[43] Statistisches Amt der DDR, ed., *Statistisches Jahrbuch der Deutschen Demokratischen Republik 1990* (Berlin: Rudolf Haufe Verlag, 1990), 144.

[44] Lothar and Helena Hepner, 87.

[45] Siedler, "Festzunageln," 71.

[46] Manuela, Wilfried and Steffi Klenner, "Auch wir bekamen irgendwann den Betonblock-Rappel," in Quiesser and Tirri, eds., *Allee der Kosmonauten*, 37.

[47] Dieter and Irmgard Reimann, "Von Architektur konnte man hier nicht redden," in Quiesser and Tirri, eds., *Allee der Kosmonauten*, 91.

[48] Dieter and Irmgard Reimann, "Von Architektur konnte man hier nicht redden," 91.

[49] Manfred Schulze, Helgard Behrendt, Günter Milde, and Volker Schielke, "Umzug. Vor den Kommunalwahlen: Glückliche Stunden in erfolgreichen Jahren," *Neue Berliner Illustrierte* (vol. 35, no. 20, 1979, 16–17).

[50] Interview with Gerlinde Paulus, Berlin, July 22, 2008.

deposit that new residents had to put down in cash and communal labor.[51] For Gisela Siedler and her husband and two children, this meant a hike from 54 marks a month in Weissensee to 212 marks. Shocked by the steep increase, the Siedlers complained to various state organs as well as *Neues Deutschland*, and eventually got it reduced to 140 marks.[52] This was more typical for Marzahn—Dieter and Irmgard Reimann paid 117 marks "warm" (meaning certain utilities were included in the monthly rent) for their three-room WBS 70 apartment on Allee der Kosmonauten in WG 2,[53] and Elisabeth Albrecht paid 92 marks for her two-bedroom WBS 70 ninth-floor apartment on Franz-Stenzer-Strasse.[54] Barbara Diehl went from paying 23 marks for the claustrophobic one-room place in Friedrichshain to paying 123 marks a month when she and her husband and son moved to their three-room apartment in a WBS 70-11 on Allee der Kosmonauten.[55] The rents were high, but could have been even higher—the state subsidized the average apartment in Marzahn to the tune of 591 marks.[56] Indeed, the cost of living in Marzahn was subsidized by the state by almost 70 percent. A similar story was repeated throughout the Republic; these subsidies, even more than the actual construction costs, were responsible for making the Housing Program the most expensive venture ever attempted by the GDR, and contributed greatly to the Republic's dire financial situation throughout the 1980s.

The way that the Housing Program reflected the goals of "real existing socialism"—to target young, married couples and families—manifested itself in the social and demographic make-up of Marzahn. According to a comprehensive sociological study of Marzahn and its residents conducted by Loni Niederländer at Humboldt University's Institute for Marxist–Leninist Sociology, 27 percent of the population of Marzahn was aged between twenty-five and thirty-five—twice the amount for the rest of Berlin. Seventeen percent were young children seven years of age and under; more than twice the percentage of East Berlin as a whole, meaning that over half the population of the new settlement were either people in their late twenties or early thirties, or young children. Conversely, only 4 percent of Marzahners were over sixty-five years of age, in contrast to just over a quarter of the population of Berlin as a whole (see Table 1).

In addition, in a republic that had the highest divorce rate in the world, Marzahners were much more likely to be married—66 percent of the population was married, 10.4 percent single, and only 4.4 percent divorced.[57] Furthermore, about 40 percent of the new residents had grown up in Berlin, 40 percent had grown up in a different city, and about 20 percent had grown up in a small village—although many, like Barbara Diehl, had moved to Berlin's inner city as

[51] Though, as Alice Kahl notes in her longitudinal study of Grünau outside of Leipzig, the rent in new apartment settlements could end up being cheaper than in old buildings, because the utilities were often included in the rent, and the heating was more efficient. See Kahl, *Erlebnis Plattenbau: eine Langzeitstudie* (Opland: Leske & Budrich, 2003), 71.

[52] Siedler, "Festzunageln," 71–2.

[53] Reimanns, "Architektur," 93.

[54] Albrecht, "Balkonblick," 36.

[55] Interview with Barbara Diehl, Berlin, February 20, 2008.

[56] Hemprich, "Hochhaus," 14.

[57] Niederländer, "Forschungsbericht," 2.

Table 1. Ages of the populations of Marzahn and East Berlin, 1980

Age range (years)	Percentage of total population of Marzahn	Percentage of total population of (East) Berlin
0–7	17.2	8.3
7–16	13.2	13.5
16–18	1.7	3.3
18–25	12.3	9.8
25–35	27	13.7
35–45	16	17.8
45–55	6	10.8
55–65	2.5	7.4
65+	4.1	15.4

Source: Niederländer, "Forschungsbericht zum 1. Intervall der Untersuchung 'Wohnen 80 – Marzahn.' Zur Entwicklung eines Neubaugebietes der Hauptstadt der DDR, Berlin." (Berlin: Humboldt University, 1981), Pt II, 2.

young adults, and counted themselves as Berliners, even if they had not grown up in Berlin.[58]

The people moving to Marzahn were indeed mostly from the working class, according to information gathering by the Stasi in a 1983 report. Of the 127,385 people who had moved to Marzahn by May 1983, 28,838 were employed (the rest were mainly children or the retired). Of these, 10,555 were employed in some form of industry, 3,345 in construction and 1,282 in forestry or agriculture. The rest worked in traditional crafts or trades, in stores ("trade"), and in transportation; and close to 10,000 worked in other areas, many likely for the state or the Party.[59] They were the mainstream of the socialist society; as East German sociologist Simone Hain has noted, Marzahn seemed to define the highest point of achievement for the typical East German couple:

> The typical marriage in the GDR was between a worker and a (female) academic. The (female) journalist and the carpenter, the painter and the (female) principal, the truck driver and the (female) historian, always with two or three small kids, and in the end, winding up in a Marzahn apartment.... It was the wish of their life, and their claim to quality of life.[60]

Several Marzahners seemed to have the impression that their neighbors were very much a part of the "system," either by being members of the security apparatus or being connected to the SED or its mass organizations in some way. Christian Domnitz, whose family lived in the village of Marzahn before 1976 and thus witnessed Marzahn's transformation from the beginning, noticed that the new children flooding into his brand-new school were "cut from a somewhat different cloth" (*teilweise anders gestricken*) to him and his friends; something he connected

[58] Bezirksmuseum Marzahn, *20 Jahre Marzahn*, 16.

[59] BStU MfS ZAIG 13751 "Erhebungsprogramm für die Ermittlung von Planstellennormativen, Bezirksverwaltung für Staatssicherheit Berlin-Marzahn," May 1983, 000316.

[60] Hain, "Marzahn, das sozialistische Projekt zwischen rational choice und Diktatur," in Quiesser and Tirri, eds., *Allee der Kosmonauten*, 12.

to the fact that some of them had fathers who were Army officers, or border guards.[61] This led to trouble one day when one of the new kids came to his house after school, and, as was their usual custom (until the buildings interrupted the signal too much), they watched West German television. The friend then told his father upon returning home, which led to an uncomfortable conversation between the two families. Still, Christian recalled that he did not find the new residents' homes to be a "den of Party big shots" (*eine Gegend von Parteibonzen*); rather, that just a handful of the new parents were "actual socialists"—the rest were just "loyal" to the state. After all, Christian noted, if you were really a big name in the socialist state, it was not to Marzahn that you moved, but to the luxury socialist housing right near the Wall on Leipziger Strasse.[62]

The proliferation of mid-level state or Party workers moving to Marzahn is confirmed by other residents, such as Irmgard Steinbach, who moved there in 1984 and found out that there were so many employees of the police and other state apparatuses in her building that it was known as the "Red House."[63] Reinhard Ladwig, a firefighter who moved to Marzahn with his wife Renate in 1979, agreed, noting that many of the people who lived in his building were from the same AWG, which contained many firefighters, police, and members of the East German Army.[64] Sybille Topp, a nurse and Comrade who moved to Marzahn from the midsized town of Neustrelitz in Brandenburg in 1978, also described her building as "overwhelmingly police and their families; among the wives many worked in health clinics" in Marzahn, like her. As was often the case, many of the police families were also Party families.[65]

Other residents of Marzahn seemed conflicted as to how many Party members were part of their new community. Aribert and Renate Bautz, who moved to the Allee der Kosmonauten in 1979, agreed that their building was not "only big shots (*Bonzen*)," and that the building committee (*Hausgemeinschaftsleitung*, HGL, discussed below) was "not partisan" (*nicht parteipolitisch*).[66] The Bartsches, Rudi and Jutta, who did not belong to a party, described themselves as "wanting nothing to do with politics," to the point of seldom voting, though Jutta was part of the state-run labor union (*Freie Deutsche Gewerksbund*, FDGB) for a time.[67] Gerda Marin, who moved to Marzahn in 1981, did not belong to the SED either and claimed that she did not feel any pressure from those around her—the "Comrades"—to join.[68] So too with Lothar Hepner, who moved to Marzahn in 1980 as a member of the power plant AWG "Elektrokohle." Heppner did not belong to the Party, and usually watched West German TV. He did, however, belong to the FDGB, but that, he claimed, was just because of the discounted travel packages that mem-

[61] Domnitz, "Packen," 42. [62] Domnitz, "Packen," 42.

[63] Irmgard Steinbach, "Diesen Zeiten sind Gott sei Dank vorbei!" in Quiesser and Tirri, eds., *Allee der Kosmnonauten*, 46.

[64] Renate and Reinhard Ladwig, "Wir haben beschlossen, dass wir hier alt werden," in Quiesser and Tierri, eds., *Allee der Kosmonauten*, 77.

[65] Sybille Topp, "Ich war mit Leib und Seele Schwester," in Quiesser and Tirri, eds., *Allee der Kosmonauten*, 41–2.

[66] Aribert and Renate Bautz, "Wir taten," 67–8.

[67] Jutta and Rudi Bartsch, "Die Häuser," 58. [68] Marin, "gelebt," 82.

bership entailed, especially at the GDR's Interhotels—that, and the fact that "everyone" was a member of the FDGB in his factory.[69]

For others, however, Marzahn and its new residents were part of a life lived though a progression of Party and state organs. Gerda Kriszunewicz, whose husband was an economist who got a job like so many other cadres with the State Planning Commission in 1979 and moved to Marzahn (later to work for the Ministers' Council), expressed this sentiment:

> Many were with the police, many were teachers' families, I worked in export (for the state), my husband for the Ministers' Council.... In my opinion, it had to do with the fact that many young people came here, who were raised in the same way and who participated in the development of socialism: Pioneers (*Junge Pioniere*, the Party's youth group for young children), FDJ (*Freie Deutsche Jugend*, Free German Youth, the Party's youth group), SED—that was the course of our lives.[70]

For Gerda, this pathway was one that led from a nineteenth-century apartment, through these Party and state organs, to a full-blown membership in the SED. An apartment in Marzahn was the proof of having been lifted out of the misery quarter, so it was infused with the state and the Party's narrative of upward mobility and social progress:

> Whoever came here from an old building fit right in automatically with us. I was a progressive person, and being a Comrade fit right in with all that. I was a Pioneer, in the FDJ, and automatically a Comrade. It was my own decision. At home, we watched (state TV news program) "Aktuelle Kamera" and even our kids watched and we answered their questions when they arose. We almost never watched West German TV.

Gerda described herself and her husband as *Betonköpfe*, literally "cement heads"—a phrase intended to describe conformists or followers, similar to the American expression "ditto head," but rich in irony considering the importance of cement in the built environment of Marzahn; the very expression of their ambition to conform to the system.

"A GIANT EMPIRE APPEARED"—ZERO HOUR ON THE GRÜNE WIESE

The first day that the new Marzahners arrived was often a bewildering, if not thrilling experience. Not only were they leaving behind everything they had known, in some cases everything their parents or grandparents had ever known, and entering a world that was new to them—they were entering a world that was new to almost

[69] Lothar and Helena Hepner, "Im Altbau," 88. It should be noted that a number of these interviewees were interviewed for a book written by a Swedish journalist and Italian photographer—in other words, "Westerners"—to whom some of the former East Germans certainly would have wanted to portray themselves as as detached from communism and the SED as possible.

[70] Gerda Kriszunewicz, "Wir waren warscheinlich Betonköpfe," in Quiesser and Tirri, eds., *Allee der Kosmonauten*, 52.

everyone. They were entering a world that was still in its becoming. They too, like the workers who first began breaking the ground for the settlement, felt like pioneers or colonists, starting a completely new life in a new urban space.[71]

After packing up their moving van—the wait for vans and movers was lengthy in the days of the Housing Program all over the GDR, with delays of up to eight weeks in some places[72]—the new arrivals drove out of the old city (or in some cases out of their old villages or from other cities), through the countryside and into a vast landscape of sand dunes, mud, construction vehicles, cranes along the *Taktstrassen*, and half- and newly finished buildings.

Gabriele Franik was unprepared for the site—she, like most of the new arrivals, "only knew Marzahn from the media. I had no idea of the scale of the construction site."[73] Still pregnant, she and Stefan drove their Wartburg from the hospital where she was due to go into labor all the way out to Marzahn, to see their apartment, which was still under construction:

> He drove and drove. We emerged in a giant construction site: our way was lined with cranes. Everywhere stood just-begun *Plattenbauten*. There were no streets to be seen anywhere. Mountains of sand towered, a gigantic wasteland of mud (*Schlammwüste*); nowhere was there a tree, or even a shrub.[74]

Like many Marzahners, in the old Berliner tradition of moving in "wet," the Franiks were given the key to their apartment on the second floor of the WBS 70–11 on 43 Ludwig-Renn-Strasse while the upper floors were still under construction. With a stomach that measured 108 cm in circumference, and so pregnant that she was barely able to waddle to the front door, Gabriele recalled:

> My heart was in my throat with excitement; my knees shook as I left the car and we walked up to the second floor together, the building still smelling of cement and paint. My husband opened the door to our new apartment and...
>
> A giant empire appeared, with enough room for five family members. Central heating, warm water from the wall, and a six-meter-long balcony! This is what happiness looks like. We fell into each other's arms, euphorically.[75]

For Gabriele, the memory of the *newness* of the experience—the barely dried cement and paint, the cranes and sand—was intertwined with the memory of her extremely advanced pregnancy. Both the 108-centimeter stomach and the large, fresh concrete space that would be their new home were "pregnant" with meaning to come, both fecund and ready to yield forth some new form of life—not a coincidence or a mere metaphor, nor an isolated incidence; Gabriele was only one of thousands of expectant or brand-new mothers to experience the twin events of a new child and a new, modern, prefabricated apartment in a still-unfinished housing

[71] Kolenc and Blotevogel, *Fremdenführer*, 27.

[72] Manfred Schulze, Helgard Behrendt, Günter Milde, and Volker Schielke, "Umzug. Vor den Kommunalwahlen: Glückliche Stunden in erfolgreichen Jahren," in *Neue Berliner Illustrierte* (vol. 36, no. 20, 1980, 12).

[73] Franik, "Gemini," 79. [74] Franik, "Gemini," 80. [75] Franik, "Gemini," 81.

settlement in those years in the GDR—a direct result of the policy of the state and the Party.

Others experienced the same kind of disorientation; something like landing on a completely new planet. Klaus Hölgermann was one. He moved his family from the small town of Ilmenau, south of Erfurt, where they had shared a house with his wife's grandparents, to Marzahn in the snowy winter of 1979. In the deep snow and ice, under the moonlight and the lights of the third shift, Klaus and his family and the movers arrived—and promptly got lost. There were still no street signs, and the snow made it even more of an alien and foreign landscape. It took the movers "four or five" trips around the settlement before they found their building.[76] His wife, Marianne, and their small daughter had never seen Marzahn, like many, except from the plans shown in the media.[77] Others specifically compared the new surroundings to a moonscape; Dr Bernd Engling, for example, penned a song in commemoration of his move to Marzahn, written in full Berliner dialect, entitled "A True Plant from Berlin" ("*'Ne Echte Pflanze aus Berlin*"):

> I've lived here in Marzahn for many years
> Right there in a newly constructed block
> Back when I moved here, there was lots of dirt
> Rubber boots fulfilled their purpose
> And all around it looked like on the Moon
> I did not get used to it so easily.[78]

The same was true of Werner Hinkel, who recalled seeing his building amidst others, all still under construction: "The tower jutted out like a post, and all around it looked like a giant wasteland (*Wüste*)." Going in, he found everything, including the cement and the paint, still wet, as had the Franiks. The experience of Joachim and Jutta Kretzschmar, who moved to 65 Heinrich-Rau-Strasse in the same snowy January of 1979 was defined the by the experience of moving into a construction zone—they could see the line of WBS 70s stretching northwards from their own building, along the *Taktstrasse,* each in a progressively less advanced state of construction. The most defining sense memory for Joachim during that first year was of cranes towering outside their window in the day, and headlights shining through their windows in the night: "And under headlights we made our start, because the deliveries of the heavy loads from the concrete panel factory also ran during the night. It took a long time until the last flatbed truck was gone from here, and the last cranes were dismantled."[79]

This "moonscape," as some new residents called it, was quickly incorporated into the new lives of the residents, and children in particular; the endless sand hills and half-finished construction projects—combined with lax safety regulations—made Marzahn in the late 1970s and early 1980s a "dreamscape" for young children. A young mason, who was one of the 1,300 FDJ members who were sent to Marzahn in apprentice-like "youth brigades" in 1977, recalled seeing "swarms of children, in

[76] Bezirksmuseum Marzahn, *20 Jahre Marzahn*, 119.
[77] Bezirksmuseum Marzahn, *20 Jahre Marzahn*, 39.
[78] Engling, "Echte Pflanze," 87. [79] Engling, "Echte Pflanze," 45.

colorful rubber boots, playing in absolutely enormous construction puddles."[80] Christian Domnitz, the child whose family lived in Marzahn before the construction, recalled the wonder of construction on a vast scale all around him:

> All around we found a gigantic adventure playground (*Abenteuerspielplatz*): pieces of cement shot out of the ground everywhere. Rough and raw towers, entirely empty of people. We played in the chaos in between. Because of the clayish soil, the water did not drain well. Giant, turgid (*aufgewühlte*) puddles formed between the construction pits, piles of earth, and gravel piles. We played at our own kind of construction (*Tiefbau*), and connected the puddles with canals. The point [of the game] was to channel as much water as possible in wide, fast streams.[81]

Here, what stands out in Domnitz's memory is not just the fact that he and other schoolchildren were finding ways to adapt their imaginative play to the massive upheavals of their physical world, but that they saw the overturned and churned earth and water much as the socialist state saw it—as infinitely plastic and malleable. This, of course, is not an unusual or specifically socialist sentiment in children. The universal appeal of sandboxes, sandcastles, or children's molding clay attest to the particular dialectic formed between sediment (sand, clay, etc.), which is both natural and malleable, and the childhood imagination. It was the project of the socialist state that dug up that soil, and created the piles and pits and puddles; a project flowing from many of the same impulses that lie at the heart of children at play in sandboxes or on the beach. In turn, the children recreated the same impulse to build anew amidst a primordial ooze, as if they were absorbing the mission of the state and recasting it into their own play worlds.

In fact, for Domnitz, the relationship between the high-rise apartment towers and the soil was filtered through a framework of nature. "All over, concrete pieces shot up out of the ground…when I was at home with my family, and I gazed out the window, I did not see trees growing, as elsewhere; I saw dwellings growing. There were more and more, they grew all around, and they grew higher and higher." This "forest" of prefabricated buildings was not politically neutral, either: "Over time, we noticed the changes that the high-rise buildings brought with them: our reception of Western TV signals grew worse. With every high-rise, the image flickered a little more."[82] The height of these housing blocks, and the steel and concrete used to build them, made them an ideological bulwark against the West.

The piles and puddles could also form the opportunity for resistance to the rigidity of cement and rebar for children, as exemplified by perhaps the most classic film about housing blocks, *Insel der Schwäne* (*Island of the Swans*), released in 1982. Based on a book by Benno Pludra, *Insel der Schwäne* follows a family's move from a small village to Marzahn, and was filmed in 1982 in the construction site of Marzahn. The father, a construction worker on the site, is thrilled to get an apartment in a WBS 70/22 for his wife, his son Stefan, and daughter Sabrina.

80 C. Metzner, "Aus Häuser wächst eine Stadt," *Marzahn Aktuell* (vol. 6, no. 6, 25 March 1982).

81 Domnitz, "Packen," 41.

82 Domnitz, "Jetzt packen wir hier alles zusammen," in Rohnstock, ed., *Keine Plattengeschichten*, 41–4, 41.

Stefan, a rebellious early adolescent, is not so thrilled.[83] The plot plays out amidst the scenes of vast dirt piles and puddles as well as half-finished living blocks and construction debris. One of the climactic scenes takes place on a large dirt hill with an equally large puddle at its base, which Stefan and his friends have claimed for their own play place, building their own tunnels into the sides of the dirt pile, reinforced with construction debris.[84]

The hill serves as a site for the issue of power—and its relation to vertical space and topography—to play out. The steep slope of the hill is the setting for the confrontation between Stefan's friend, Hubert, and the bully of the new settlement, distinguished by his fancy windbreaker. Hubert recognizes the importance of always having the high ground, and is able to use his position further up the slope of the hill to push the bigger and stronger bully into the puddle, thus turning the table on the social hierarchy of the buildings' children.[85]

In another scene, Stefan's father demands the children stop building tunnels into the hill, because they are dangerous, and is pelted with rocks by the children.[86] He responds by having the hill bulldozed, and in response the children, led by his rebellious son, make their own placards with crayons and markers that say "We don't want cement! We want fields and tunnels!" "What do you have against fields?" Stefan asks at dinner, confrontationally, to which his father replies, summing up the very raison d'etre of the history of the German working class and the socialist state's massive building program: "I don't have anything against fields. But the plan is for a big city to be built here. I'm a construction worker. My father was a carpenter. His father was a mason. We build, *everywhere*!"[87]

In the end, Stefan's father makes the only gesture of reconciliation that he can, which is to begin construction of a playground on the spot of the hill, which begins, of course, with the pouring of a large area of cement. "What is that?" Stefan's girlfriend asks, to which he replies "It's our field." The children, in a Truffaut-esque moment, proceed to find construction debris and branches and "plant" them in the still-wet cement, thus continuing to turn the malleability of the materials used in shaping the environment to their own advantage.[88]

As the children made use of the "moonscape" outdoors, some families found that, indoors, their euphoria quickly turned to aggravation as numerous flaws in the construction were immediately apparent to the new residents. In particular, residents found that the seams between the concrete panels were not adequately insulated, with a kind of plastic insulation on the interior side of the panels, which led to moisture bleeding through the concrete, running down the interior seams

[83] "Lieber Tasso, heute ist Sonntag, da will ich Dir mal schreiben," *Insel der Schwäne*, directed by Herrmann Zschoche (1983; Berlin: DVD, Icestorm Entertainment GmbH, 2006).

[84] "Na, Hubertschen, müssen Vater und Muttern wieder arbieten?" *Insel der Schwäne*.

[85] "Na, Hubertschen, müssen Vater und Muttern wieder arbieten?" *Insel der Schwäne*.

[86] "Na, Hubertschen, müssen Vater und Muttern wieder arbieten?" *Insel der Schwäne*.

[87] "Wir wollen keinen Beton! Sondern Tunnel und Wiesen..." *Insel der Schwäne*.

[88] "Sie betonieren den Spielplatz! Lasst die Bäume stehen!" *Insel der Schwäne*. It should be noted that because of this and other scenes, *Insel der Schwäne* was heavily criticized in the official media by representatives of the Party, who felt that it portrayed the building of prefabricated construction blocks in a negative light.

and causing damage whenever there was heavy precipitation. A report from Berlin Party secretary Konrad Naumann himself blamed the design of the WBS 70/5 and/11, as well as failures of the construction teams to insulate properly. This was a particular problem during the severe weather of August 1978, which led to "visible water damage" in 800 of the 1,100 apartments inhabited in Marzahn up to that point.[89] The second section (*Bauabschnitt*) of WG1 had also experienced flooding in its basement as a result of shoddy construction.[90]

For those who occupied a top-floor apartment, the problem was even worse. The Mayor himself, Gerd Cyske, who occupied the top floor of one of the first towers built in WG1, found it rained through his ceiling shortly after moving in—a major embarrassment for both the montage brigade and the panel factory.[91] The roofs were often not built to withstand heavy snow—especially the multiple blizzards of the "catastrophic winter" of 1978–9—leading to snow falling into the crawlspace layer between the top floor and the ceiling (called a *Trampelgeschoss* or *Drempelgeschoss*), saturating the insulation fiberglass (*Kamelitwolle*) and causing water damage to the apartments below, as well as a loss of insulation and thus heat in the top-floor apartments.[92] Joachim Kretzschmar recalled that one of the first memories of moving in, less than a week after the first of the heavy blizzards (December 29–31, 1978), was of the two feet (around 60 cm) of snow on the roof—which he claimed was made of panels "only loosely laid upon each other"—melting through into their new apartment. "There were many like us," he claimed.[93]

Indeed, as soon as people began to move into apartments in Marzahn, the infamous *Eingaben* (petitions or complaints) began flowing out and flooding into Party and state offices. Other frequent complaints included, in the WBS 70/5 units, that a faulty pump for warm water and warm air was responsible for apartments losing heat and warm water when the temperature fell below 15 °C.[94] Other *Eingaben* focused on windows with faulty seals, defective doors that would not stay closed or which jammed, the slowness of repair services, and in general the delays in being able to move into the apartments people had been promised—or to enroll their children in KiKos or use other facilities they needed because the buildings could not be opened due to faulty construction.[95]

MUD AND RAINBOWS: A NEW WORLD OF THE SENSES

The vast scene of repeating blocks, construction equipment, and mud that greeted new arrivals to Marzahn was more than just a new place, and more than just a

[89] BStU, MfS BV Berlin AKG 1373: Konrad Naumann, "Information über einige Probleme, die vom VEB WBK Berlin im Stadtbezirk Berlin-Marzahn fertiggestellte Wohnungen betreffen," April 11, 1979.

[90] Naumann, "Information."

[91] Cyske, "Mit der Bummi-Bahn in den Kindergarten," in Rohnstock, ed., *Keine Plattengeschichten*, 26.

[92] Naumann, "Information," 5.

[93] Verein Kids & Co., *Südspitze*, 39.

[94] Naumann, "Information," 5.

[95] BStU MfS HA XVIII file no. 6869.

matter of adjusting to a new home. It was, on the most intimate and psychological level, a fundamental change in the kinds of sensory perceptions experienced by the new residents—signals, and patterns of signals, to their eyes, ears, noses, and even tongues. Through their skin, through the soles of their shoes, through their inner ears and their senses of balance and distance, and even through their sense of time itself, the world as it came to be represented in their minds, in the neocortexes of hundreds of thousands of people (and, counting the rest of the country, millions—and counting the rest of the Eastern Bloc and the USSR, tens of millions) began to fundamentally change. This was not necessarily the plan of the state, but in adopting the holistic building approach which stemmed from Le Corbusier, in which all aspects of the life of a city were created anew on a (supposedly) blank slate, the state found that construction and architecture could in fact change the very inner psyches of people in ways that traditional methods of propaganda and education could not, since these were channeled through at most one or two sensory inputs. This was, of course, the kind of geomancy that Le Corbusier had foreseen: rebuilt cities would produce rebuilt subjects.

The first and most immediate change in the sensory world was, as mentioned above, the ubiquitous dirt, which, because of the poor drainage of the clayey soil in places, turned to an omnipresent mud whenever it rained.[96] So it was in the accounts of building and moving into Marzahn: "Whenever there was rainy weather, the soil of Marzahn, churned up by all the construction, turned to a gooey pulp (*zähflüssiges Brei*)," recalled Mayor Cyske.[97] Shoes would often get stuck in the mud, causing people to step out of them. Smaller children would actually sink so deep in the mud they would get stuck and have to be rescued; as Anneliese Suck recalled, one day in 1980 saw a three-year-old crying for help outside her window, stuck waist deep in the mud and unable to move.[98] The mud was so bad, it threatened the construction itself—an entire brigade of workers had to be devoted to clearing the mud from the main supply road.[99]

For Marzahners, it meant that mud itself became a central theme of their new life. The "fight against mud" was "daily" according to Harald Buttler, a resident of Marzahn who became Mayor in 1995.[100] Rainer Nordmann, who moved to Marzahn with his wife and child in 1979, found the mud made transporting children almost impossible: "I remember I had this fold-up stroller, you know the kind? But where could it roll? I ended up carrying my kid in one arm and the damn thing in the other arm—it was not easy to get around."[101]

In fact, the early years of Marzahn were so dominated by this one defining environmental characteristic—mud—that for most of the new arrivals those years

[96] The continual reappearance of mud as a theme in the attempts of Germans to control the nature around them is prominent in Blackbourn's *Conquest of Nature*, (see, e.g. p. 15).

[97] Marte Kühling, "Weisse Fahnen, Hohe Prozente—Anekdoten," in Bezirksamt Marzahn, ed., *1979–1999*, 63.

[98] Suck, "Knirpsenrettung," in Bezirksamt Marzahn, ed., *1979–1999*, 45.

[99] Kühling, "Weisse Fahnen."

[100] Bärbel Felber, *1979–1999. 20 Jahre Marzahn* (Berlin: Pressesetelle Bezirksamt Marzahn, 1999), 9.

[101] Interview with Rainer Nordmann, March 22, 2008, Berlin-Marzahn.

became an era unto themselves, bound together by the pervasive idea of mud, and specifically the ubiquitous and identical rubber boots that almost everyone owned to deal with it.[102] "The era of rubber boots [*Gummistiefelzeit*], [is what] we all called the first years here," recalled Renate Bautz, who moved into the Allee der Kosmonauten in 1979, and the term is how most original Marzahners refer to their first days and months after moving there.[103] The rubber boots—sometimes called "Marzahn foot condoms"[104]—became part of the identity of Marzahn; as much as the mud itself. "You can tell Marzahners by their shoes" was a common saying at the time, according to Cyske.[105] Renate Bautz remembered similarly: "you could tell from where we came by what was on our shoes."[106]

The mud and the construction noises and smells would pass away, eventually. But there were changes to Marzahners' sensory world that were permanent. Many of these were framed by the new spatial matrix within which they suddenly found themselves, a matrix defined by a new sense of vertical and horizontal space. More plainly: many of the new residents lived higher off the ground than they (or anyone they knew or anyone in their previous generations) ever had before. Relatively few buildings in Germany stood taller than five stories. Even if people lived on an upper story of a tenement, they often lived in the first or second courtyard or in a "passageway" apartment, in which the view from the window (assuming there was one) looked out on another wall of the courtyard immediately opposite. There was little view even of the sky, or the sun, except at high noon, and no view whatsoever of the horizon or the surrounding geography. And in general, East German territory, with the exception of some areas in Thuringia and Saxony, is mostly dominated by the glacial sea plain, no more than a few meters above sea level, of Brandenburg, Anhalt, and Mecklenburg/Pomerania. Many East Germans, further, were former refugees or descendants of former refugees from lands further to the east, the former Prussian lands, even lower-lying than Brandenburg and Mecklenburg. These were flatlanders, for whom verticality had never played much of a role in their socio-spatial dialectic.

So living in a high rise now meant the opening of a new world of the senses—exactly, it must be noted, as Le Corbusier had intended. Marzahners often first picked the word "sunny" to describe their new apartments, again, following the CIAM's prescriptions, and manifesting the intentions of the WBS 70's architects. Sunshine in Marzahn itself became a new and major facet of life, (even if north-eastern Germany was and is notorious for long stretches of overcast weather, especially in the winter). Living vertically opened up new phenomena of the natural world that were either not visible or, at best, highly obscured for those living in rental barracks. Johann and Sofia Schöring experienced this when they moved to Marzahn from Pankow in 1983, where they had lived in a passageway apartment with no windows that they described as "miserable." They had very much grown up with war, fascism, and the misery of the working-class movement casting a shadow on the narrative arc of their lives. Johann's father,

[102] Buttler, 9. [103] Bautz, "Wir taten es für uns," 67. [104] Peters, *Platten*, 108.
[105] Kühling, "Weisse Fahnen," 63. [106] Bautz, "Wir taten es für uns," 67.

opposed to the regime and the War, deserted and was sentenced to death in absentia, surviving in hiding to return to the family later, but penniless. Johann, born in 1940, was trained as a wooden boat-builder in the 1950s and early 1960s. Sofia was born to a father who was a member of the KPD, who "grew up red," and spent much of the war in Sachsenhausen, managing to survive and return to the family after the liberation.

Living on the seventh floor of a QP 71 building, with windows and a balcony facing towards the East, they saw sunrises and rainbows—not for the first time, but on a daily basis, and from a majestic and unfettered vantage point. They documented these with their camera and saved the images in a photo album.[107] They were not the only ones to incorporate a record of a new *Sinnwelt*, a new sense of meteorology and altitude, within the arc of their lives; other Marzahners did the same, such as Evelyn Marquardt, who also documented the stunning displays of rainbows from her WBS 70 balcony, which faced south-east (see Figure 8).[108]

For in Northern Europe, the jet stream usually takes weather on a straight west-to-east trajectory. Weather systems, such as storms and rainclouds, sweep across northern Germany, across Berlin and Brandenburg, and then continue across Poland. In particular, short, intense rain and thunderstorms—squalls—define the weather in the spring, summer, and fall in north-eastern Germany, with the sun often making several appearances in between fast-moving and short-lived bursts of rain. As with many severe weather systems, these storms often occur later in the day, once the sun has warmed up the surface enough to fuel the systems. The combination of late afternoon/early evening sun shining at an angle from the western horizon through the gaps between curtains of showers moving away to the east produces the ideal conditions for rainbows—if one has a clear and unobstructed view of the eastern horizon. The later in the day, the lower the angle of the western sun, and the more likely it is that rainbows will be produced; also the less likely a dweller within a cramped urban environment will be able to see the rainbows. So new Marzahners, being in a position where they could see rainbows regularly, not only experienced a sensory artifact new to their everyday worlds; their new sense of verticality also introduced a new sense of orientation, in Germany, in Europe, on a strict east–west axis defined by the weather and the sun as much as by political geography. All of this orientation was made possible by the elevation of Marzahners out of the cramped inner cities, which had been defined by a very different form of orientation. Not everyone had an eastern view, of course, but there were other sources of verticality in Marzahn, including the Kienberg and the Ahrensfelder Berg, both of which stood high enough (between 70 and 100 m) that they offered anyone who climbed them stunning views of the Barnim Plain stretching to the Oder Valley to the east.

For those with western views, the sunsets were often the first things they thought of when asked what was the best part of their new apartments. "The best are the sunsets," commented Renate Bautz, reflecting on her twenty-five years in Marzahn.

[107] Interview with Johann and Sofia Schöring, Berlin, May 23, 2008.
[108] Interview with Evelyn Marquardt, Berlin, May 26, 2008.

"You don't have to go to Capri. Every night we enjoy the view right from our window."[109] For others, the view was what helped mitigate the ambivalence they felt leaving their familiar surroundings in the city, such as Helena Hepner: "We weren't terribly excited [to move to Marzahn] because we lived in the city. It was like a little town here [*Dörfli*] for us—everything was just farmland. But we moved into a building with a beautiful easterly view, and when the weather was clear, we could see all the way to the Müggelturm [a modern recreation of a historic tower at on the Müggelsee, a popular vacation outing destination, 20 km south-east of Marzahn]."[110] Renate and Reinhard Ludwig also described their view of the distant Müggelberge (hills near the Müggelsee) and the Schönefeld airport even further south, and a sweeping vista "from Hoppegarten to Neukölln."[111] The new vertical axis of their lives gave them a new sense of orientation within the horizontal geography of the Berlin–Brandenburg eastern landscape, especially if they had a building built on a north–south axis and an apartment that spanned from the east-facing side to the west-facing side, like Gerd Jütte, a machinist who was one of the first residents of WG 1 along with his wife Carola and one-year-old daughter Ilka. Upon moving in, he found that "on the one side we saw Biesdorf, and behind that far-reaching fields on which sheep were grazing, and on the other side, we had an unfettered view of the city center, out of which the TV tower rose."[112]

For others, the change in vertical orientation was too radical. Some people simply grumbled from time to time about the height of the buildings, complaining that they were simply too tall.[113] Others found the new heights to be such a change from their previous lives that they experienced vertigo. This was the case with the elderly Wandreys, who had at first to be carefully escorted to the windows of their twenty-second-story apartment by their *Hausmeister*, who had become familiar with this kind of disorientation from people who had come "from the cramped living quarters of the inner city."[114]

As much as prefabricated housing settlements like Marzahn were reorientations on a vertical axis, they were also a reordering of horizontal space. For some, it was a matter of simple convenience—crucial to the design of Marzahn was, as mentioned earlier, a maximum distance of 600 m between residences and other facilities such as schools and transit points. Publications in the GDR such as the *Neue Berliner Illustrierte* naturally highlighted this particular issue. In an article about new arrivals to Marzahn, *NBI* quoted Marianne and Dieter Fornfeist on the convenient proximity of the facilities and shops nearby:

> Our apartment tower is in a really good location. To go shopping it's just a few steps. And also, the service center is right nearby; same thing with the post office and the

[109] Bautz, "Wir taten es für uns," 67. [110] Lothar and Helena Hepner, "Im Altbau," 87.

[111] Renate and Reinhard Ladwig, "Wir haben beschlossen, dass wir hier alt werden," in Quiesser and Tirri, eds., *Allee der Kosmonauten*, 77.

[112] Manfred Otto, "Berliner Journal: Wo einst Schafherden weideten," *Neue Berliner Illustrierte* (no. 50, 1980, 2).

[113] Dieter and Irmgard Reimann, "Von Architektur konnte man hier nicht reden," in Quiesser and Tirri, eds., *Allee der Kosmonauten*, 93.

[114] Dieter and Irmgard Reimann, "Architektur," 93.

restaurants. And for the kids? There are two playgrounds right behind the building. At the bigger one there is a youth club, just around the corner.[115]

Others clearly read the social and ideological goals of the GDR as inscribed into the horizontal space of the settlement, such as Gerda Kriszunewicz:

> It was a signature [*Aushängeschild*] of the GDR: many apartments, a Kindergarten, day care [*Krippe*], and a school in each living sector. People did not have far to go to get to the Kindergarten, nor to the S-Bahn to get to work.[116]

Others, like Domnitz, also saw the broad meaning of modernity and socialism inscribed in the very re-ordering of space produced in Marzahn. For the young Domnitz, the physical reality of the relationships between the living towers, the pathways, and the schools shaped his own inner self into a "socialist personality:"

> When I went to school, I could choose between two paths. Both were about equal in length and both paved with asphalt, so I could keep my feet dry. One led straight along the edge of the new housing settlement. That was the way that almost all the kids used. Every morning there was a kind of procession. To the left the new housing settlement stood tall and proud, and in front of us lay the school. When I took this path, I felt as if I were developing a socialist personality, which would fit into a huge socialist project.[117]

But there was another side for Domnitz, who had always been conflicted about the transformation of his home village. The environment, both built and "natural," was the medium through which the socialist state was creating this "socialist personality" inside him. But the "environment" was essentially a neutral substrate—it could just as well be manipulated in ways that ran counter to the state's intentional or implicit designs. Simply by finding a second path to school, whether a short cut or not, he could reclaim or preserve a part of him that was not turning into the "socialist personality:"

> The other way snaked through the small garden colony. There, I could linger [*nachhängen*] in peace and alone with my thoughts. In the summer, plum trees grew over the fences, dogs ran barking through the gardens, and on one corner there was a crazy old man who carved wooden figurines. The figurines were colorfully painted, and funny to look at, and then there was a small water mill that still turned round and round. That was really the path of *self-discovery* [emphasis added].[118]

Domnitz straddled both worlds—the world of the straight path with a clear destination, and the world of whimsy, nature, and chance—by walking both paths: "Sometimes," he recalled "I took one, and sometimes the other. I liked both of them."[119]

Walking amidst green space was another new way in which a socio-spatial dialectic was created in Marzahn. One of the first things Sofia and Johann Schöring did when they got to Marzahn in 1984 was to wander out to the Kienberg, walk

115 Hemprich, "Hochhaus," 17.
116 Kriszunewicz, "Betonköpfe," 51.
117 Domnitz, "Packen," 43.
118 Domnitz, "Packen," 43.
119 Domnitz, "Packen," 43.

along the Wuhle, and get lost in the vastness of the green meadows all around them. In what could have been a testimonial to the original intentions of the Athens Charter, Leo Mitschke remarked, "The air is good here." Gerlinde Paulus added, "It's a green city district [*Stadtbezirk*]...you really have to get out of your apartment and go for walks."[120]

In a way, the fact that Marzahn was created to be so walkable, and the fact that all the buildings were surrounded by large amounts of green space gave residents the ability to produce their own space in a way that would not have been possible in a cramped older neighborhood. This is because the green spaces in between buildings allowed for residents to create their own "desire paths;" cutovers between parallel paths and sidewalks, which are still there and in use in Marzahn. Thus, a Mr Preußing remarked in giving a tour to two visitors of WG III, that the distances between any two points in Marzahn are often not connected as the crow flies, but rather one has to zig and zag through the concentric rings surrounding each subsection, and this is the reason for the vast network of worn footpaths through the green space. "If you know your way around, you can use the shortcuts," he remarked.[121] Essentially, the green spaces between buildings became interstitial space that functioned, again, like a blank slate, allowing residents to shape nature and space to their own collective destinies, refracting yet again the same dynamic of space and ideology that "thoroughly dominated" the building of Marzahn in the first place.

There was a flipside to the emptiness and vastness of the new settlements, however. The move to places like Marzahn entailed a radical break with the past in all the ways documented above, true enough, but because the new environment was so sterile, so empty, and such a blank slate, it did not entirely break the connections held in the memories of the new arrivals. There was a scarcity of sense memory cues—rarely did Marzahners see a sight, smell a scent, hear a noise, or traverse a pathway that sparked a Proustian moment of recall of their and their families' old lives. But those memories continued to live on like an echo in a racquetball chamber, dying away only slowly, or like the ghost pains of amputated limbs. Thus for a time, Marzahn was, for many, two worlds—the immediate world of prefabricated buildings, construction teams, mud, fields, open spaces, and rainbows, and a *ghost* world, consisting of old neighborhoods, shops, stoops, courtyards, parks, cobblestone streets—and all the history of the world before socialism that was inscribed in those places—superimposed like a fading watermark on the bright and hard world around them.

"You missed the *Kiez* culture," Leo Mitschke recalled. "You missed rambling down the street, peering in shop windows; familiar cafes on the sidewalk; long walks; getting ice cream at the corner with the neighborhood kids."[122] Aribert and Renate Bautz agreed, with Renate remarking that they missed strolling down the Karl-Marx-Allee, which was a few blocks from their old apartment in Mitte: "Even

[120] Interview with Mitschke and Paulus, July 22, 2008.
[121] Kolenc and Blotevogel, *Fremdenführer*, 22–5.
[122] Interview with Leo Mitschke, July 22, 2008.

today, we miss the window shopping [*Schaufensterbummeln*];[123] here, there is mainly the one shopping center."[124]

The concentration of shops into one-stop "shopping centers," similar to large, Western-style shopping marts, was another feature of life in prefabricated housing settlements like Marzahn. As in the West, such centers were to make life more convenient and rationalized, especially for East German women, in this case through shopping, thus reducing their "double burden" of work and housework. Rather than there being several small neighborhood stores, such as the grocer, the butcher, the bakery, the beverage/liquor store, and so on, lining old city streets, all these would be concentrated in one place; a modern store with a produce aisle, a bread aisle, and so on, usually with goods such as breads and pastries made remotely and shipped to the store. This was key to the design of such settlements, going back to Le Corbusier, who called for the "death of the street" as a place in which transportation, work, shopping, and living mixed. Concentrating all the food shopping, and often all the shopping, in one place enabled the rest of the design of the settlement to work—it was the only way to ensure that an economy of scale could be produced and that the requirement of walkable distances from all residential locations could be met.

But, more than almost any other facet of the old *Kiez*, the neighborhood shops and businesses were what produced space. This was something that the DBA-ISA repeatedly found to be a chief complaint of residents moving into new housing settlements like Marzahn. As one woman remarked, responding in a 1975 survey of 3,747 residents of prefabricated housing settlements, "I like it here, but the smell of fresh *Brötchen* [small rolls, usually baked fresh in the morning and consumed with various toppings or plain for breakfast] at my baker in my former living area is something I really miss."[125] This smell of *Brötchen* baking in the early morning which filled the old city neighborhoods was gone, leaving only the memory of the smell in its absence. In general, in most studies carried out in the new housing settlements, people consistently ranked the shopping possibilities, especially their preference for the old neighborhood shops, as one of the least satisfactory aspects of their new lives—even though, the new centralized marts saved residents an average of 2.3 hours a week.[126] The study's author, Alfred Schwandt, remarked that there had been a "loss of certain qualities of the earlier shopping experience" which, "as a necessary consequence of the centralized shopping system,

[123] The shop windows in socialism were highly significant in the context of the state's ideologically driven consumer society. See Pence, "Schaufenster des sozialistischen Konsums: Texte der ostdeutschen 'Consumer Culture'," in Alf Lüdtke and Peter Becker eds., *Akten. Eingaben. Schaufenster. Die DDR und ihre Texte: Erkundungen zu Herrschaft und Alltag* (Berlin: Akademie Verlag), 91–118.

[124] Aribert and Renate Bautz, "Taten," 67.

[125] BA-L DH2 23447 Dr-Ing. Dip. Phil Alfred Schwandt. "Neubauwohngebiete im Urteil der Bewohner: Soziologische Analyse einer Umrage in zwölf Neubauwohngebieten der DDR September–Oktober 1975," Bauakademie der DDR, Inst. F. Städtebau und Architektur; Abt. Theorie und Geschichte; Themengruppe Städtebausoziologie (March 1977), 25.

[126] Schwandt, "Neubauwohngebiete," 19; the study refers to two previous studies that produced these findings, a study by the Leipzig-based Institute for Market Research in 1970 and one by the University of Rostock in 1974 which confirmed it. In the 1975 IBA study, only 47% rated the shopping experience as "good," while 33% rated it as "satisfactory," and 19% as "unsatisfactory."

have been lost for all time." Despite the fact that old *Kiez* with its corner bakery was (at least for the new residents of the settlements) gone forever, consigned to an old and forgettable era of history, Schwandt observed that "it is always still surprising to determine how strongly the absence of (for example) a baker, the immediate relationship between the bakery and the customer, impacts the satsfaction level of the living milieu overall."[127]

The magazine *Kultur im Heim*, in its full-issue exposé on Marzahn in 1986, conceded that the comfortable, familiar haunts of the old neighborhoods, such as bakeries, cafés, and beer stalls, were the one thing still missing nine years into the construction of Marzahn, remarking: "There is still a lack of small, individual stores, a proper shopping street, or in the realm of gastronomy, the experience of being served in a small, cozy café or at a beer stand on the corner." Still, *Kultur im Heim* noted, these traditions would develop, given enough time.[128]

The old world of the *Kiez*, created by nineteenth-century capitalism and twentieth-century fascism and war was a space defined, like all produced spaces, by the sensations it produced in its residents, the memories linked in their minds to those sensations, and ways in which their own life stories were interwoven with and through that matrix of space and sense memories. The old ways were embedded in the darkness, the dampness, the angles and the widths between walls; the smells from the corner bakery and from the countless lignite ovens; the views (or lack thereof) of the landscape and the horizon. The building of holistic, self-contained, socialist cities like Marzahn did more than just solve a practical problem—the housing shortage—they erased the sensory world that was the casement of that space–sense–memory–history matrix. Those worlds continued to live on in people's memories, especially because their new world was still so blank and new—but like all memories deprived of real sensory cues, they faded, as a new matrix of sense, space, and lifespan took shape, part of the creation of a new community, and the subject of the next chapter.

[127] Schwandt, "Neubauwohngebiete," 25.
[128] "Leben in Marzahn," *Kultur im Heim* (no. 2, 1986, 2).

4

Growing with Marzahn

Childhood, Community, and the Space of Socialism's Future

"With the apartments being completed, came the moving vans. And with the moving vans, came ever more children." This was the recollection of Anke S., who had moved to Marzahn in 1977 to teach ninth grade. Anke experienced the construction of Marzahn around her in terms of a flood of children, with the newly constructed KiKos, Kindergartens, and schools, and their newly hired teachers and principals, unable to keep up with this deluge of kids. As mentioned in the previous chapter, Marzahn quickly became the district with the highest proportion of children in the entire country—over 30 percent of its residents were under the age of eighteen. This was because having a child, or children, was often a prerequisite for getting the desirable Plattenbau apartments, in Marzahn and throughout East Germany; a direct result of the intertwined policies of "real existing socialism" and the Housing Program. Nor did children only come to Marzahn in moving vans—storks, it would seem, were in a holding pattern above the new concrete utopia in the late 1970s and 1980s, when 22,000 additional babies were born, with over 3,000 born in 1985 alone.[1]

These children born in the 1970s and early 1980s were part of the second East German generation, those born to the founding "GDR generation." The GDR generation—which included people like Sofia and Johann Schöring, or Barbara Diehl—was the first not to have any personal memories of life before socialism (or only the vaguest). They were, as Dorothee Wierling writes, "born in Year One."[2] But they lived and grew up in a world physically made in, and thus inscribed with the memories of, the history of Germany before the GDR. They were a bridge generation; an "indigo" generation which contained within it the traces of the old and the new world, but which had to live through the rupture between old and new itself. It was *their* children, the second GDR generation, who were the first to have no connection to that old world, shaped by capitalism and fascism and war. They were to be the first generation to grow up completely in socialism, not as part of a transition to it or a building up of it. They were to be the first generation in over century not to have to experience any ruptures.

Thus, this chapter is about childhood in Marzahn, and the spaces that formed that childhood. But it is also about community, because that childhood was not

[1] Bezirksmuseum Marzahn, *20 Jahre Marzahn*, 29.

[2] See Wierling, *Geboren im Jahr Eins*.

lived in a vacuum. It was the way in which a new community—a new *Kiez*—was created, often through direct force of the state or Party, and always within the parameters of the state, that created the new memories which adhered to the new spaces. Here too was a dialectic, for as much as memories were formed "in" a space, they were often created and brought about by that space itself; or the memories and the spaces were coeval, springing from the same root, forever ontologically linked. It was into this new community and spaces that a new kind of socialist childhood took shape, physically and figuratively. It was in the formation of a new community that new memories, rituals, friendships, and experiences would take root, and adhere themselves to the saplings, young grass, concrete walls, and radial paths which would form the fabric of memory and meaning for the new generation in Marzahn.

At the same time, this chapter is also concerned with aspects of the inner, domestic space of these new apartments, for this was the real space in which the new generation grew and thrived. Again, the relationship between the children and their families, prefabricated apartments and, ultimately, the state and Party, was a complex and dialectical one. One could say it represented an example of Foucauldian "biopower." In most cases, children were the reason for the apartment in the first place, and the same was true for much of what went into the apartment, in terms of furnishings and appliances—made possible by both the biological fact of a baby being born, and the SED's largesse. Thus, the apartments were both of and for the children themselves. As mentioned in the previous chapter, however, in many cases couples had babies *just so that* they could get an apartment in a Plattensiedlung like Marzahn. In which case, the debt was reversed—the family did not owe the modern comforts of their WBS 70 or QP 71 three-room home to their children and the Party; instead, the children themselves owed an existential debt to the apartment itself—had it not been offered, they'd never have existed—a debt impossible to pay. Either way, children and the apartments in which they grew up in Marzahn and similar places were inextricably linked.

The marshlands outside Berlin had long before been drained of their water to make fertile soil on which to grow crops. In the 1970s and 1980s, it seemed like that fertile soil now sustained buildings and children instead. Children and concrete—the two pillars of socialism's future—seemed to take root and sprout, *together*, linked. This chapter charts how they grew together, and how time itself came to be experienced, measured, and remembered in terms of the ways children, concrete, and trees can grow.

ARRIVAL IN A NEW *KIEZ*

Most buildings in the GDR required that residents belong to a building communal association called *Hausgemeinschaft* (HG), typically run by a (usually) five-person committee, or *Hausgemeinschaftsleitung* (HGL). HGs were a legal extension of the National Front, which was a political organ of the state that organized citizen participation and a key reason why Fulbrook has called the GDR a "participatory democracy."[3] They received a budget directly from the National Front, which they used to promote a sense of community. So, in Marzahn, they became especially important as a way of creating a new community, and did so under the direct aegis of the state. In Isolde Baumgarten's building, for example, the HGL maintained a clubroom in the cellar, with a bar and tables, where they held parties. The association leadership in her Allee der Kosmonauten QP 71 ten-story building "did a lot," she recalled, even if she "only participated during the building's summer festival and the Christmas festival."[4]

The spatial ordering of the buildings, inside and out, played a role. In the summer, outdoor parties, with grilled meat, cold beer, and lots of children took place on the open greenways in front of the buildings—something that would not have been possible in the old *Kiez*.[5] In cold weather, the communal associations held parties in the communal rooms built into specific levels of the prefabricated towers—in Jutta Wormbs' case, she recalled celebrating Carnival (called *Fasching* in Germany) in the communal room on the ninth floor of her WBS 70/11 every year.[6] Elisabeth Albrecht recalled her association throwing a children's festival to celebrate International Children's Day every June 1 on the greenway outside her eleven-story WBS 70 building.[7] Ursula Weber's communal association held festivals especially for seniors in Advent.[8]

The associations would also hold celebrations for birthdays, for name-giving ceremonies (*Namensgebung*, a kind of atheist replacement for traditional baptism ceremonies in the socialist GDR), and for *Jugendweihe* ceremonies, or throw welcome-home parties for young men returning after completing their mandatory year in the East German military,[9] generally using the building fund for party supplies and an appropriate gift.[10] They coordinated with sporting clubs and the traditional charitable service known as the *Volkssolidarität* (People's Solidarity) by holding charity auctions and singing competitions with an entry fee to raise money for the "Solidarity," as Marzahner Jasper Oelze recalled.[11] They coordinated with, among other mass organizations, the German-Soviet Friendship organization to organize meet-and-greet events with Soviet officials and soldiers.[12] They also organized field trips to memorials to the KPD (*Kommunistische Partei Deutschlands*, the German Communist Party, forerunner to the SED), the Soviet Union, and the anti-fascist resistance during World War Two.[13]

Connected as it was to the political system as a part of the National Front, the association at 86 Allee der Kosmonauten, like many others, held biannual residential meetings, to which their *Volkskammer* (parliamentary) representatives were

[3] Fulbrook, *The People's State*. [4] Baumgarten, "Küche," 31.
[5] Jutta and Wolfgang Wormbs, "Astronauten," 18.
[6] Jutta and Wolfgang Wormbs, "Astronauten," 18.
[7] Albrecht, "Balkonblick," 38. [8] Weber, "Zuzug," 41.
[9] Wohnbezirksausschüss 103, "Hausgemeinschaften," 4.
[10] Renate and Reinhard Ladwig, "Wir haben beschlossen," 78.
[11] Bezirksmuseum Marzahn, *20 Jahre Marzahn*, 121.
[12] Wohnbezirksausschüss 103, "Hausgemeinschaften," 4.
[13] Wohnbezirksausschüss 103, "Hausgemeinschaften," 4.

invited to hear residents' concerns.[14] It held discussions with each one of the 200-plus families in the building to get a sense of their concerns and complaints, which it helped filter to officials in the government and in the economic planning apparatus. Significantly, the communal association also maintained a house book (*Hausbuch*), in which all the names of the buildings' residents had to be entered, along with key bits of information about them, including any visits by citizens of non-Socialist countries.[15] This book was available to the police and the Stasi upon demand.[16]

The communal association's coordination of building activities culminated in their conducting of the *Mach Mit!* ("Join In!") program, a National Front program run through residential committees to get residents to participate in the beautification of their neighborhoods and buildings, another form of the twenty-five hours of "People's Economic Mass Initiative" (VMI) labor required yearly of all East Germans.[17] *Mach Mit!* was, as Paul Betts has argued, an example of the "dilation of the state into family and private life" in the Honecker years, in the years of the Unity of Social and Economic Policy.[18] Even though *Mach Mit!* was not exclusive to the *Plattenbau* settlements, it did have a particularly unique meaning there.[19] Not only was *Mach Mit!* used as a focus to socialize new residents into a new community, but one of the main tasks that it accomplished in new settlements like Marzahn was the landscaping and decorating of the newly built areas around the buildings. Much landscaping, from planting grass and trees to building playgrounds, was accomplished through *Mach Mit!* initiatives—initiatives that took place every two weeks in the planting season, and were coordinated between the communal associations, the Berlin Magistrat, and the VEB Office of Green Space (VEB *Grünflächenamt*, part of the WBK overseeing the whole project), accounting for "many thousands of square meters of green space," according to one official with the Green Space Office.[20] If *Mach Mit!* represented a "dilation" of the state and the family, *Mach Mit!* events in Marzahn and similar places drew the act of co-creation into that process as well.

Thus, one of Torsten Preußing's first memories of moving into Marzahn was of a placard posted by his building's communal association in the lobby, which read "Tomorrow topsoil is coming. All men outside, with shovels in hand!" "It worked," Preußing recalled. "We stood there [the next day], and we spread out the topsoil. And we designed the garden in front of our building ourselves. It was a time which

[14] Wohnbezirksausschüss 103, "Hausgemeinschaften," 4.

[15] Dieter and Irmgard Reimann, "Architektur," 91. See chapter 5 for more on the house book.

[16] Renate and Reinhard Ladwig, "Wir haben beschlossen," 78.

[17] In some cases, communal associations had contracts with the communal residential government (WBK, mentioned above) in which they received money for extra *Mach Mit!* Work—money which they put into the building's communal fund for parties and celebrations, according to resident Dagmar Pohle. See Bezirksmuseum Marzahn, *20 Jahre Marzahn*, 51.

[18] Betts, *Within Walls*, 145.

[19] See Palmowski, *Socialist Nation*, chapter 5, for a more in-depth discussion of the role of *Mach Mit!* in creating—or not—a sense of community or *Heimat*.

[20] Manfred Bluhme, "Erinnerungen," Bezirksamt Marzahn, ed., *1979–1999*, 54.

can be described with a phrase that was often thrown around back then: 'From 'I' to 'we.''"[21]

Klaus Hölgermann recalled the *Mach Mit!* days as a kind of foundational myth, with honest labor yielding results and a well-deserved reward:

> The residents were ready to join in. One didn't need a lot of convincing. The tasks were organized here, in the building. On this or that day, for example in May, it would be announced: "In 14 days we're getting bushes and trees delivered. You are to see to it that they are planted." And it worked. We got started at eight in the morning, and we worked straight through to 11:30 am. And when we finished something, we went and grabbed a case of seltzer, or two, and also perhaps a crate of beer. It was all work, sweat, and beer![22]

The residents of buildings also used the *Mach Mit!* events as a chance to play the "resource game"—the real economy of socialism. That was Wilfried Klenner's memory of his communal association's building of a small playground outside his WHH SK 25 building on the Allee der Kosmonauten, most of the materials for which residents simply took from nearby construction sites. The benches were "outright stolen" from the state-owned gardening company where one of the residents worked, Klenner recalled, but since the company was a "People's Own Factory" (*Volkseigener Betrieb*, VEB, officially denoting a state-owned enterprise), "it was all people's property (*Volkseigentum*), and anyway, it was for the building."[23]

In some cases, the residents participating in *Mach Mit!* were confronted with the physical reality that Marzahn was in fact not really a *tabula rasa*; that it contained within its soil the very past, often ugly, of Berlin and Germany's northeast lands that it was supposed to be breaking away from—an experience similar to those of the planners and construction workers themselves. Elisabeth Albrecht recalled that in her apartment building in WG 3, the northernmost of the main WGs in Marzahn, the soil was too contaminated for the trees and bushes planted by her communal association. Twice they tried to plant the saplings—poplars and birches—and twice the young trees died. The reason was that WG 3 lay the closest (except for Marzahn Nord, built a few years later and even closer) to the old sewage farms, where the sewer pipes built under the auspices of Virchow's urban sanitation reforms emptied out.[24] For Albrecht, it was also a bitter irony, since she had escaped the crumbling inner city due to her and her child being sickened by the poor ventilation and the build-up of carbon monoxide inside their rental barracks—the pollution of capitalism seemed to follow her wherever she went. Nor was she the only one to be confronted with the legacy of the sewage farms—Ursula Weber also noticed the foul smells arising from the overturned soil in WG 3 every time it rained.[25] Eventually, however, on the third attempt, Albrecht's communal association had luck—the poplars and birches

[21] Preußing, "Fluchtversuch," 17–18.

[22] Bezirksmuseum Marzahn, *20 Jahre Marzahn*, 119.

[23] Manuela, Wilfried and Steffi Klenner, "Auch wir bekamen irgendwann den Betonblock-Rappel," in Quiesser and Tirri, eds., *Allee der Kosmonauten*, 38.

[24] Albrecht, "Balkonblick," 37.

[25] Weber, "Zuzug," 39.

took, including one poplar in particular that Albrecht planted directly under her window, nine stories up—a tree that would "grow" in importance for her, which is discussed below.[26]

In fact, in the end Albrecht's building association managed to do such a good job with their landscaping—Albrecht's poplar, she recalled proudly, nicely framed the entranceway in photographs of the building's front—that they were awarded a "golden house number." This award was handed out by the National Front to buildings which particularly distinguished themselves in *Mach Mit!* work; a reward for creating a kind of socialist "curb appeal" (though in a world designed quite consciously with no curbs).[27] The award, given to over 300 buildings a year by 1989,[28] was generally a plaque affixed to the front entrance of the building, other residents, such as Ursula Weber, remembering it as a central event in their new lives in their new buildings.[29] The golden house number commendation was not only an honorific—it also carried a cash award, which could be added to the communal association's building fund for a couple of extra parties or more lavish festivals. Not everyone took it that seriously, however, seeing it as a petty and anachronistic gimmick typical of the late GDR, as Wilfried Klenner remembered—his building in Marzahn Nord won a golden house number but he and the other residents saw it as something of a joke. They gladly took the cash, but never bothered to affix the golden plaque to their front entrance.[30]

In general, the existence and activities of the building communal associations helped create a very real sense of community and *esprit d'corps* in most of the buildings. This sense of solidarity reflected a kind of Lüdtkean "*Eigen-Sinn*" in that, although it was ultimately a result of the National Front (as well as the overall project of the Housing Program), the presence of the National Front was rarely felt, and residents' interests began and ended with their own building, mostly. According to Niederländer's study, 72 percent of Marzahners had no idea who their National Front *Volkskammer* representative was, and 50 percent responded that whoever they were, they were totally useless. At the same time, a large majority of Marzahners studied had a strong interest in the activities of the communal association, with 84 percent reporting a definite interest in helping with celebrations and festivals and 67 percent reporting a definite interest in helping with VMI labor (such as *Mach Mit!*).[31]

Those who did not pull their weight or shirked communal duties were subjected to a certain amount of social pressure—Werner Hinkel recalled muttering nasty comments such as "You haven't done squat so far" to people who had conveniently slipped out of *Mach Mit!* events, when he passed them in the hallway, claiming that usually a few "reminders" like that and the people could be counted on to show up at the next event.[32] Wilifried Klenner remarked that in some buildings, failure to

[26] Albrecht, "Balkonblick," 37. [27] Albrecht, "Balkonblick," 37.

[28] Bezirksmuseum Marzahn, *20 Jahren Marzahn*, 34. [29] Weber, "Zuzug," 41."

[30] Manuela, Wilfried, and Steffi Klenner, "Betonblock," 38.

[31] Niederländer, "Wohnen Marzahn '80," 27.

[32] Bezirksmuseum Marzahn, *20 Jahre Marzahn*, 120.

attend communal festivals could hurt one's career (*rufschädigend war*).[33] It certainly did not go unnoticed by the Stasi, which was well connected with the HGLs and local National Front branches to pick up on gossip, as the next chapter discusses. This would suggest that the buildings housed a kind of Foucauldian microphysics of power or "governmentality," in which the National Front (or SED or Stasi, for that matter) needed not be visible or even consciously respected—the whole machinery of the buildings and the social structures bound up with them set in motion a group dynamic that naturally replicated the collectivist enforcement of the communist regime.

However, other Marzahners recalled that they generally forgave people who did not participate in communal activities. Jasper Oelze related an incident in 1983 in which the communal association leadership was planning a building party at the Biesdorfer Kreuz pub, and suggested that only those residents who had participated in the year's communal duties should be invited, but were voted down by a majority of association members: "The majority said, 'No! Whoever wants to come, let them come. Some did more, some did less, but let's just invite everyone.'"[34] The "vibe" (*Stimmung*) at these events was, Oelze recalled, "great, and we had lots of fun."[35] Jutta and Joachim Kretzschmar agreed, saying "When it came to communal festivals, it didn't matter if you had helped clean the stairwell or not, every doorbell was rung. There were a few people who organized it all...we had a cook in the building, as well as the director of the shopping mart, and that was reason enough to throw a party."[36]

Indeed, most Marzahners recalled a sense of neighborliness that did not result from any sense of pressure or official or political initiative. Karin Hinkel remembered the residents of the twentieth floor where she lived having spontaneous parties:

> Overall, we partied a lot. Never planned it, just did it. We'd meet up in the hallway on the 20th floor, and that's how it would start. Everyone brought a chair, and with the kids we'd do something for Carnival (*Fasching*), or we'd organize dance parties for the older kids (*jugendlichen Diskos*). Or, right in front on the greenway, there would be kids' parties, sometimes in conjunction with the school nearby. And there would be a lot of baked treats. There was a real sense of togetherness and sociability (*geselliges Zusammensein*) in the building.[37]

According to Niederländer, most families had close relationships with between three and five other families, with only 14 percent of the residents having no close relationships with any other residents. Two-thirds of the residents overall reported that they would leave their key with at least one neighbor, and in the five-story WBS buildings the atmosphere was even more trusting—95 percent reported they

[33] Manuela, Wilfried, and Steffi Klenner, "Auch wir bekamen irgendwann den Betonblock-Rappel," in Quiesser and Tirri, eds., *Allee der Kosmonauten*, 38.
[34] Bezirksmuseum Marzahn, *20 Jahre Marzahn*, 121.
[35] Bezirksmuseum Marzahn, *20 Jahre Marzahn*, 121.
[36] Verein Kids & Co., *Südspitze*, 54.
[37] Bezirksmuseum Marzahn, *20 Jahre Marzahn*, 121.

trusted their neighbors enough to leave a key with them.[38] Overall, 60 percent of the residents studied reported that mutual help between neighbors was "common."[39] Katrin Brandtstadt recalled that her building was a "great community," and Elisabeth Westermann described her twenty-second floor as "definitely having a *Kiez* feeling; people would meet in the hallway or in the stairwells, say hello, and we had trust, we'd look after each others' kids."[40]

Ingeborg Hämmerling, an economist and single mother who moved to Marzahn with her daughter, described the experience of living in her five-story WBS 70 building as one of collective effort and communalism. It was almost a utopia, she recalled, in which everyone pitched in, creating a sense of egalitarianism, meaning, and safety; again, a utopia as much of the grassroots as anything imposed from above:

> The renters were blue-collar and white-collar workers, and intellectuals, although these intellectuals had come originally from the working class, taking advantage of the many educational opportunities they had, as I had in earning my degree in economics. So, there was no division into social classes. And we residents took over responsibility for maintaining the building and the landscaping, and for upholding order and security in the building, including observing the fire code.... With us, the professor lived next to the cleaning woman, and we all used the informal form of address (*Du*)....
>
> The residents supported absolutely their duty to take care of the living area. We maintained the apartment, the building, the landscaping in the front, and we made sure all the kids in the building were respectful of the property. Because all the residents were employed, including women and young adults, the communities in these buildings were not environments where petty criminality, drug addiction, vandalism, or a seedy atmosphere could take root. Outside of a few cellar break-ins, I don't recall any criminality at all.[41]

The creation of a new sense of community was not limited to the spaces within and immediately outside of the prefabricated buildings themselves, however. Marzahn's designers had built open spaces into the city center, to be used for communal purposes, a kind of blank canvas for the new rituals of a new community. Sensing the need to fill this void, District Mayor Cyske helped found an event called the "Marzahn Spring," in 1980; a community festival intended so that, according to Cyske, the new municipal district could create "its own traditions,"[42] and "so that people will identify with their new surroundings and feel at home there."[43] In the space of a few years, the Marzahn Spring became one of the most popular festivals in the country, drawing visitors from across the GDR.[44]

Jan Palmowski has argued that attempts by the "regime" to encourage neighborhood festivals in such "new towns" failed to "take root in any significant degree," partially, he writes, because there were "few communal structures" in existence in

[38] Niederländer, "Wohnen Marzahn '80," 28.
[39] Niederländer, "Wohnen Marzahn '80," 39.
[40] Interview with Katrin Brandtstadt and Elisabeth Westermann, Berlin, 22 April 2008.
[41] Letter from Ingeborg Hämmerling to author, April 2008.
[42] Cyske, "Nerven," 59. [43] Cyske, "Bummibahn," 27.
[44] Cyske, "Bummibahn," 27.

such places.[45] There were, however, spaces specifically built for communal events such as these festivals, and in Marzahn they very quickly became large successes. During the festival, the open spaces built into Marzahn's design filled up with food stalls, beer taps, and rows of picnic benches. The Marzahn Spring was especially noted for the amount of flowers available in the marketplace—in part because of the huge demand that existed from Marzahners to be able to buy flowers to adorn their balconies. In fact, the Marzahn Spring became a spring flower festival as much as anything else, with people coming from around the country to buy flowers for their buildings as well.[46]

In addition, there were poetry contests at the Marzahn Spring, announced over East Berlin radio stations,[47] and pony rides, petting zoos, magic shows, horse-drawn carriage rides, and even open-air boxing matches took place.[48] Live music acts, including some of the biggest-name rock bands in the GDR such as the Puhdys and Karat played the Marzahn Spring.[49] For the teenager Alexandra Günter, the concerts made the Marzahn Spring "the big event" of the year in Marzahn.[50] The district government even managed to leverage the popularity of the festival into extra deliveries of the vital rubber boots, always in demand and often scarce in Marzahn, especially in children's sizes.[51]

Even more significantly, residents were allowed to set up their own stalls and sell home-made goods, ranging from baked treats to knick-knacks to fabrics; a kind of *Eigen-Sinn* and micro-capitalism which could thrive in the space created by the Marzahn Spring. Heidi Elgt, for example, had always dreamed of being a fashion designer, though the state-run fashion institute where she worked was not the venue for individual expression or creativity. So, using her own sewing machine, she made her own sweaters, jackets, and skirts, always with her signature logo—a stylized bird of paradise. These items were given to friends and neighbors, or traded for other goods or services. They had a kind of "buzz" about them—they were something authentic and unique; you had to know someone in Marzahn to get an Elgt skirt—and when she got her license to set up a stall at the Spring, her designs sold out by 10:00 a.m. From her stall at the Marzahn Spring, she also sold purses that she had sewn, and so too did many others.[52]

What should we make of this evidence? On one hand, the residents of Marzahn played an active role in creating a new social world, a new *Kiez*, through their own initiative. Often, the world they created seemed to have little or nothing to do with

[45] Palmowski, *Inventing a Socialist Nation*, 191. Palmowski also claims that the evidence that the regime no longer tried to foster a sense of community drawn purely from within the "new towns" was that they stopped giving them utilitarian names like "Halle Neustadt" turning instead to older standing names like "Lütten Klein" in Rostock, or Marzahn or Hellersdorf. But as we have seen, this was indicative of very little in the way of respect or inclusion of local traditions or histories, which were essentially swept away by the massive planning and construction apparatus.

[46] Cyske, "Bummibahn," 27, confirmed in an email from Dorothee Ifland to author, January 16, 2015.

[47] Ursula Schwabe, "Marzahner Frühling," Bezirksamt Marzahn, ed., *1979–1999*, 76.

[48] Verein Kids & Co., *Südspitze* 52–3.

[49] Ursula Günter, "Marzahn war ein potemkinsches Dorf," in Quiesser and Tirri, eds., *Allee der Kosmonauten*, 28.

[50] Günter, "potemkinsches Dorf," 28.

[51] Cyske, "Bummibahn," 28.

[52] Günter, "potemkinsches Dorf," 28.

politics or the state—holiday and birthday celebrations; home-made baked goods and fashion items sold on the side; an overwhelming willingness to pitch in with landscaping and building chores; resourcefulness in "acquiring" materials and tools for landscaping and repairs; acceptance and tolerance even of the free-riders and wallflowers in the building; and all these combined with an unapologetic disregard for national politics. If anything came from "above" it was not from a very high level—the municipal District Mayor, or communal residential commission, or the local National Front branch at the most. It would seem to lend credence to views of everyday life in socialism as apolitical, "normalized," or somehow defined by a niche carved out through the exercise of *Eigen-Sinn*.

This was all true, except for the fact that, almost as soon as this *Wende* took place, and the organs of the state and Party vanished, so too did most of the sense of community. Most residents—and this is not limited to Marzahn or even to other *Neubausiedlungen*—describe the loss of communal trust and collective feeling as part of their narrative of the changes they have witnessed in the years since 1989–90. As Wilfried Klenner put it, "this us-feeling is gone today. Now, there are borders, which didn't used to be there."[53] What was it that could be lost in this way, yet remain unseen? State power, and the power of socialism, was truly diffuse in the GDR, and in Marzahn in particular it must be viewed with a very wide-angle lens. Marzahn was a physical manifestation not only of socialism, but of socialism as an iteration of a kind of modernity; an all-encompassing Enlightenment project that thought only in terms of complete and closed *systems*. The physical spaces, the political ideology running the economy, and the people themselves, along with their social dynamics all combined in an interdependent matrix. Remove one thing from the equation, and the system breaks down.

Thus, what may look like a niche, a "private" sphere, a "colony of Eigen-Sinn" as one book has described,[54] when viewed in terms of a larger system becomes something quite different. The communities formed around the cleaning of stairwells or holding *Jugendweihe* celebrations in the clubrooms, or the playing of soccer and drinking beer on the greenways, cannot be understood removed from the stairwells, the clubrooms, and the greenways. The spaces are the key—they are the convection, the pathway through which the power of the state and Party travelled and diffused into everyday life, so unseen we might be almost be forgiven for mistaking this as a "normal" or "bottom-up" world.

PLATTENBAU INTERIORITY: ABSENCE, PRESENCE, AND MODERNITY

As this chapter has argued, the creation of a new community within a new space was one of the critical steps in severing links with the past. New memories in the

[53] Klenner, "Betonblock," 38.

[54] Regina Bittner, *Kolonien des Eigensinns: Ethnographie einer Ostdeutschen Industrieregion* (Frankfurt/New York: Campus Verlag, 1998).

new spaces were generated by new events, new rituals, and new friends. This took place in the hallways, the greenways, and the open squares of the promenade; but above all it took place in the interiors of the apartments themselves—the inner spaces of the new lives begun in the settlement.

The people who moved to Marzahn often had little or nothing with which to furnish and equip their new domestic spaces. This was for a number of reasons. First, many were young adults, in their twenties, just beginning their lives together as married couples, usually with young children in tow or on the way. Second, many of these people had come from places that were too small and cramped to fit very much furniture, and moving to a WBS 70, QP 71, or WHHT meant, among other things, having much more space to fill. Or, the material realities of living in a nineteenth-century domestic space meant a different relationship to domestic goods—no windows meant there had been no need for curtains; without a bathroom, there had been no point in owning a toilet-paper dispenser or a bath mat. In many cases, these young people were not even living in their own spaces, but rather living with relatives, so that they had nothing at all in the way of their own furnishings to bring to the settlement.

So, for example, when Sofia and Johann Schöring came to Marzahn, they came with almost nothing that bore any link to the past—especially their own past. As mentioned in the previous chapter, Sofia's father was a communist who spent much of the Third Reich and the War in Sachsenhausen, and Johann's father had been a deserter who spent the War in hiding, with a death sentence hanging over his head. By the end of the War, neither family had anything—Johann's family was given an apartment that had belonged to a Nazi family, which had fled. But when the daughter of the family came back, Johann and his family had to leave again. In the end, between the two of them, the only heirloom they had was a black Bakelite coffee tin from the 1920s that had belonged to Sofia's mother, and some old photographs.[55] Barbara Diehl inherited nothing from her mother, who had nothing to give her and likely would not have given her anything if she did; only some photographs and letters from her father from when she was an infant, during the War, before he was killed.[56]

Rainer Nordmann only inherited an old table from his father, who had served in France during the War and had become a miner in Thuringia after it. His father would not even share with him any of his memories of the War, refusing to speak of any of his experiences, except to say: "boy, just be glad there's no war on now."[57] In this way, Nordmann's father had already precipitated a break with the past for his son that went beyond the material realm and extended into the realm of memory—and amnesia. Gerlinde Paulus only inherited an old pocket watch, and some photos from her mother and grandmother, who lost their apartment and were forced out on the street, when it was given to refugees immediately after the War. Gerlinde's mother had once had heirloom jewelry, but she sold it all in 1945 to

[55] Interview with Johann and Sofia Schöring, Berlin, May 23, 2008.
[56] Interview with Barbara Diehl, Berlin, March 6, 2008.
[57] Interview with Rainer Nordmann, Berlin, April 22, 2008.

help the family survive.[58] Elisabeth Westermann's parents had been refugees from Pomerania, where they had owned a farm. She came to Marzahn with one piece of furniture—a floor-to-ceiling shelving case called a *Schrankwand*.[59]

Research done almost a decade earlier by the state-run Institute for Market Research (*Institut für Marktforschung*) confirmed that most people in East Germany who moved into a new apartment were in need of furniture—and that many of them, especially the youngest, had virtually nothing at all with which to furnish their new apartments. Earlier research, done in 1966 by the same Institute, showed that 81 percent of all East Germans who moved to a modern apartment were in the market for new furniture in the first year of their move.[60] Indeed, the same study found that, of the families who had just "established a household," that is, gotten married, and were moving into a prefabricated apartment, 92 percent had no furniture of their own to bring to the apartment from a previous abode.[61] Overall, the study found, just under a quarter of all East Germans had absolutely no furniture to their name when they moved to a new apartment.[62]

In particular, Marzahners moving into new apartments knew what they wanted, and they knew how the system worked and where they fit into it. Niederländer's study found that half of the residents of Marzahn preferred floor-to-ceiling furnishings, and that 40 percent wanted "open space" as their most valued characteristic in a living room, something that a floor-to-ceiling *Schrankwand* made possible.[63] A report from the state-run "Institute for Market Research" issued a report as early as 1974 advising that a home furnishing store be placed strategically in the shopping area of Marzahn, because "many families moving into new apartments wish to furnish them with new furniture."[64] And they understood that they were taking part in a bigger "system" by furnishing their new homes in Marzahn, as Gerda Marin recalled: "The furniture [in my apartment] is still from the GDR: Hellerau furniture—I swear by it. Those were good architects, the ones that used Bauhaus ideas. They made really unadorned [*Schlicht*—meant as "minimalist" in a positive way] things . . . I like plain walls and unadorned things."[65]

Almost as soon as they moved in, Marzahners began furnishing their new apartments, which, as a general rule, came with nothing included; not even kitchen or toilet cabinets, nor wallpaper or flooring. All of this had to be purchased and installed, often by the residents themselves—like with the *Mach Mit!*, residents helped to co-create their domestic space, often with friends and new neighbors

[58] Interview with Gerlinde Paulus, Berlin, July 22, 2008.

[59] Interview with Katrin Brandtstadt and Elisabeth Westermann, Berlin, April 22, 2008.

[60] BArch-L DL 102 208 Dr Harald Zappe and Dr Annelies Albrecht, "Der Einfluß des Bezuges einer Neubauwohnung auf die Anschaffung von Wohnraummöbeln und Beleuchtungskörpern—Analyse einer Konsumentbefragung," 3.

[61] Zappe and Albrecht, "Einfluß," 9. This particular group amounted to 14.3% of the total surveyed, but it goes to illustrate the amount of furniture most newlyweds had in the GDR on the date of their move to a prefabricated apartment, which was usually nothing.

[62] Zappe and Albrecht, "Einfluß," 9.

[63] Niederländer, "Wohnen Marzahn '80," 104 (appendix 79).

[64] BArch-L DL 102 800 "Stellungnahme zur Entwicklung des Bedarfs an Konsumgutern im Neubaugebiet Berlin-Biesdorf-Marzahn 1974," February 13, 1974, 26.

[65] Marin, "gerne gelebt," 81.

coming to help them put up wallpaper and install carpeting. Barbara Diehl, for example, spent almost three months setting up her apartment, putting up wallpaper in some rooms and painting different rooms different colors, with various friends coming to help.[66]

Usually, most of these new expenses were paid for with marriage credit. Gerlinde Paulus furnished her apartment mostly on the credit, mostly with items from the department store at Alexanderplatz, except for her Hellerau *Schrankwand*, which she purchased (also using her state credit) at a store on Spandauerstrasse.[67] Katrin Brandtstadt, who moved to Marzahn from a quasi-shack on the site of a former orchard along the Baumschulenweg, had literally nothing, other than a few items her parents and her sisters gave her. She too also bought most of her furniture upon moving to Marzahn in 1979, including a washing machine and a *Schrankwand*.[68] Elisabeth Westermann, her friend, who moved in around the same time, purchased an entire kitchen set and an entire bedroom set, though she was able to pay for it all up front, without needing the credit.[69]

The furniture was not cheap. The "Carat" brand *Schrankwand* cost 3,500 marks when Lidia Leinart bought it from the home furnishing store in Marzahn on Marchwitzastrasse. The bedroom set, which she also bought on credit, cost 2,000 marks.[70] In comparison, she made 400 marks a month, and her husband, who worked in a cement factory, made 900 a month.[71] Rainer Nordmann recalled buying a dining room table set that cost 700 marks on credit; he made 350 marks a month.[72] And of course, like almost every other major purchase in socialist economies, there was often a wait, though Nordmann recalled it was more like six to nine months, as opposed to the wait for Trabants, which could extend to ten years or more.[73] He got around this wait by taking a different model of sofa than what he had wanted, and buying the store's floor model for his *Schrankwand*.[74] Others used the infamous "Vitamin B" (B for *Beziehungen* or "connections") to get sweetheart deals on furniture; such as Astrid Gottwald, who personally knew a furniture seller who lived on Schönhauser Allee, and managed to buy a "Carat" *Schrankwand* for only 50 marks, essentially getting it for free.[75]

GROWING WITH MARZAHN: CHILDHOOD SPACES

One of the most important ways in which the new spaces inside the apartments shaped new lives was for the children who moved in at an early age to, or who were

[66] Interview with Barbara Diehl, Berlin, February 20, 2008.
[67] Interview with Gerlinde Paulus, Berlin, July 22, 2008.
[68] Interview with Katrin Brandtstadt and Elisabeth Westermann, Berlin, April 22, 2008.
[69] Interview with Katrin Brandtstadt and Elisabeth Westermann, Berlin, April 22, 2008.
[70] Lenart, "Wozu brauche ich," 62. [71] Lenart, "Wozu brauche ich," 61–2.
[72] Interview with Rainer Nordmann, Berlin, April 22, 2008.
[73] Interview with Rainer Nordmann, Berlin, April 22, 2008.
[74] Interview with Rainer Nordmann, Berlin, April 22, 2008.
[75] Astrid Gottwald, "Ich habe die anderen zu Erich laufen lassen!" in Quiesser and Tierri, eds., *Allee der Kosmonauten*, 21.

born in, Marzahn. The phenomenologist Gaston Bachelard has written about the importance of the spaces of one's childhood abode—the almost mystical power that the spatiality of childhood has on one later in life, and on one's perception of the world. What a child's room, for instance, looked like (if a child had their own room, or space, at all); whether there was a cellar, and whether the cellar was dark and scary or a space of safety and magic; whether there was light, and what the views out the window were, views which populated the long hours of childhood ennui on rainy or lazy summer days; what kind of furniture existed in relationship to the angles and dimensions of the home; how a child's parents and siblings existed in relation to all these factors—all come to fundamentally shape a childhood and a personality.[76] For young children, the home, along with a very limited number of other spaces (Kindergartens, nearby parks or lawns, and sidewalks outside the home) come to form the entirety of the world, of the whole universe. A wall, or a corner, or a sill can take on a kind of valence that adults often do not understand. Spaces can be friends, or enemies—a room can be an "ally" or a hallway can be charged with foreboding and threat. They can have their own geography: carpet pile can be a tossing ocean traversed by a plastic boat, or it can be a wild grassland populated by toy animals; PVC flooring can become an ice rink for small figurines, and so on. The "architectonics" of home spaces are therefore magnified exponentially for children, far more than they are for adults.

For the children of Marzahn, a place with more children per capita than anywhere else in East Germany, the architectonics of their world were even more important, because they were the first generation not to experience a childhood home that was built before socialism. They were the generation that was going to grow "with" Marzahn—they were going to be coeval with the prefabricated housing settlement, and so in a way, they were going to merge and become as one with the place around them. They would hear about the old working-class heroes and street fighters, and the old rental barracks, but only in textbooks or during field trips for school or the SED's youth organization, the Ernst Thälmann Young Pioneers (for younger children), or the Free German Youth (for older children). Socialism to them would be the whole universe, as natural as air and belonging entirely unto itself, not defined in reaction to past wounds, injustices, or oppression.

Many of the memories and experiences of the young children in Marzahn were tied to the spaces that suddenly became available to them, since those children born before the move usually did not have a space of their own. For Barbara and Rolf Diehl, moving into their three-room WBS 70 apartment on Allee der Kosmonauten in 1980 was a huge relief for many reasons, but chief among them was the fact that now their difficult son Dieter had his own bedroom, and Barbara and Rolf had theirs. Dieter, who was naturally withdrawn and had obvious social deficits, thrived in having his own private space. His room was furnished with a children's bedroom set, including a bed, a dresser, a writing desk and toys bought

[76] See Bachelard, *The Poetics of Space*, trans. Maria Jolas (Boston: Beacon, 1969).

using Barbara's state credit.[77] It was a space populated with plastic toys typical of the GDR, purchased at the state-run "House of Children" in Strausberg, just outside Berlin. Books (especially the popular illustrated series *Max und Moritz*), plastic animals, plastic blocks similar to Lego, and his favorite, a plastic dump truck, formed his new world.[78] Elisabeth Albrecht's son, Steffen, also counted his plastic dump truck, which he liked to load up with his other toys, as one of his most prized possessions.[79]

Detlef Habrom remembered that the almost ten-meter-long corridor of his new four-room apartment became a perfect place for his stepchildren to play with toy cars: "The corridor soon became a racing strip for the boys' plastic trucks. The three- and five-year-olds cruised their (for the times) modern cars here and there for hours at a time."[80] Isolde Baumgarten also recalled that one of the advantages of her new QP 71 apartment's long and spacious corridor was that it was beloved by her kids as a place to play.[81] So too with Hardy Stahl, eleven, son of Regina and Helmut, who now had space to play with his model train on a lazy Sunday morning, when a reporter from *Marzahn Aktuell* visited the family, in April 1979.[82] For teenagers, too, it was important—perhaps even more important—to have their own room. This was something which made the move to Marzahn special for the Hepners, whose fifteen-year-old son "finally" had his own room,[83] or the Marquardt's daughter Daniela, who also had her own room, finally, as a teenager.

One of the best examples of a young child growing with Marzahn was that of Ilke Jütte, born in late 1975 to Gerd and Carola Jütte. Gerd, in his twenties, was a drill press operator at the machine tool factory in Marzahn, and Carola worked in the state export organ. They were the ideal socialist family of the 1970s—both were Party members, working class, young, recently married and with a small child, and they were living in an old, one-room apartment in Weißensee. Gerd was upwardly mobile, in the socialist sense—he participated in the Party group in his factory, the "Salvador Allende Collective" which had sent him away in 1977 for a three-month retreat at the district Party school (*Bezirksparteischule*).[84] The AWG at the VEB Berlin Machine Tool Factory was one of the first to get apartments for Marzahn, and, unsurprisingly, the Jüttes were the first to get an apartment in Marzahn, on the ninth floor of a ten-story QP 71 building on Marchwitzastrasse, in December 1977—with the help of Gerd's comrades from the Allende Collective, who all pitched in with the move and the setting-up of the apartment.[85]

Der Neunte, understandably, picked the Jüttes to profile in February 1978. What is interesting about the newspaper's article is its angle—it focused on Ilka as much as her parents, the theme being that she and Marzahn were "growing

[77] Interview with Barbara Diehl, Berlin, February 20, 2008.

[78] Interview with Barbara Diehl, Berlin, June 3, 2008. [79] Albrecht, "Balkonblick," 36.

[80] Habrom, "Orangen," 64. [81] Baumgarten, "Küche," 31.

[82] Hans Habermann, "Bilanz Stimmt im Großen wie im Kleinen," *Marzahn Aktuell* (vol. 3, no. 7, 12 April 1979, 4).

[83] Lothat and Helena Hepner, "Im Altbau," 87.

[84] Rudolf Bensel, "Ilka Wächst Mit: Arbeiterfamilie Jütte hielt Einzug in Berlin-Marzahn," *Der Neunte* (vol. 2, no. 3, 2 February 1978, 1).

[85] Bensel, "Ilka Wächst Mit," 1.

together;" a double meaning in that both the girl and the new city district were both just beginning their lives, but also that the girl and the city district were becoming one as they aged. Entitled "Ilka Grows Too" [*Ilka Wächst Mit*], the newspaper found her at home, in her room which her parents had decorated for her with stuffed animals, a small table and chairs, and art supplies. The article noted that the first Kindergarten would be finished soon, directly opposite the Jüttes' building, and that hers would be among the first tiny feet to traverse the newly paved pathway linking the building entrance to the preschool. For Ilka, this too would create a new pathway, as had in fact the many new spaces and sensations absorbed by the blonde two-year-old in the previous few months. "Ilka has grown sleepy," the article stated; "from playing, and from the many new impressions. From children grow great people. In time, perhaps, she will tell her own children about the district Berlin–Marzahn and its origins. Ultimately, the two of them are growing up together!" (see Figure 9).[86]

The newspaper returned at the end of the year, in December 1978, to write a follow-up piece on the Jüttes. The picture under the headline showed Ilka, now three, in her room drawing on her easel with her stuffed animals and dolls watching her, and a caption that read: "The little Ilka, of the Jütte family, is growing with Berlin–Marzahn."[87] "How do things look, for Gerd Jütte... and his wife Carola at the end of the year?" the article asked. "How has their little three-year-old daughter changed?" The first thing to come out of Gerd's mouth was, in fact, a comment on how impossibly short the walk from their front door to the Kindergarten was, and how this gave the family "a great deal" more free time. The free time, the article intoned, was, for Ilka, spent in her room, filling it with herself (in a Bachelardian sense), and clearly her room and her Kindergarten had come to fill her world:

> Ilka, who got out of bed not long ago, has begun to draw from her imagination on her chalkboard [*Schiefertafel*]. She begins to babble excitedly, and tells us how Santa already came to her Kindergarten with a sleigh, two horses and bi-i-i-ig sack, and gave gifts to all the children, because they had all been so good; and how they had gone to the senior center and sung to the grandmas and grandpas, who loved it, and—and—and!! Happy childhood; it makes a visitor happy to be able to share the experience.[88]

The Jüttes were profiled again by the magazine *Kultur im Heim* in a 1986 issue devoted almost entirely to Marzahn, as the first renters, and thus as a kind of mirror of Marzahn's development. By then, Gerd had become a representative in the district council (*Stadtbezirksversammlung*), Carola was actively engaged in the school's PTA (*Elternaktiv*), and Ilka, now 11, was now playing volleyball with one of Marzahn's sport clubs, TSC.[89]

The local newspaper also followed the lives of Constance and Christian Hämmerling, the first babies born to residents of the Marzahn settlement, to their mother Karin and father Detlev, on March 13, 1978, only a month after moving

[86] Bensel, "Ilka Wächst Mit," 1.

[87] Lilo Erbstößer, "1 Jahr Danach ..." *Marzahn Aktuell* (vol. 2, no. 17, 21 December 1978, 4).

[88] Erbstößer, "1 Jahr Danach," 4.

[89] "Leben in Marzahn," *Kultur im Heim* (no. 2, 1986, 3).

to their new apartment in the *Südspitze* on Marchwitzastrasse.[90] The twins were local "celebrities" because they were the first babies born in Marzahn, thus the perfect symbol for Marzahn as a place of birth as well as rebirth, and, like the Jüttes, an excellent propaganda piece for Honecker's policy of "real existing socialism." But the fact that they were twins was also important. In addition to being the district with the most children per capita, Marzahn was also the East German district that had the most twins and triplets per capita, because, as Mayor Cyske recalled, having twins or triplets propelled you to the front of the waiting list, something Gabrielle Franik experienced.[91] There were so many twins and triplets in Marzahn that there was a special celebration of them organized at each year's Marzahn Spring festival.[92]

There was, in effect, a strange symmetry between the children and the buildings; since it was the fact that above all else, in the GDR, it was *production* that mattered. In an echo of Nazi population policy, the East German state rewarded its citizens for having as many children as possible through instruments like Marzahn, as well as marriage credit. And having twins or triplets made mothers into a kind of Adolf Haennicke or Alexei Stakhanov of fertility—doubling or tripling their output in the same amount of time. The symmetry went further, since the East German state's embrace of the method of mass-producing identical consumer goods, and buildings, including the WBS 70, lay behind the same *Tonnenideologie* that motivated the encouragement of babies, especially twins and triplets (the motto of Marzahn's construction brigades was, after all, *Jeden Tag Guten Bilanz*, or "Good Output Every Day"). Thus there was a kind of link between the identical copies of children (twins and triplets) in Marzahn and the identical copies of buildings stretching to the horizon in which they came in droves to live—symmetry within symmetry, as it were.

Constance and Christian's milestones were, like Ilka's, according to *Der Neunte*, a mirror of the early milestones of the great construction project of Marzahn. Visiting the twins just before their first birthday, in March 1979, reporter Volkhard Kühl wrote:

> The first twins in Berlin-Marzahn are already standing on their own two feet. Constance and Christian Hämmerling will be one year old on March 13th. But in the intervening time, more twins have arrived [in Marzahn].
>
> The residential district, in which the little ones will now grow up, is also already able to stand on its own two feet. On March 8th and 15th, 1978, the first Residential District Committee of the National Front was constituted; and on the 18th of March, the residents of Marchwitzastrasse began planting the first garden in front of their building...
>
> Soon, Constance and the already very adventurous Christian will discover the neighborhood they call home (*Heimat*).[93]

[90] "Das Glück ist perfekt," *Der Neunte* (vol. 2, no. 7, 20 March 1978, 4). Also see Hübner, Nicolaus, and Teresiak, *20 Jahre Marzahn*, 21.

[91] Cyske, "Bummibahn," 28. [92] Cyske, "Bummibahn," 28.

[93] Volkhard Kühl, "Gutes Gedeihen," *Der Neunte* (vol. 3, no. 5, 8 March 1979, 4).

The newspaper visited the Hämmerlings one more time, in October of 1979, showing Constance and Christian already walking and enrolled in the Kindergarten across the pathway, the same that Ilka Jütte was attending.

These stories were obviously done with bias, to portray the new residents in the most optimistic light, but they also reflected a theme of rebirth and new beginnings that was very real, which many of the residents in retrospect still cling to. For the families featured, the articles were important life events—they made them a "somebody"—and some, like Gerd Jütte, have them saved in their family albums to this day.[94]

For example, Elisabeth Albrecht's poplar tree, planted in 1982 directly below her ninth-story apartment (after two previous attempts had failed), came to symbolize for her the rebirth of her own life and especially that of her very young son. The poplar, barely 2 m tall when she planted it, had grown within four years—around the time her son began school—to be "a proper tree," as she reminisced. The tree grew as her son grew; as it put down its roots, so did she and he. Eventually, her son grew up and moved away, "but in the meantime, the poplar that I planted during those days [when he was a child] has reached all the way to me, almost growing into my window. It is now twenty-one years old." It was as if Albrecht's poplar had taken the place of her son. It also points to the ways in which, as people grew "with" the Marzahn settlement, their sense of verticality and nature and time all seemed to interact with each other. Buildings (especially those based on Le Corbusier's "towers in a park"), children, and trees all grow vertically, though at different rates. In Albrecht's mind, time could be measured in different scales: son, poplar, or WBS 70. Each scale was a way of marking time—the building went up first, the children followed, and once they were gone, the trees marked the longest time and deepest roots, so, there was "construction-time," "son-time," and "tree-time." But in every case, the time was the state's, and the growth began in the soil of Marzahn, and time was marked from that space too—not underneath the soil, despite the traces of older worlds and poisoned pasts, and not before, but with the topsoil as year zero on multiple registers. This was, again, a topography formed of space, time, and memory, all set in motion by the state's policies.

Another article, this time in *NBI* in 1979, captured a further combination of tree, child, and building as a metaphor for socialism's future. The article was entitled "Our Boom in Marzahn," which was a pun on the word "tree," *Baum*, pronounced "Boom" in Berliner dialect, with the doubled meaning of "construction boom," in this case borrowed from English. The article focused on a willow tree, planted amongst the chaos of the construction site. "Our tree is rooted in Berlin-Marzahn. Berliners might say what they always say when they aren't familiar with someplace: 'the boonies (*Jottwedee*)'. But they might get guff from other Berliners, who would say back: 'Heinz Graffunder, Chief Architect. He, who knows his way around palaces... Berlin-Marzahn, the largest construction site in the Republic, a home for 100,000 people, as large as Schwerin."[95] After further enumerating the statistics about Marzahn, the magazine alluded to the many, many trees that had already

[94] Email from Ilka Jütte to author, January 8, 2008.

[95] Christa Otten, "Unsere Boom in Marzahn," *Neue Berliner Illustrierte* (vol. 35, no. 40, 1979, 35).

been planted, by the state and by residents, again using the trees as a metaphor both for individual lives and the layout of the city itself. It pointed to a particular stand of trees, planted between a Kindergarten and a senior home, remarking that the trees stood "right in the center of life" (as in a "lifespan"). "In its truest sense," the article continued, "Marzahn is not just a construction project, but also a garden, not just for trees, but for children as well; a real 'Kinder Garten.'"[96]

In fact, the growth of vegetation in general became an important means of measuring time and plotting the narrative arcs of lives in Marzahn. "The poplars we planted will be here, as long as we live," remarked Marianne Franzel, reminiscing about the trees she planted in her first months in the prefabricated housing settlement.[97] The Schörings also recalled the transformation from "green fields" to mud, to weeds growing in the mud piles, and then again to green again as marking off the first few years in their new home. And with all the new vegetation, especially shrubs and thickets, came animals: Johann especially remembered the first appearances of rabbits, deer, and ermine, and foxes following them, as a sign that a certain level or stage of growth had been completed.[98] Katrin Brandtstadt, who did not initially want to move out of her ramshackle house on Baumschulenweg, but was forced to move out and to Marzahn when it was condemned, claimed that the fact that things eventually became green was "very important" for her, as far as learning to feel at home there was concerned.[99] Karl-Heinz Gärtner described this passage of "green-time" in a poem written in honor of Marzahn's twentieth anniversary in 1999:

> The ground looked frightful, far and wide
> The first residents often think of the time of rubber boots;
> For many of them, Marzahn was truly a horror
> Unimaginable: here they want to construct a city?
> The time of cornflowers[100] is now over
> Importing flora was not just an afterthought to the planners;
> The tender little seedlings—you barely saw them—
> Are now the green of shrubs and trees.[101]

Manfred Bluhme, who was an official with the VEB Green Space Office, overseeing the *Mach Mit!* initiatives to plant grass, shrubs, and trees, had a unique sense of this timescale, as his family had been one of those from Berlin that had vacationed in Marzahn in the 1950s:

> In the mid 1950s, I often rode out to Marzahn on weekends on the double-decker bus from Friedrichshain, which cost 20 pfennigs. The last stop was the church in the center of the village. A few steps beyond that, began the fields and meadows and gentle hills.... Not seldom would I see a herd of sheep. For a city kid, it was pure nature![102]

96 Otten, "Unsere Boom," 36. 97 Verein Kids & Co., 50.

98 Interview with Johann and Sofia Schöring, Berlin, May 23, 2008.

99 Interview with Katrin Brandtstadt and Elisabeth Westermann, Berlin, April 22, 2008.

100 A cornflower is a weed common in agricultural areas, presumably here one that covered the mud hills at the construction site.

101 Gärtner, "Marzahn—Ein Bezirk Wird 20," in Bezirksamt Marzahn, ed., *1979–1999*, 70.

102 Bluhme, "Erinnerungen," 54.

Thirty-five years later, the young boy Bluhme had grown into a man, and returned to a Marzahn where the construction had created "an environment that looked like a wasteland, and one could honestly say that it was chaos for the residents," but he returned as one of the key officials responsible for helping that state and its citizens restore the green spaces that he remembered from his youth. The difference was that this time the greenery would be planted anew, in conjunction with the construction project; indeed, as an extension of it. Bluhme noted that the differing timescales presented a problem, because "The construction of apartment buildings was so fast that the construction of greenways and landscaping could not keep up. Often, residents had to wait up to two years for their green spaces."[103]

In an unpublished novel she wrote after moving to Marzahn and before the greenery had filled in, Maja Maria Christian imagined an even longer narrative arc for the settlement, stretching into the future, as the green spaces would eventually outlive and outgrow the concrete blocks:

> A white, damp haze lies over the city district-to-be. The land protests, does not want to become a city. It protests against streets, buildings, and asphalt.
>
> It is good earth, here, that is being violated [*vergewältigt*]. Earth upon which green fields, meadows and forests blossomed for centuries. But this land will not see another farmer for a long time. Instead, the bulldozers come to clear space for a new seed; one of cement.
>
> Sleeping Beauty had to sleep for a hundred years. How long will this earth have to wait? Fifty years, a hundred, or longer? But one day, this new city will crumble, the cement will erode from the weather, and then nature will awaken, full of triumph and strength, and flowers will bloom and grass will become verdant, like the very beginning of time itself.[104]

In her novel, the protagonist, Eva, who has just moved to Marzahn and is living in a newly built tower, looks out at the meadows on the edge of the construction site, knowing they and the world they incorporate are not long for this world. It is only through her planting of a tree in front of her building and her daily care for it in what she calls the "stony desert" that she is able to bear the depression of the old world she once loved being torn asunder; able to begin marking new time so she can imagine her future in this new place.[105]

DIFFERENCE AND REPETITION: THE PHENOMENOLOGY OF CHILDHOOD IN MARZAHN

The near omnipresence of children was one of the defining features of life in the new settlement. By 1988 there were 33,000 schoolchildren, and a further 18,000 in Kindergartens or KiKos. A visitor wandering the recently constructed buildings

[103] Bluhme, "Erinnerungen," 54.
[104] Christian, "Ich will sehen, wie dieser Baum wächst..." in Bezirksamt Marzahn, ed., *1979–1999*, 32.
[105] Christian, "Ich will sehen," 33.

and newly planted greenways would see children and their traces everywhere. It was, in contemporary parlance, a "family-friendly" space, creating an obvious sense of dissonance with the—at first glance—distinctly unimaginative, and frankly unfriendly, rows of prefabricated buildings. As Elisabeth Albrecht recalled, there were forty-two children in her wing of her building (her "entrance") alone, a fact that "created quite a tumult" in the mornings and afternoons before and after school, in the entrance and lobby.[106] Eleanor Gast recalled that in the Marchwitzastrasse area (*Viertel*), "all the KiKos were overburdened. We had so many kids that the buildings were on the verge of falling apart."[107]

In fact, there were so many children in Marzahn that the construction brigades could not keep pace with the influx, and the Kindergartens, KiKos, and schools were not able to accommodate all the children—in this case, a conflict between "child" time and "construction" time.[108] To handle the shortfall, in the fall of 1983, Mayor Cyske and other Berlin city officials arranged for a special tram to carry all the children 19 km to the neighboring districts of Lichtenberg and Hohenschönhausen, which were also being developedwith *Plattenbau* in the name of the Housing Program.[109] Called the "Bummi train" (*Bummibahn*), named after the popular East German children's comic book cartoon bear, Bummi, the Tatra streetcar train would carry hordes of children outside Marzahn until the remaining schools and Kindergartens/KiKos were finished.[110]

Indeed, the concrete blocks and spaces were shaped to conform to a child's world. Often, *Mach Mit!* events would involve not only landscaping, but building playgrounds. The Klenners recalled doing this, and so did the Bautzes, who found out it was going to take two years for a playground to be built outside their building, due to the fact that the AWG, communal leadership, and *Hausmeister* could not seem to get their act together. In this case, the building's residents simply took it upon themselves to stage a mini tennis-court oath, walking out of a communal association committee meeting to the school across the street, where they elected a new leadership committee; one capable of getting at least an interim playground built. This at least led to an area of "a few play structures and a sandbox," which served until a better, more permanent one could be built.[111]

Often, residents would take it upon themselves to paint the entrances of their buildings with figures or scenes from well-known fairy tales or popular East German children's cartoons and shows, including Bummi the bear, and the ever-popular Sandman.[112] Kindergartens and KiKos were also designed by the artist brigade working with Marzahn's planners, who employed different motifs,

[106] Albrecht, "Balkonblick," 38. [107] Verein Kids & Co., *Südspitze*, 41.

[108] Cyske, "Bummibahn," 31. Cyske also intimates here that the shortfall of schools was a planning defect, the general rule of thumb for planners in the GDR being one school per 100 families. Because of the unusually high concentration of children in Marzahn, this had to be recalibrated to one school per 60 families—a fact which did not become clear to the district government until the early 1980s.

[109] Bezirksmuseum Marzahn, ed., *20 Jahre Marzahn*, 30.

[110] Bezirksmuseum Marzahn, ed., *20 Jahre Marzahn*, 30.

[111] Aribert and Renate Bautz, "Wir taten es für uns," 68. [112] Albrecht, "Balkonblick," 38.

such as "the circus," "fairy tales," "birds," "cactus," "beetle," or "caterpillar," the latter being the motif of the first KiKo, on 47/49 Marchwitzastrasse,[113] the one attended by Ilka Jütte and Christian and Constance Hämmerling. Their "Caterpillar" KiKo had a large plastic caterpillar affixed to both entrances. Officially, the "Caterpillar" KiKo was simply known as "Building [*Objekt*] 230."[114] In both cases, the point was to make a more "kid-friendly" environment for children amidst the near-identical apartment blocks and Kindergarten/school buildings. But it was also pragmatic, especially for younger children, who either could not read numbers or had trouble remembering their building's address—the differentiated symbols helped them find their way to school or home again.[115]

The child-friendly design of spaces such as KiKos and schools extended to their interiors, or at least was supposed to. The massive team assembled to build Marzahn also included pedagogical experts from the Ministry of Education (*Volksbildung*), who participated in the planning and the construction of the schools. The magazine *für dich*, for example, showcased the "Little Caterpillar" KiKo in a 1978 issue about children in Marzahn, describing an official from the Education Ministry, Liselotte Berger, as overseeing a collective of teachers, parents, and engineers to make sure that the school was built properly—inspecting the plastic flooring, making sure that the walls were insulated for sound (so that the infants and toddlers in one half could nap while the pre-Kindergarten and Kindergarten-aged children played in another half), and so on.

The article described the main accoutrements to be delivered to the school, including a set of "Bummi" (the bear) tableware for every child, toys, cozy corners, playground equipment, etc. Most importantly, the article showcased a three-year-old named Claudia Schreiber who was to go to the KiKo when it opened in late April of 1978, picturing her next to one of the dump trucks used in the construction of the school, and then later in the school itself, to show how she was part of the creation of the school. Because the KiKo was being built directly opposite the building into which the Schreibers had just moved, Claudia could watch the construction process, her own earliest memories being of the construction of the world that was to become her world.[116]

In some cases, children themselves shaped their new world. Inspired by the example of the new housing settlement in Leipzig-Süd, in which the gray concrete panels used to build everything including bus stops were painted with sunflowers, Mayor Cyske enlisted Marzahn's school directors and children to add color to the gray concrete world of Marzahn by painting each of Marzahn's fifty-eight bus stops with a specific motif.[117] The plan, begun in the mid 1980s, was a success, except for one case in which the children encountered the "limits of the dictatorship" (to borrow Lindenberger's notion). The tenth graders from the fourth High School

[113] Marianne Kühling, "Bildhafte Hausnummern für Vorschulkinder," in *Links Rechts der Wuhle,* 2003, 57–8.

[114] Inge Kertzscher, "Die Raupe als Haustier: Wie die erste kombinierte Kindereinrichtung auf unserer größten Baustelle der DDR in Berlin-Marzahn fertig wurde," *für dich*, (no. 22, 1978, 13).

[115] Both Albrecht in "Balkonblick" and Kühling in "Vorschulkinder" make this claim.

[116] Kertzscher, "Die Raupe," 13.

[117] Cyske, "Bummibahn," 29.

(*Oberschule*) painted one bus stop with a satire of firemen, presumably because the new volunteer fire station was nearby. In one image, a fireman sprayed water from his fire hose in the opposite direction to a fire; in another, a fireman was depicted at the top of his ladder on the eleventh story of a WBS 70 building, peering pruriently into an open window at a woman undressing.[118]

Though residents thought the raunchy images wonderful, and apparently the firemen were also good-humored about being spoofed by teenagers, the police chief of Marzahn was not amused in the slightest. He enlisted the representatives of the district council, the First Secretary of the SED in Marzahn, and the Fire Marshall of Marzahn to vehemently condemn the images, stating that anyone who depicted the firefighters, as an organ of the People's Police, in a satirical way could only have been influenced by the "Class Enemy."[119] (He also objected to the fact that some of the equipment depicted was outdated, and Marzahn's fire department among other things was the most modern and well equipped in the country.) He ordered the bus stop to be whitewashed, and though the parents' council at the school (*Elternbeirat*) objected, nothing could be done about it. Cyske apologized in person at the school for whole to-do. It was an object lesson for the tenth graders on how far their creativity was allowed to stretch in the socialist state, and especially in the "narrow-mindedness" of many officials in the GDR, a phrase used by Cyske in retrospect.[120] But mostly, the "fireman" incident showed to what extent the state and the Party valued Marzahn as a prestige object, and how sensitive they were to any perceived criticism of it, even from adolescents.

Other spaces in Marzahn were also designed specifically for children. These included two fountain playgrounds; open concrete areas with fountains for children to run in—often naked—on warm days, while parents shopped or simply sat nearby. Evelyn Marquardt could let her four- and five-year-old children run out to the fountain playground because she could see it clearly from her balcony, and because, following the Corbusian model, the children did not need to cross any streets when walking in Marzahn.[121] The fountains were turned on in the morning and left on until the evening, according to Jutta Wormbs.[122]

The fact that Marzahners like Evelyn could see their children from their high-rise windows or balconies was another aspect in which the spatial tectonics of Marzahn and the WBS 70/QP 71 shaped the experience of childhood—and, by extension, parenthood. Most of the living towers were designed with playgrounds directly adjoining them, so that almost every resident could see the playground from their window—this was especially true in the early years when most of the trees planted outside the buildings were still saplings (today some of the playgrounds are obscured by trees, during the warm months). In many cases, the plan for Marzahn placed KiKos, elementary schools (*Grundschulen*), and high schools

[118] Klaus Rebelsky and Renate Schröder, "Es war Einmal..." in Bezirksmuseum Marzahn, *20 Jahre Marzahn*, 123–5. Cyske also discusses this incident in "Bummibahn," and it is likewise recorded in Verein Kids & Co., *Südspitze*.

[119] Rebelsky and Schröder, 124–5. [120] Cyske, "Bummibahn," 29.

[121] Interview with Evelyn Marquardt, Berlin, May 26, 2008.

[122] Verein Kids & Co., *Südspitze*, 58.

(*Oberschulen*) within clear sight lines of the residential buildings that framed them. (Because many of the WBS 70 apartments spanned the width of the buildings, residents had views out of both sides of the building, so regardless of which side the school or KiKo was on, they could see it.) In many cases, this meant that parents could, if they were home during the day, look out over their kids during recess hour and at other outdoor activity times. *Kultur im Heim*, in its 1986 feature on Marzahn, noted that this was one of the primary advantages that attracted families to Marzahn: "The great majority of Marzahners feel good in their apartment and their environs... they value the comfort of their apartment, [and] the opportunity for their children to play in wide-open spaces that are still easily overseen [*doch überschaubares*] and safe."[123]

This proved vital for Barbara Diehl, whose son Dieter had had so much trouble integrating at the Kita where he had been in Friedrichshain. Her apartment on Allee der Kosmonauten afforded her a clear line of sight into the schoolyard of the elementary school where Dieter was to go (see Figure 10). She could see, during recess, that at first he continued to experience isolation and trouble integrating with his new classmates, often standing alone and sucking his thumb. (She was home in this first year on maternity leave with Stefan, born just after their move to Marzahn in 1981.) Towards the end of that first year, however, things began to improve for Dieter. Like so many other families, he had moved from someplace else, and had no friends in his new, concrete *Heimat*. Most children faced the same anxieties, which made it somewhat easier to make friends, considering that there were not a lot of pre-existing friendships or cliques at school, especially in the very early years. As it happened, Dieter met a girl his own age, whose family, through a rather amazing coincidence, hailed from the same village that Barbara had grown up in—Magdeborn, no longer in existence—and who lived in the same building and went to the same school as he. Dieter made his first friend in Marzahn, and gradually he eased out of his shell, playing with his friend and then with other kids at school—a process Barbara could observe day by day because of the views her building afforded her (see Figure 11).[124]

Along with a sense of community, of course, came a kind of conformism that perhaps was not always present in the older districts, especially for children. "Everyone was in the Young Pioneers and the Free German Youth," recalled Evelyn Marquardt, reminiscing about her daughter Daniela's experience as a preteen and teenager in Marzahn in the 1980s (see Figure 12). Though children did not always wear their Pioneer uniforms or blue scarves, they did all wear them on special days, including the last day of school.[125] Even beyond Party-run groups like the Young Pioneers there was little else for children to do in Marzahn other than join the proscribed social groups in the physical spaces set aside for them. So, for example, while Dieter Diehl made incremental progress in his social life with his one friend, his younger brother Stefan proved to be an extrovert as he grew into a schoolboy,

[123] "Leben in Marzahn," 2.
[124] Interview with Barbara Diehl, Berlin, February 20, 2008.
[125] Interview with Evelyn Marquardt, Berlin, May 26, 2008.

spending most of his free time, like most other kids in Marzahn, at the *Jugendklub*. This was also true of Ingeborg Hämmerling's daughter, as well as the other twenty-two children in her building, who went to school together "like siblings and spent their free time together at the playground, athletic fields, and later at the *Jugendclub*. Vandalism or graffiti was unknown to them." Not only that, but Hämmerling could rely on friendly neighbors to take care of her daughter if necessary, recalling "Kids were friends with all the families. As a single mother, I got so much support from my neighbors. If I was ever late to get home, I knew one of my neighbors would watch my daughter."[126]

There was no urban jungle to wander, with snaking alleyways, abandoned apartments to enter, windows to break, or rooftops which could be ascended and views enjoyed. There were no street corners to hang out on and start trouble, especially since any teenager thinking of scrawling graffiti, surreptitiously smoking or drinking, lighting a fire, or otherwise causing mischief knew they could be seen from a thousand windows at any time. There were few, if any, secret hideouts built into Le Corbusier's designs. It was not an urban childhood, but a more pure, modern, socialist one. It was both utopia and dystopia, and the dark side was the power or hegemony of the state built into the spaces, technologies, and social structures of the place; fundamental but invisible, like dark matter.

[126] Letter from Hämmerling to author, April 2008.

5

Plattenbau Panopticon

The Stasi, *Durchherrschung*, and the New Housing Settlements

Publicly, the Honecker regime based its legacy and legitimacy on the massive expansion of the Housing Program, and other aspects of "real existing socialism." But this was not the only important expansion happening in the 1970s and 1980s; it was during these two decades that the Ministry for State Security (*Ministerium für Staatssicherheit*; MfS or "Stasi") ballooned in size and scope. In the 1950s, the Stasi employed between 10,000 and 16,000 agents, and utilized between 20,000 and 30,000 collaborators (known as "informal cooperators," *Informale Mitarbeiter*, IM).[1] By the 1980s, the Stasi employed around 91,000 East Germans directly, many as officers or agents, and utilized 173,000 IMs.[2] Conceiving of itself as the "sword and shield" of the SED, the Stasi aimed to achieve "blanket" (*flachendeckend*) surveillance in the Republic. Its ratio of one secret police agent to every 180 citizens was vastly higher than other communist countries such as Czechoslovakia (1:867), Poland (1:1,574) and even the USSR itself (1:595), and much higher than the feared Gestapo, which had about 7,000 agents in the Third Reich, in a country of 61 million citizens.[3]

As is well known now, the MfS had hidden cameras and microphones seemingly everywhere, highly developed training methods in its academy, and even an archive of the smells of its own citizens. It had the power to harass, arrest, and even torture perceived enemies of the regime—but more than that, it was an all-seeing eye, arguably the most advanced surveillance state the world has ever witnessed. As Paul Betts, among many others, has noted, the Stasi produced more files, most of them on ordinary East Germans, than all the files produced by all the governments in German history since the Middle Ages—an estimated six million of them.[4] For this reason, Betts has compared the entire GDR to a "panopticon;"[5] the prison proposed by Jeremy Bentham and made famous by Michel Foucault as a kind of

[1] Jens Gieseke, *The History of the Stasi: East Germany's Secret Police, 1945–1990*, trans. David Burnett (New York: Berghahn, 2014), 36 and 81. Also see Gieseke, *Die hauptamtlichen Mitarbeiter der Staatssicherheit. Personalstruktur und Lebenswelt 1950–1989/90* (Berlin: Ch. Links, 2000), 293–4, and Helmut Müller-Enbergs, ed. *Inoffizielle Mitarbeiter des Ministeriums für Staatssicherheit: Richtlinien und Durchführungsbestimmungen* (Berlin: Ch. Links, 1996).

[2] Gary Bruce, *The Firm: The Inside Story of the Stasi* (New York: Oxford University Press, 2010), 10.

[3] Bruce, *The Firm*, 10–12. Also see Betts, *Within Walls*, 24.

[4] Betts, *Within Walls*, 22.

[5] Betts, *Within Walls*, 21.

manifestation and metaphor of the link in modernity between knowledge (especially visual knowledge) and power.[6] Even though many parts of East German society, especially in the domestic sphere, felt "private," that "private life...was never a world apart, but was always shot through by the forces of state and society."[7]

Of course, as Gary Bruce and others have noted, discussions and debates about the Stasi penetrate right to the deep divide within and beyond academic circles as to whether the GDR was a "thoroughly dominated" (*durchherrschte*) society. Some have argued that, despite the numbers of informants and the fancy surveillance technology, it was not true that GDR society was a dystopia of panopticism. Jens Gieseke, for example, has debunked the myth that children informed on or even denounced their parents.[8] And of course, Mary Fulbrook and a number of her protégés have famously argued that there was a degree of "normality" in the GDR, which coexisted alongside the Stasi and its "blanket surveillance." The Stasi was like a "scratchy undershirt," as dissident Jens Reich described it in 1988: omnipresent, yes, but no worse than a mild irritation or hassle, certainly not a looming threat.[9] For those whose lives were ruined by the Stasi, of course, these academic exercises and metaphors ring hollow, a legacy of "ostalgie" or Western academics with their own post-Cold War political agendas. As Bruce remarks, quite often the sides in this debate have become too entrenched, and as a result a more nuanced understanding of the complex role of the Stasi in everyday East German life has been difficult to achieve.[10] And as Gieseke notes, there are still numerous areas of East German society that have yet to be explored in terms of the level of Stasi penetration or *Durchherrschung*.[11]

It is that nuance that this chapter aims to find, by examining the role of the Stasi in everyday life through the prism of the socio-spatial dialectic. Specifically, it explores what role the Stasi played in the design and construction of Marzahn, and what the *spaces* created by Marzahn and other prefabricated housing settlements in the GDR meant to the Stasi—how a new kind of space shaped not only new kinds of surveillance, but acted dialectically on the heart of the notion of surveillance in a modern, socialist state like East Germany. The point here is that the Stasi was

[6] Foucault, *Discipline and Punish: The Birth of the Prison*, trans. Alan Sheridan (New York: Vintage Books, 1995). See esp. p. 214.

[7] Betts, *Within Walls*, 13.

[8] Gieseke, *The Stasi*, 119.

[9] Reich, "Sicherheit und Feigheit—der Käfer im Brennglas," in Walter Süß and Siegfried Suckut, eds., *Staatspartei und Staatssicherheit. Zum Verhältnis von SED und MfS*, (Ch. Links: Berlin, 1997), 25–37, first published in 1989 under the pseudonym Thomas Asperger in *Lettre international*. This is quoted in many places; here from Konrad Jarausch, "Between Myth and Reality: The Stasi Legacy in German History" in *Bulletin of the German Historical Institute* (Supplement 9, 2014, "Stasi at Home and Abroad: Domestic Order and Foreign Intelligence," edited by Uwe Spiekermann), 73–86; 76.

[10] Bruce, *The Firm*, 11. For a good recent overview that makes a similar plea for nuance in the study of the MfS, see Gieseke, "The Stasi and East German Society: Some Remarks on Current Research" in *Bulletin of the German Historical Institute* (Supplement 9, 2014,) 59–72, and Gieseke, "Staatssicherheit und Gesellschaft—Plädoyer für einen Brückenschlag," in Gieseke ed., *Staatssicherheit und Gesellschaft*, 7–22.

[11] Gieseke, *The Stasi*, 105.

intimately involved with the Housing Program from the beginning, and the fact that settlements like Marzahn were entirely new, built on a blank slate, and that the Stasi was there in some way watching them be built, meant that the secret police in East Germany knew these spaces inside and out. They knew them when they were just imaginary spaces and blueprints; they were there when each foundation was laid; they knew every access point, every piece of technology, every sight line, every angle. They were there when the first families moved in, and in fact, many if not most Stasi officers' families lived amongst the other residents in places like Marzahn, Lichtenberg, and Hohenschönhausen. The MfS knew the spaces of Marzahn better than the residents themselves, and this gave them a kind of spatial knowledge that translated, in a Foucauldian sense, to power more complete than any other space in the GDR.

Not only that: the contention here is that the Corbusian model of "towers in a park" created the perfect kind of panopticon effect in which there was nowhere to hide; no dark corners or basements or back alleys in which subversive activity could take place, as there was in older parts of the city, dating back to a more tumultuous time. The previous chapters explored the ways in which vertical living produced new sensations—especially new views, of sunsets, rainbows, or the *märkische* landscape. The new verticality, combined with the large empty green spaces and parking lots also produced new views of other people—a near-perfect window, so to speak, on the question that Stasi agents and their informers always began with: *Wer ist wer*, or "who is who;" or, more accurately, "who is *where*?" In a way, they echoed James Scott's condemnation of Corbusian "high modernist" architecture as emanating from Le Corbusier's love for authoritarianism, and abhorrence of the chaos, crime, and subversion present in early modern or industrial-era cities and slums—a reason that Scott gives for Le Corbusier's affinity with the authoritarian Soviet Union in the early Stalinist period.[12]

The previous chapters have made clear that the experience of Marzahn for most families was one of upward mobility, new beginnings, and general happiness. This chapter shows the darker side—that the prefabricated housing settlements were thoroughly dominated by the Stasi, and really, even more than that, they were of the same root—the Housing Program and the Stasi grew together in the same way children like Ilke Jütta or Constance and Christian Hämmerling grew together, or along with, the housing settlement. There was a "normality" (to borrow from Fulbrook) to everyday life in Marzahn. But behind the scenes, the Stasi was the glue that held everything together; it was often the reason for the production of this "normality." Of course, that "glue" was not benign. As the case of Marzahn and other settlements of the Housing Program show, the Stasi's involvement in the building of utopia was deeply connected to its ability to know spaces and thus have power within and over spaces.

[12] Scott, *Seeing Like a State*, 113 and 117.

THE CLANDESTINE HAND: THE STASI AND THE BUILDING OF MARZAHN

The Stasi, and its chief Erich Mielke, had long been interested in the economy. Mielke reasoned that one way to keep the Stasi relevant, and indispensable, was to use its surveillance and information-gathering abilities to help the GDR's planned economy function more smoothly. One of the biggest shortcomings of planned economies was, of course, that the system could not easily correct itself in the case of shortfalls or bottlenecks, in the way that a free market system could. And since job security was far greater than in capitalist economies, directors of enterprises or factories often did not have great leverage to prevent poor-quality work or bad behavior. But the Stasi realized that it could do that—it could be the eyes and ears of the economic control structure, reporting on shortages, gluts, and quality issues, and it could be the enforcer on the shop floor in a way other organizations could not. In lieu of the "invisible hand" the MfS provided a "clandestine hand."[13] Indeed, as Jens Gieseke writes, there was little need for such a massive a secret police force in the GDR—there simply were not that many dissidents or threats to the regime. The real threat to the regime, and thus to the party, he writes, was sloppy, lazy, careless, or often drunken workers—or outdated and broken equipment.[14] Thus, the MfS became an "ersatz public sphere" which became crucial for mediating between the public, the economy, and the regime.

By 1959, Mielke had already decided that the focus of the MfS would be to secure the material economy from sabotage attempts by enemy forces,[15] and by 1969 the MfS had dramatically expanded to cover all areas of the economy,[16] including concentrations of informers and agents in crucial factories such as the chemical factories in Leuna and Buna,[17] as well as a whole Department (XVIII) dedicated to the economy.[18] Once Honecker took over in 1971, and instituted "real existing socialism," the Stasi expanded its work in the economy even further, following the prevailing political winds. And these winds blew especially strongly through the Housing Program, as the cornerstone of the policy of "real existing socialism."[19]

And Marzahn was central to that Housing Program—thus, it was of great interest to the Stasi. As a 1974 report by the Berlin branch of the MfS on the early stages of the planning process stated: the Marzahn project had a "certain specific model character for the socialist living milieu in the GDR as an alternative to the

[13] The term "clandestine hand" is my own, but the point has been made in much more detail by Jens Gieseke in *The Stasi*, 107–9, and elsewhere in his work on the MfS.

[14] Gieseke, *The Stasi*, 105.

[15] Maria Haendcke-Hoppe-Arndt, *Die Hauptabteilung XVIII: Volkswirtschaft (MfS-Handbuch)* (Berlin: BStU, 1997), 13.

[16] Gieseke, *The Stasi*, 102.

[17] Gieseke, 105, and also see Georg Wagner-Kyora, "Spione der Arbeit—Zur Methodik der Alltagsgeschichte im IM Berichten aus Industriebetrieben" in Gieseke, ed., *Staatssicherheit und Gesellschaft*, 209–52.

[18] Gieseke, 104, and Haendcke-Hoppe-Arndt, *Die Hauptabteilung XVIII.*

[19] See Haendcke-Hoppe-Arndt, *Hauptabteilung XVIII*, 57–9; on 59 specifically about the Housing Program.

mass construction of apartments in capitalist cities."[20] It had to be a success, and when anything had to be a success, the Stasi was there behind the scenes.

From the beginning, then the Stasi was watching the project closely, obtaining copies of every planning document available on the project, from the minutes of meetings in the Politburo and the Magistrat, to reports on the soil and geology, to blueprints of all the buildings, utilities, and roads, to extensive photographs of the construction site.[21] In a number of cases, the Stasi also collected detailed blueprints on the WBS 70 models themselves.[22] From the beginning, they acted as a feedback mechanism for the Party to know exactly what was and was not working. The plans, the Stasi reported, were not adequate in terms of the proposed utility lines—especially water and sewage—[23] and the electric cables were not buried deep enough. The Stasi predicted that large-scale utility (especially electric) failures would result.[24] In one report from 1974, the Stasi foresaw the problems that would arise in this enormous project, remarking that "the complexity of planning and building demanded by the Biesdorf/Marzahn construction project is not feasible using the traditional methods of city planning and architecture."[25]

The Stasi began building its clandestine infrastructure in Marzahn early on, beginning with a "working group" for Marzahn, led by Major Knut Danicke,[26] which was expanded to a formal District Office on orders directly from Erich Mielke himself.[27] This central base, brought into existence in late 1978/early 1979, was made of twenty-five small offices.[28] The MfS would be well staffed in the new prefabricated housing settlement. From these offices, the MfS aimed to be the "clandestine hand" that made the whole project come together economically. The District Office set up a special organ for economics [*Referat Volkswirtschaft*], which conceived of its task as coordinating the construction process, and making sure that it came to a successful conclusion.[29] The Stasi was like a shadow in the

[20] BStU MfS BV AKG 1019, MfS Verwaltung Groß-Berlin "Information über Probleme des Standes der Vorbereitung des komplexen Wohnungsbaues im Gebiet Biesdorf/Marzahn," December, 4, 1974, 1.

[21] The Stasi archives are full of files that contain copies of construction diagrams, planning "harmonogramms," and other information related to the construction of Marzahn. See among others, BStU MfS HA XIX 4500; HA VIII 5090; VRD 792 "Informationen zu den Standorten des Kompleken Wohnungsbaus," and VRD 7784.

[22] BStU MfS HA VIII 5090, 16–20.

[23] BStU MfS BV Berlin AKG 1419, 3, and BStU MfS BV Berlin AKG 1511, "Information über einige Probleme bei der Erarbeitung des Bezirksharmonogramms für den komplexen Wohnungsbau, insbesondere in Berlin-Marzahn, 1981/1982 sowie des Plans 1981 für das WBK Berlin (Sekretariatssitzung am 1.12.1980)."

[24] BStU MfS BV Berlin AKG 1494 "Information über einige Probleme, die die Inbetriebnahme und Nutzung der Sammelkanäle im Neubaugebiet Berlin-Marzahn betreffen," September 11,1980, 2.

[25] BStU MfS BV AKG 1019, MfS Verwaltung Groß-Berlin "Information über Probleme des Standes der Vorbereitung des komplexen Wohnungsbaues im Gebiet Biesdorf/Marzahn," December 4, 1974, 1.

[26] BStU HA KuSchu 24953 "Vorschlag zur Bildung der neuen Kreisdienststelle Berlin-Marzahn," from the Bezirksverwaltung für Staatssicherheit, Berlin, Leiter, Generalmajor Schwanitz, to the MfS HAKuSchu Leiter, Genossen Generalmajor Otto, October 17, 1978.

[27] BStU BdL 006834—refers to Mielke Befehl 8/79.

[28] BStU MfS BdL 006834.

[29] BStU MfS BV Berlin BV Leitung 84; Bezirksverwaltung für Staatssicherheit Berlin, Kreisdienststelle Marzahn, November 7, 1985, 9.

construction site—it kept a running commentary on the shortfalls, missteps, safety violations, and other problems that arose both at the construction site itself and at the concrete panel factory. It focused, for example, on the lack of coordination in the WBK—the organ responsible for bringing together the many different state companies and enterprises involved in constructing an entirely new socialist city. The contractors (*Bedarfsträger*) involved, claimed one Stasi report, felt "no responsibility" towards each other, and thus there was "no coordination" within the WBK.[30] Several WBK factories were already behind schedule, the Stasi noted as of 1974, three years before actual construction of the apartments was to begin.[31]

Furthermore, the Stasi reported, discipline among the workers at the construction site was a real problem. As described above, the construction site had a "Wild East" feel to it, as the workers were removed from their ordinary circumstances and put moved to barracks in the middle of nowhere. Not all workers were happy about it, grumbling about the conditions in the barracks.[32] This was especially true of those forced to move to the crucible of Marzahn, including older and more experienced workers such as Joachim Kretzschmar, who already had a job in a factory in Dresden that made kitchen equipment, and who was "sentenced" (*verdonnert*) to move to Marzahn with his wife, and others from Dresden, to help construct kitchens for the WBS 70 housing.[33] In one case, of concern to the Stasi, a masonry brigade led by Klaus Laubner had decided to celebrate the birthday of one of the brigade's workers by consuming numerous entire bottles of brandy, vodka, and beer at 6:30 in the morning while singing "rowdy songs." When confronted on the site by an authority of the *Aufbauleitung* around mid-morning, Laubner and a couple other workers, still drunk, swung at the official and accused him of being a "snooper" and a "Stasi-informer," and complained that it was "impossible to celebrate a birthday in this fucked-up country."[34]

The sense of laxity had more serious consequences, as well—workers routinely left electric cables lying on the ground in puddles,[35] smoked near open fuel sources, and committed other violations without care, resulting in a high number of fires and accidents, including the death of a worker named Hartmuth Schleicher in December 1979.[36] Security around the site was lax—construction materials disappeared from unguarded storage areas, and children were allowed to play in and

[30] BStU MfS BV AKG 1019, MfS Verwaltung Groß-Berlin, "Information," 2.

[31] BStU MfS BV AKG 1019, MfS Verwaltung Groß-Berlin, "Information," 2–3.

[32] BStU MfS BV Berlin AKG 1281, letter from Konrad Naumann dated May 3, 1977: "Information über einige Probleme im Zusammenhang mit der nachrightentechnische Erschließung und Versorgung des 9. Stadtbezirks."

[33] Kretzschmar, "FDJ nach Berlin," in Verein KIDS & Co., ed., *Südspitze*, 28.

[34] BStU MfS ZAIG 3294, "Information über ein Vorkommnis mit Bauarbeitern auf der Baustelle in Berlin-Marzahn, Karl-Holtz-Strasse, am 17. Juni 1983."

[35] BStU MfS BV Berlin AKG 1489 "Bildbericht: Bildband zum Bericht vom 20.02.1980 über die Kontrolle der elektrotechnischen Anlagen der Baustelle Berlin-Marzahn des VEB WBK Berlin, Baustelleneinrichtung im Bereich der Apotheke, Allee der Kosmonauten," 28.

[36] BStU MfS BV Berlin AKG 1459 "Information über Mängel und Hämmnisse im Zusammenhang mit der Planerfüllung des komplexen Wohnungsbaus im I. Quartal 1980 sowie einigen die Sicherheit und Ordnung auf den Baustellen in Berlin-Marzahn beeinträchtigende Faktoren (Sekretariatssitzungitzung am 7.4.1980).

around the construction site, including in puddles that were also in contact with live electric cables.[37] This was a problem in other major housing settlement construction sites, such as in Leipzig-Grünau, where the Stasi was also deeply concerned about laxity and improper storage of construction materials.[38]

In 1980, as the Hohenschönhausen panel factory fell further behind its quotas, the Stasi singled out the factory director, Comrade Böttcher, along with other managers, calling their leadership "chaotic" and blaming them for poor discipline at the factory and ultimately for the shortfalls in production and quality. They were called in to meet with the Berlin branch of the Stasi and the State Attorney to face possible charges for their failure to carry out their duties.[39]

The Stasi was concerned early on with the spatial organization of the construction site, especially where it concerned properly connecting buildings to utilities. Often, one report noted, buildings were placed where utility connections had not been placed, or had been placed improperly, so that the gas, heat, electricity, etc. could not actually be activated inside the buildings, rendering them useless. Even the barracks built to house construction workers in Marzahn and just off-site in nearby Friedrichsfelde-Ost had themselves no connection to the main utility canal and thus no warm air or electricity, and in some cases no toilets, rendering the living conditions during the winter of 1979–80 "completely insufficient."[40] Many buildings built by the montage brigades stood empty for a lengthy time, including KiKo #243, which had been built in the early summer of 1979 but still had no utilities connected at the end of the year.

In fact, the Stasi claimed, though the Berlin WBK claimed to have produced 1,090 dwelling units in the month of September, which would have been fifty-six over the quota, only seventy-six dwelling units had been made available to residents; the rest had no heat, water, electricity, or sewage services.[41] This utter lack of coordination had led factory and construction workers to openly refer to the plan as a "disharmonogram."[42] Even when utilities were connected, and people began moving in, there were problems with the services and with numerous construction flaws.

The leadership of the Stasi was, at least at times, not happy about the fact that they had become the catch-all, the "fixers," of the entire planned economy—as Mielke himself said, "you wouldn't believe the trifles we had to deal with!... If it was raining through the roof of a hospital, that's when they called on us."[43] But in way, there was a trade-off involved; for the Stasi, being the "fixers," spending most of their time writing reports about faulty equipment or unsecured utility cables was a price they

[37] BStU MfS BV Berlin AKG 1489, "Bildbericht," 39.

[38] BStU Außenstelle Leipzig, BVfS Leipzig KDfS Leipzig-Stadt 03593. "Information zu Verstößen gegen die Ordnung und Sicherheit im Neubaugebiet Leipzig-Grünau," March 19, 1981.

[39] BStU MfS BV Berlin AKG 1459 "Information über Mängel und Hämmnisse im Zusammenhang mit der Planerfüllung des komplexen Wohnungsbaus im I. Quartal 1980 sowie einigen die Sicherheit und Ordnung auf den Baustellen in Berlin-Marzahn beeinträchtigende Faktoren (Sekretariatssitzung am 7.4.1980)," 4.

[40] BStU MfS BV Berlin AKG 1419, 3.

[41] BStU MfS BV Berlin AKG 1419, 2.

[42] BStU MfS BV Berlin AKG 1419, 1.

[43] This is from Gieseke, *The Stasi,* frontmatter.

had to pay for ever-greater access to the spaces, structures, technologies, and organizations that created the architecture of everyday life. Being the "glue" that made sure the construction teams ultimately did their jobs also entitled the Stasi to know the buildings and the residents who moved into them better than almost anyone, and to use that knowledge to expand their surveillance empire. They were, as historian Klau-Dietmar Henke called them, at once a stabilizing and destabilizing force.[44] Thus, we must look at the other side of the coin—the role of the Stasi as a surveillance organization and how it utilized the spaces of Marzahn to its advantage.

SEEING LIKE A *PLATTENBAU*: SURVEILLANCE IN THE WBS 70 AND THE SPACES IN BETWEEN

The new world of the prefabricated housing settlement, especially the building types WBS 70 and QP 71, was of great interest to the Stasi. Because these buildings constituted the vast majority of the new settlements being built around the country, the Stasi could train its agents on one or two models of building, and these agents could then be ready to conduct surveillance and espionage anywhere throughout the country—the need for local knowledge, normally a major obstacle in police work, ceased to present such a problem. More than anything, this was the main reason for the Stasi's interest in the blueprints and planning documents—so its agents could familiarize themselves with the new spaces and technologies that would shape the future of surveillance in socialism. Indeed, the Stasi studied not only Marzahn, but also other settlements, such as those outside Leipzig, Karl Marx City, Rostock, and elsewhere, to develop a new surveillance methodology appropriate for these new socialist spaces.[45]

In fact, the rise of the housing settlements in East Germany mirrored the massive growth in surveillance by the Stasi—not just in settlements, but everywhere—which was centered on the Stasi's Department VIII, dedicated to surveillance. Beginning in the 1970s, Department VIII sought to create a highly professionalized core of agents with finely tuned surveillance skills, initially developing 1,000 and later expanding to 3,000 such experts by the late 1980s.[46] To this end, Department VIII created its own "academy" to provide intensive training in all kinds of surveillance—from tailing, to staking out, to using technology—in all kinds of situations.[47]

[44] This is quoted in Gieseke, *The Stasi,* 96.

[45] BStU Archiv der Aussenstelle Chemnitz, MfS BV Karl Marx Stadt 26–168; MfS BV Karl Marx Stadt W- 23, "Konzeption für den Einsatz der Linie B in Wohnbauten der Typenreihe P2," From Referat II, Abt. 26 Oct. 1972; also BStU Außenstelle Leipzig, MfS BV Leipzig VIII 367 "Die Erarbeitung einer Dokumentation und einer grafischen Darstellung zur Nutzung operative Sicht- und Aufenthaltsstützpunkte in den Wohnkomplexen Leipzig-Grünau."

[46] Angela Schmole, *Hauptabteilung VIII. Beobachtung, Ermittlung, Durchsuchung, Festnahme. (MfS-Handbuch)* (Berlin: BStU, 2011), 48.

[47] Schmole, *Hauptabteilung VIII,* 18. Also see BStU MfS, HA VIII, Nr. 1875/2, HA VIII/Schule: Studienmaterial zum Thema: Die Erarbeitung von Varianten zur Maskierung von operativen Kräften und Tarnung operativ-technischer Mittel—Aspekte ihrer Anwendung in der operativen Beobachtung v. Juni 1981, 72–130.

Popular notions of the Stasi focus very much on this aspect of the MfS, but place too much emphasis on the Stasi's use of technology, such as hidden cameras and "bugs," as demonstrated by the film *The Lives of Others* or the popular Stasi Museum in Berlin. And while technology was not unimportant to Department VIII (and other departments), it was not the main focus of surveillance taught in the Department and in its school. In reality, *footwork* was the main method of surveillance. A great deal of what surveillance really meant was understanding space and place, understanding distances, angles, and sight lines, and always having a map of a space in one's head. For this reason, the motto of Department VIII was "By foot, by car, or by public transit—always use the right distance from your object."[48] The aim of Department VIII was to create a highly trained cadre of agents and informers who could use the spatial environment to their advantage, including knowing where to hide, how to blend in, how to access rooftops or balconies, and where to take shortcuts. They wanted both Stasi officers and IMs to be able to quickly develop the skills of a Jason Bourne or a Carrie Matheson, and that meant, in the case of Marzahn, developing a mental map of this newly created space.

So as part of the same project that led to the surveillance academy, Department VIII began creating a series of manuals that could be used as instructional material in the academy and as part of the "training-up" of IMs and other field agents to get them ready for the footwork of surveillance in specific places and situations.[49] And there were several created for prefabricated housing settlements, including Leipzig–Grünau[50] and Marzahn.[51] The Marzahn manual is perhaps the most complete, offering fascinating insight into the Stasi's full repertoire of thinking and tactics regarding conducting surveillance in Marzahn and its WBS 70 buildings. This manual was to be standard reading for any agents or unofficial collaborators engaged in clandestine operations in Marzahn or in any similar settlements—in fact, the Stasi recommended it be carried along on any missions in Marzahn. Stasi agents could use the manual for their own field operations, or use them to train IMs which they had recruited for clandestine work in Marzahn (see Figure 13).[52]

Agents or collaborators conducting surveillance in the settlement needed to understand this new place as a space and a technology; they needed to understand not only how to "see like a state" (to quote Scott), but more specifically how to "see" like a *Plattenbau.* Their training, included in manuals such as those for Marzahn and Grünau, involved three general steps: first, gaining a basic sense of orientation in such a radically different space; second, understanding the new advantages and disadvantages that vertical space, that is, the "towers in a park" concept, posed for surveillance; and finally, learning and mastering the models of

[48] Schmole, *Hauptabteilung VIII,* 49. [49] Schmole, *Hauptabeilung VIII,* 49.

[50] BStU Außenstelle Leipzig, MfS BV Leipzig VIII 367; "Die Erarbeitung einer Dokumentation und einer grafischen Darstellung zur Nutzung operative Sicht- und Aufenthaltsstützpunkte in den Wohnkomplexen Leipzig-Grünau."

[51] BStU MfS HA VIII 5192; Jugendkollektiv des Referates 4 der Abteilung 3, "Dokumentation über den Stadtbezirk Berlin-Marzahn."

[52] BStU MfS HA VIII 5192; "Berlin-Marzahn," 3.

the apartments used in prefabricated settlements, especially the WBS 70, as a space and a technology.

Orienting oneself in a new place was key to any kind of clandestine work, claimed the Stasi's Marzahn manual.[53] This was especially true of the prefabricated satellite settlements, which were so radically different to the old city or town. In particular, the manual stated, the secret police agent needed to reorient themselves to the sheer size of Marzahn, a settlement the size of Gera (a small city in the GDR).[54] That, combined with the special nature of the settlement, meant that "orientation for a person unfamiliar with this place is difficult," and that people unfamiliar with the place often found themselves repeatedly asking for directions, especially while on foot.[55] The Marzahn manual contained information and a map describing forty-five locations throughout the settlement that could be used as temporary cover and as surveillance posts for tracking suspects outside their apartment buildings. These buildings included schools, KiKos, police stations, restaurants and pubs, and health clinics; the main post office, the Biesdorfer Kreuz, and even the Stasi District Office itself.[56] Other manuals, such as that for Leipzig–Grünau, contained similar orientation guides, detailing where important intersections, public telephones, or clandestine meeting locations were to be found; these included the Hermann Matern 80th Polytechnical High School on Grünauerallee and the "Gertrude Frank" retirement home.[57]

But beyond gaining a sense of where buildings were, relative to one another, surveillance in places like Marzahn meant understanding how the "towers in a park" concept around which prefabricated settlements were built redefined the power dynamics between buildings and the spaces between them. There was a great deal of open space between buildings, and the verticality of the buildings meant that the sightlines from their windows and balconies extended a great distance. All residents had at least a view of one side of their buildings; not all had a balcony, but those who did had the ability to extend their vision around the sides and corners of the building and all the way down to ground level. Most of the buildings had two entrances, and so most apartments offered a clear view of who came in and out of the building. Especially in the early years of Marzahn, when the saplings and other plants were still young, there was little to no cover when approaching buildings, even from a great distance (today, the trees planted in the late 1970s and early 1980s are mature, and when they have leaves they partially obscure the balcony view of some sidewalks and pathways in between buildings). This is different to life in the old courtyard apartments of the inner city, where only those with a street-view apartment could see who entered the building, and even then it was difficult to see a long way, since the sight lines usually stopped at the façade of the building on the direct opposite side of the street. In Marzahn there were no streets, and everyone had a panopticon-like view of the surroundings.

[53] BStU MfS HA VIII 5192, "Berlin-Marzahn," 4.

[54] BStU MfS HA VIII 5192, "Berlin-Marzahn," 14 and 17.

[55] BStU MfS HA VIII 5192, "Berlin-Marzahn," 14.

[56] BStU MfS HA VIII 5192, "Berlin-Marzahn," 20–1.

[57] BStU Außenstelle Leipzig, MfS BV Leipzig VIII 367, "Leipzig-Grünau," 12, 18.

This meant that a secret agent had to be very careful about when and how they tried to enter a building. Furthermore, Marzahn was constructed so that every resident could walk to either work or school, or could walk easily to a public transit stop. There were very few who left their building and hopped into a car to drive away, in contrast to the older neighborhoods. And in the "large green areas" between buildings, the manual noted, the important thing to bear in mind was that there was "heavy foot traffic only during the morning and evening time—people going to and coming from work."[58] The implication was clear—it was much harder in a model community like Marzahn, with no physical cover, to remain unseen and anonymous during the middle of the day, or at any other time. Nor were people necessarily out and about, and thus easy to follow, during any other time. If an agent needed to move about, it would have to be a matter of getting lost in the crowd during the morning or afternoon rush hours.

The parking of cars was a particular bedevilment for the Stasi, as the manual noted. There were only centralized parking lots, usually near the periphery of the settlements; residents did not drive with great frequency if they did own cars, and there were only a couple of main arteries leading in and out of Marzahn. On one hand, this meant it was easier to follow a potential suspect by car—if in fact they were driving—at least until they were out of Marzahn. On the other hand, however, it meant that there was no way to park a car and use it as a safe place from which to observe or stake out a suspect, since the parking lots were consciously separated from the buildings, and those which were near buildings were in easy view of almost every resident.[59] Unlike on older city streets, people rarely sat in their cars for extended periods of time—if you were waiting for someone to come out of their building or a shop or office, presumably you would be waiting outside the building itself, which meant waiting on foot. Thus, there was little in the way of plausibility for a police stake out in a car, the manual noted.[60]

In fact, the manual stated, it was even more difficult for the Stasi, since one of the preferred methods of surveillance was the parking of a van or a small truck, presumably a delivery or service vehicle of some kind, outside an apartment building; something entirely plausible in a mixed-use urban space. But in Marzahn and in other settlements, where commercial space was largely separated from residential space, there was little reason for a delivery van or truck to be parked near an apartment building. Such vehicles were rarely seen—unless they were moving vans, (but the moving vans usually only came to a particular area as it was being built; once it was, generally speaking most of the people who were going to move in had done so already), and thus the presence of such a vehicle was bound to "arouse the suspicions of the citizenry," according to the Stasi.[61] Undercover police work was just very hard to conduct outdoors in a place like Marzahn, as the Stasi manual explicitly stated: "Observing from the windows of the residential buildings

58 BStU MfS HA VIII 5192 "Berlin-Marzahn," 17.
59 BStU MfS HA VIII 5192 "Berlin-Marzahn," 14.
60 BStU MfS HA VIII 5192 "Berlin-Marzahn," 14.
61 BStU MfS HA VIII 5192 "Berlin-Marzahn," 17–18.

presents the opportunity to overlook very large areas, and therefore to be able to recognize clandestine surveillance as such."[62]

Indeed, the difficulties presented by the "towers in a park" concept in terms of law enforcement and social control were already becoming known in the West, in the *banlieues* of Paris, for example, and especially in the housing projects of American cities. As sociologist Sudhir Venkatesh has described in his research, the high-rise towers of housing projects such as the Robert Taylor Homes in Chicago have proved to be bastions of criminal gangs, and ultimately impenetrable to the police (or rival gangs, for that matter) because, quite simply, lookouts working for the gangs could see the cops coming from a mile away—literally. Once the police lost control *within* the towers, there was no way to control the community and urban space that surrounded them.[63] The towers, isolated amongst open spaces, became both the figurative *and* the literal high ground in the battle for state control. Whether in Chicago or in East Berlin, high-rise housing settlements "raised" the stakes of control and power—control one building, and you control the ground for many miles around it.

Thus, it is not surprising that the Stasi sought to establish control within such high-rise towers, especially through the acquisition of "clandestine" apartments or the recruitment of residents as IMs whose apartments overlooked strategic points of interest. Best of all were retirees or homemakers with upper-story windows overlooking those strategic spaces—because they would be home a lot and able to keep up continuous surveillance, or at least be able to give entry to MfS agents. These included, for example, a retired policeman with an apartment in a WBS 70 building in the new Lütten Klein prefabricated settlement outside Rostock, as well as a retired elderly woman in the Südstadt settlement, also outside Rostock, both of whom were recruited successfully as IMs by the Stasi because of the views their apartments afforded.[64]

In Leipzig-Grünau, for example, the Stasi recruited several collaborators along a specific street, securing their permission to use their apartments as clandestine meeting places or central surveillance points (*Stutzpünkte*), because their windows and balconies overlooked the two churches that were part of the settlement. The apartments in the WBS 70 buildings along Potschkaustrasse, facing west, had a clear view of the Lutheran Paulus and Catholic St. Martin's churches, making them valuable vantage points (*Sichtpünkte*) for the Stasi to keep detailed notes on who went in and came out of these churches[65]—which were notorious for being among the only places in the GDR where dissidents could escape the watchfulness of the

62 BStU MfS HA VIII 5192 "Berlin-Marzahn," 18.

63 Venkatesh, *American Project: The Rise and Fall of a Modern Ghetto* (Cambridge, MA: Harvard University Press, 2002), 72. See also his *Gang Leader for a Day: A Rogue Sociologist Takes to the Streets* (New York: Penguin, 2008) for a more in-depth look at the inner workings of power and surveillance (on behalf of criminals, not police) in high-rise housing projects in Chicago.

64 BStU Außenstelle Rostock, MfS BV Rostock 53–93 Bd 1 "Bekanntwerden des Kandidates," and MfS BV Rostock 345–93 Bd. 1 "Bericht über durchgeführte Wohngebietsermittlung zur Person Koepsell, Ursula geb. Jeschke."

65 BStU Außenstelle Leipzig, MfS BV Leipzig VIII 367 "Aufenthaltsstützpunkte in den Wohnkomplexen Leipzig-Grünau," 11, 15.

state.[66] It was, in particular, the apartment of the Kreisel Family—apartment 403 at 30 Potschkaustrasse—that the Stasi used to look down on the Catholic church, and that of the Ungewitter family at number 74 to oversee the Lutheran church.[67]

Another example from the Schönau section of Leipzig–Grünau illustrates both the danger and the opportunities that the "verticality" and the spacing between the buildings presented to the Stasi. Schönau lay, like so many such settlements, beyond the edge of Leipzig, built on the *tabula rasa* of the "green fields" outside the city. It also lay directly opposite a Soviet military base and training ground in which a sizeable number of Red Army tanks and armored vehicles were kept. A report filed by an IM code-named "Joker" in 1985 caught the Stasi's attention: apparently, some residents of an apartment with a view of the Soviet base were using binoculars to observe the military exercises of Soviet armored vehicles.[68] In particular, a husband and wife on an upper floor of the building at 114 Uranusstrasse were observing tank movements from their balcony, reporting to each other. The Stasi then opened an "OV" (*operative Vorgang*, a formal surveillance operation) and, using the housebook, determined the identity of the residents. They then began recruiting their neighbors, especially those with apartments across from their building, as IMs.[69] In another case a few years later, also in Schönau, a couple was noticed using binoculars to observe the tank movements at the Soviet base.[70] In both cases, the observers themselves were observable; through its IMs the Stasi watched, photographed, and filmed the suspects even as they were watching the base,[71] their verticality and open sight lines being both an advantage and a disadvantage (see Figure 14).

Of course, there was only so much that could be observed from a window; the Stasi and its collaborators needed to be able to follow suspects into buildings, without blowing their cover, and for this reason they needed to learn the internal workings of the WBS 70 (and other models like the QP 71 and P2) like the back of their hand. What was the best way to follow a suspect into such a building, and track their destination, without revealing the presence of the agent or informer? It began, according to the Stasi, with understanding the elevator, and the floor-by-floor blueprints of the WBS 70. To follow a suspect into a WBS 70 building meant, first of all, finding a way to get past the locked lobby door, because, generally speaking, it raised suspicion if an agent waited for the suspect to open the door themselves (or have themselves buzzed through) and followed right behind. Here, the fact that the buildings were so large, and the residents in them often still quite

[66] See Betts, *Within Walls*, chapter 2 for an excellent overview of the role of churches in affording privacy in the GDR.

[67] BStU Außenstelle Leipzig, MfS BV Leipzig VIII 367 "Aufenthaltsstützpunkte in den Wohnkomplexen Leipzig-Grünau," 15.

[68] BStU Außenstelle Leipzig, BV Leipzig KD Leipzig Stadt 388–02, "Vorschlag zum gemeinsamen Aufklären der Personen, die vermutungsweise nachrichtendienstliche Beobachtung des GSSD-Objektes Schönau durchführen," December 1985.

[69] BStU Außenstelle Leipzig, BV Leipzig KD Leipzig Stadt 388–02, "Wohngebietsermittlung," May 23, 1986.

[70] BStU Außenstelle Leipzig, MfS BV Leipzig KD Leipzig Stadt, 101, "Bericht über die Arbeit des Beobachtungsstützpunkt der GSSD Schönau (betr. Den Balkon im 2. Stock, Schönauring)."

[71] BStU Außenstelle Leipzig, MfS BV Leipzig KD Leipzig Stadt, 101, "Bericht," 10–25.

new, and yet that the place enjoyed a kind of neighborly sense of communal trust, was a great advantage for the Stasi. It was not uncommon for residents to ring a random bell and ask to be buzzed in because they had forgotten their key or because they needed to use a telephone, which many of Marzahn's buildings had in their lobbies, the MfS noted.[72] This had to happen fast, though—because once the target got on the elevator on the other side of the glass, it was too late to follow them. The agent had to make sure they got on the elevator with the target.[73] Once in the elevator with them, the agent needed to make sure that their target was allowed to press their button first—even if the agent needed to stall in some way.[74] Here too the relative anonymity of the buildings meant that people were used to sharing the elevators with strangers, and often did not strike up conversations with those they did not know in the elevator, making it easier to maintain cover (although all agents needed a plausible cover story at all times, just in case).[75]

But it was dangerous, the manual continued, to simply get out at the same floor as the suspect. This might arouse too much suspicion—people often did not know all the residents of their building, but they often *did* know the residents of their own floor (assuming that they were going to their own abode, or to one where they spent a large amount of time, which was not always the case). Instead, the manual advised, agents would do well to push the button for the floor one story below the target's, and because the elevators in these buildings had doors that closed quite slowly, it should be possible to make it to the stairwells, usually positioned quite close to the elevator shafts, and swiftly make it up one story, arriving just after the suspect had exited the elevator, and just in time to espy into which door they had gone.[76] This got a bit more difficult if the target was going to the eleventh floor, as the elevators in WBS 70/11 buildings only went to the tenth.[77] Of course, the manual explained, the agent had to reckon with the fact that the target might already be taking general precautions to shake any potential surveillance, and in this case it was important to understand a unique feature of the WBS 70, which was that with several buildings linked together in different patterns there were throughways that connected the buildings—on the ninth floor and often in the cellar, where the communal rooms were located (although the ninth floor throughways were also frequently used as communal rooms). This meant that a careful suspect could enter at one address, take the elevator to the ninth floor, and follow the throughway to a building several addresses down (each elevator shaft or stairwell was separated by about 15 m), and agents needed to be aware of this.[78]

Furthermore, the fact that these buildings had two entrances/exits, a main one and a "back" one, made it difficult for clandestine operations to succeed inside the buildings. A clever suspect, or one that had been alerted to the fact that they were

[72] BStU MfS HA VIII 5192; Jugendkollektiv des Referates 4 der Abteilung 3, "Dokumentation über den Stadtbezirk Berlin-Marzahn," 10.

[73] BStU MfS HA VIII 5192, "Berlin-Marzahn," 10.

[74] BStU MfS HA VIII 5192, "Berlin-Marzahn," 10.

[75] BStU MfS HA VIII 5192, "Berlin-Marzahn," 10.

[76] BStU MfS HA VIII 5192, "Berlin-Marzahn," 12.

[77] BStU MfS HA VIII 5192, "Berlin-Marzahn," 15.

[78] BStU MfS HA VIII 5192, "Berlin-Marzahn," 12, 14, and 15.

being watched, could give the Stasi the slip by using the communal rooms or the ninth floor to go down a different elevator shaft than they had used coming up, and/or they could go out the opposite side of the building than they had entered on.[79] For this reason, among others, the Stasi recommended at least two agents be involved in the following of any suspect into a WBS 70 building with an elevator.[80]

DEFENDING UTOPIA: THE STASI IN THE FABRIC OF THE NEW COMMUNITY

As with the construction of the physical spaces and structures of settlements like it, the Stasi was the secret midwife to the construction of the new communities in Marzahn. From the beginning, The Stasi's new District Office made sure the right people were chosen for the local political leadership, from the Mayor all the way down to the leaders of the HGLs and "other communal political activities," through the use of specifically targeted task forces.[81] It was their business, according to Stasi documents, to know how many people were in each building, who they were, and who was in charge of them.[82]

Perhaps most important among the new residents was the *Hausmeister* that each building had. Dating back to at least the nineteenth century, the *Hausmeister* (literally "house master") was traditionally a resident of an apartment building who also worked for the landlord of the building, taking care of routine or basic maintenance, overseeing issues of basic orderliness such as noise or cleaning, and lending a helping hand where needed—usually in exchange for reduced rent. The *Hausmeister* could also be a useful instrument of surveillance and the "microphysics" of state power. This was especially true in the Third Reich, where the *Hausmeister* was useful for the Gestapo in keeping an eye—or an ear—out for anything suspicious.[83]

In the GDR, the *Hausmeister* became an even more important figure in the State's ability to penetrate the domestic sphere. Beginning in the early 1950s, a *Hausmeister* was expected to maintain a register of the residents of their building called a "housebook" with the names and apartments of the building's residents, their occupations, sometimes their comings and goings, and their visitors, including especially any visitors from a non-socialist country. These books were checked by the Stasi.[84] In Marzahn too, the *Hausmeister* was a central part of the life of the building and its new residents, and Marzahners recall the fact that their *Hausmeister* not only helped with stuck windows or carrying groceries, but also kept close tabs

[79] BStU MfS HA VIII 5192, "Berlin-Marzahn," 15.
[80] BStU MfS HA VIII 5192, "Berlin-Marzahn," 13.
[81] BStU MfS HA II 31363 "Information zur Gemeinschaftsantennenanlagen," 4.
[82] BStU MfS HA II 31363 "Gemeinschaftsantennenanlagen," 5.
[83] Betts, *Walls*, 28–9. Betts also notes that a similar system was used in the early USSR.
[84] Betts, *Within Walls*, 28–9.

on them. Renate and Reinhard Ladwig[85] and Ursula Weber [86] all recalled that their *Hausmeister* kept detailed records of residents in their building's housebook. Records included any potentially suspicious details, including, in one case, the fact that a resident wore a crucifix as a necklace.[87]

Indeed, *Hausmeister* were among the most important targets for recruitment as IMs for the Stasi. This was *especially* true in the new prefabricated housing settlements; a 1980 report from Department VIII stated that the fact that in the new settlements the bonds were less strong between the residents because they were new to the area meant that they were more reliant on the *Hausmeister* and less likely to trust neighbors, at least initially.[88] In fact, the report stated that it was actually easier to recruit IMs in older neighborhoods with more established relationships than in the new settlements[89]—in part because neighbors knew more about each other and thus had, presumably, more "dirt" on and possibly bones to pick with their neighbors. In the settlement, that often meant that the *Hausmeister* was everyone's best friend.[90]

There was another reason why recruiting the *Hausmeister* as an IM was crucial for the Stasi: the WBS 70 and QP 71 buildings had central antennae, which could not receive Western television channels, and which were governed by a switching device (usually) in the cellar, to which only the *Hausmeister* had the key. Thus the MfS kept a detailed list of each building in Marzahn, along with the names of each building's *Hausmeister*, and the location of the antenna and switching device, presumably to make sure that there was no risk of the devices being altered—for example, to receive Western television signals.[91]

In addition to the *Hausmeister*, however, the Stasi also believed it was crucial to get eyes and ears inside the social structures of the new settlement, including the HGL, but also the local National Front and *Volkssolidarität* branches.[92] Collaborators within state organizations, including such "mass organizations" were often termed "social cooperators" (*Gesellschaftliche Mitarbeiter*, GMs) and to the Stasi they were valuable as central nodes of gossip and information.[93] Also, presumably, this was a way to keep an eye on who was *not* participating in official events, such as "*Mach Mit!*" activities (something that we have seen was sometimes noted with disapproval by neighbors); or visits by VIPs; or elections, which were

[85] Renate and Reinhard Ladwig, "Beschlossen," *Allee der Kosmonauten*, 78.

[86] Weber, "Zuzug," *1979–1999*, 40.

[87] Weber, "Zuzug," *1979–1999*, 40.

[88] BStU MfS HA VIII 8278, "Forschungsergebnisse zum Thema Grundfragen der Qualifizierung operative Ermittlungen in Wohngebieten durch die Linie VIII und die Kreisdienststellen entsprechend der Erfordernissen und den wachsenden Möglichkeiten der entwickelten sozialistischen Gesellschaft zur Erhöhung der Wirksamkeit der vorbeugenden Verhinderung, Aufdeckung und Bekämpfung feindlich-negativer Aktivitäten," May 1980; 110 and 30.

[89] BStU MfS HA VIII 8278 "Forschungsergebnisse," 30.

[90] Specifically on the importance of the *Hausmeister* in the new Marzahn settlement, there is good material in Peter Militzer, "Praktikum für Hausmeister: Enge Kontakte mit künftigen Mietern wurden geknüpft" *Der Neunte* (vol. 1. no. 12, 7 July 1977, 4), as well as Manfred Hemprich, "Zu Hause im Hochhaus: Über Marzahner Kinder und ihre Eltern," *Neue Berliner Illustrierte* (no. 14, 1980, 12–17; 13–16).

[91] BStU MfS HA II 31363 "Gemeinschaftsantennenanlagen," 1.

[92] BStU MfS, HA VIII 8278, "Forschungsergebnisse," 110.

[93] BStU MfS, HA VIII 8278, "Forschungsergebnisse," 110.

often communal activities replete with fanfare and National Front members going door to door to solicit votes.[94] And because these local organizations were just being built in this new community, it was a perfect moment for the Stasi to get in, while people were still relatively unknown to each other—and thus had less loyalty, perhaps, to their *Kiez* than to the state.

One might wonder why the Stasi would be so concerned with this model community, one in which, clearly, one could not get an apartment as a dissident or a person who had run afoul of the Stasi. Not only did most people need to have a clean record to get into Marzahn, there was an enormous concentration of employees of the state, many of who were also members of the Party, including many families connected to the organs of state repression—military families (especially those connected to elite military units such as the border patrol), police families, and a good number of Stasi agents and their families lived in Marzahn, too. Based on records in Stasi files on apartments given to Stasi employees, it is estimated here that there were at least 1,500 Stasi families in Marzahn.[95] None of the families were openly identified as belonging to the Stasi, but, according to Ursula Weber, you could always tell which ones they were because they always listed their occupation as simply *Angestellter* ("employee," often specifically denoting "white-collar worker") and they all listed the same state-owned factory as their place of work in the building's housebook.[96]

The concentration of residents and families connected to the organs of state power in Marzahn made the Stasi more, rather than less, concerned about keeping an eye on things there. This was simply because the people of Marzahn were, generally speaking, better connected, and closer to the organs of power, and enjoyed more privileges, than the average GDR citizen—certainly more than the dissidents who more often than not chose to (or were forced to by dint of their subversive activities) remain in the dilapidated inner-city neighborhoods. According to this way of thinking, Marzahn would be a more attractive place for an enemy agent to try to infiltrate the GDR, than for example an older district, because in Marzahn there was a much greater concentration of East Germans who worked for the regime, with access to sensitive political and military information: "Many citizens have moved into this settlement [Marzahn] who also have contacts in foreign countries in the West, and therefore the possibility cannot be ruled out that the enemy will try to set up centers [*Stützpünkte*] for its subversive attacks against the GDR here."[97]

Indeed, prefabricated housing settlements were ideal for concentrating families of those who worked for the most sensitive state organs, especially the police and

[94] Here see Hedwig Richter, "Mass Obedience: Practices and Functions of Elections in the German Democratic Republic," in Richter and Ralph Jessen, eds., *Voting for Hitler and Stalin: Elections Under 20th Century Dictatorships* (Frankfurt am Main: Campus, 2011), 103–25.

[95] BStU MfS VRD 2234: Correspondence from the Rat des Stadtbezirks Berlin-Marzahn, Stellvertreter des Stadtbezirksbürgermeisters für Wohnungspolitik und Wohnungswirtschaft.

[96] Weber, "Zuzug," 40.

[97] BStU MfS HA VIII 5192; Jugendkollektiv des Referates 4 der Abteilung 3, "Dokumentation über den Stadtbezirk Berlin-Marzahn," 3. Gieseke, *The Stasi* 100–1 and Bruce, *The Firm,* 86–7 both comment on this phenomenon.

the Stasi itself, not only to provide them with new WBS 70 apartments, but also as a means of keeping total control and surveillance on them. It was a priority for the Stasi to keep tabs on those with access to power and privilege, even more so than those deemed to be dissidents and thus "outsiders," who had relatively little power or privilege. The Stasi even had a subsection of Department VIII, *Arbeitsbereich* (working area) 15, "Observation and Investigation of Army and Border Patrol Personnel."[98]

So for example the vast majority of the Stasi officers who worked at the MfS headquarters in East Berlin lived in a single residential section, WG 6, of the prefabricated settlement Hohenschönhausen North, just a short drive west from Marzahn, in Weißensee. WG 6 of Hohenschönhausen North was separated from the rest of the Hohenschönhausen North settlement. Bordered by the Josef-Höhnstrasse, Gehrenseestrasse, and Wartenbergerstrasse, the settlement was described by the Stasi as the "central residential area of the MfS."[99] Out of the 966 apartments in WG 6, 872 were occupied by families of Stasi officers—the other 96 were either employees of a special Stasi-run construction firm (People's Own Enterprise "Special Construction," *Volkseigener Betrieb Spezialhochbau*, or VEB SHB), used for building top-secret structures;[100] or the Dynamo firm, which ran the popular football side in Berlin (as well as in Dresden).[101] The WG had its own schools, shopping mart, restaurant, and pub, and from the moment the first Stasi families moved in, reports began filing in as residents immediately set to work watching each other. A similar situation existed with the police force (*Deutsche Volkspolizei*, DVP) whose families were largely concentrated into a prefabricated settlement along Leninallee (today Landsberger allee) and bordered by Plauenerstrasse and Arendtstrasse; here too, the Stasi was highly interested in knowing who was acting suspicious—who might be accumulating gambling debts, drinking too much, or having extramarital affairs—as it might make them vulnerable to blackmail from Western agents.[102]

In Marzahn, the Stasi targeted an army general named Koch, who was suspicious simply because he was a general with relatives in the Harz mountains in West Germany.[103] Other cases of Marzahners under surveillance included a former editor of the Party newspaper, *Neues Deutschland*, as we will see shortly, and factory workers such as Bärbel Adamsberger who, simply because they were favored by the regime were allowed to travel to places such as Hungary, and then used that as a chance to escape to the West. Adamsberger had applied for an exit visa for "family

[98] Schmole, *Hauptabeilung VIII*, 32–3.

[99] BStU MfS HAII 40214 "Abwehrarbeit im zentralen Wohngebiet des MfS Hohenschönhausen-Nord (WG-6)," May 8, 1981.

[100] See Roger Engelman, et. al., *Das MfS Lexicon: Begriffen, Personen und Strukturen der Staatssicherheit der DDR* (Berlin: Ch. Links, 2012), 313.

[101] See Mike Dennis, *The Stasi: Myth and Reality* (London: Pearson, 2003), 132–7.

[102] BStU MfS HAVII 2504 "Plan zur Qualifizierung der politisch-perativen Abwehrarbeit in der Wohnkonzentration von Angehörigen des Verantwortungsbereiches im Bereich Plauenerstrasse für den Zeitraum von 1981–1991." Also see Gieseke, *Hauptamtlichen Mitarbeiter.*

[103] BStU MfS HA VII 4460 IM report on General Koch, 1988. The location of this file is somewhat problematic, because it is labeled HA VII but it was located within BdL, and thus turned up more or less accidentally.

reasons" but because she worked at a sensitive site—the VEB Economic Research Center for Domestic Trade—her visa was rejected.[104] After that point, in 1988, the Stasi began an OV against her—although she nevertheless managed to get out of the GDR through Hungary in September 1989.[105]

Indeed, the Stasi was busy in Marzahn. As of 1983, the Stasi had made 535 arrests for security reasons in Marzahn. It had checked over 10,000 letters.[106] It had conducted three full-blown investigations (*Operativer Personenkontrolle*, OPK—a variation of the OV especially for those who were members of state or Party organs or those suspected of engaging in espionage—and therefore operations that required special sensitivity and sophistication), and was preparing OPKs for another twenty-eight suspects.[107] Two-hundred and fifty-eight people in Marzahn were discovered preparing to leave for the West, illegally, of whom 248 were already under suspicion. One-hundred and fifty-seven Marzahners actually attempted to flee, 105 of whom concocted their plans in Marzahn, and thirty-nine of whom succeeded.[108] (In all, 4,445 Marzahners fled to the West,[109] more than half of those in 1989 alone.[110]) In addition, there had been seventy-two cases of "negative–antagonistic" written or verbal statements made that had come to the attention of the MfS.[111] And the Stasi was plenty busy doing what it did best—recruiting informers, which, as Bruce describes, was raised to something like an art form in East Germany. As of the middle of 1983, there had been 149 informers of various kinds recruited in Marzahn.[112] By 1986, this had increased to 287.[113] In 1983, there had been 623 clandestine meetings to deliver secret reports by informers (as well as to conduct other secret actions with informers) within Marzahn; by 1986 this had risen to 2,226.[114] The Stasi was especially active in spying on the apartments of those Marzahners who were employed by the border patrol, perhaps the most sensitive security unit in the country, with 580 "security checks" of border patrol troops in Marzahn in 1984, 850 in 1985, and 530 in the first half of 1986 alone.[115]

In addition to the large concentration of employees of security organs and other politically and economically sensitive organizations, the MfS was concerned about the high concentration of children in Marzahn. The fact that Marzahn was the youngest district in the country, the most "child-rich" (*kinderreichste*), was not lost on the Stasi, who noted both hopefully and ominously that by 1990 there would

[104] BStU MfS HA XVIII 12126. [105] BStU MfS HA XVIII 12126.

[106] BStU MfS ZAIG 13751 "Erhebungsprogramm für die Ermittlung von Planstellennormativen, Bezirksverwaltung für Staatssicherheit Berlin-Marzahn," May 1983, 342.

[107] BStU MfS ZAIG 13751 "Erhebungsprogramm," 341.

[108] BStU MfS ZAIG 13751 "Erhebungsprogramm," 333–4.

[109] Bezirksmuseum Marzahn, *20 Jahre Marzahn*, 37.

[110] Bezirksmuseum Marzahn, *20 Jahre Marzahn*, 42.

[111] BStU MfS ZAIG 13751 "Erhebungsprogramm für die Ermittlung von Planstellennormativen, Bezirksverwaltung für Staatssicherheit Berlin-Marzahn" May 1983, 335.

[112] BStU MfS BV Berlin Leitung 75, Leiter der Kreisdienststelle Oberstleutnant Bartels, "Bericht über die Entwicklung des politisch-moralischen Zustandes in der Kreisdienststelle Marzahn," July 7, 1986, p. 9, "Anlage: Zu einigen Arbeitsergebnissen des 1. Halbjahres 1986 im Vergleich mit den Vorjahren."

[113] BStU MfS BV Berlin Leitung 75, "Kreisdienststelle Marzahn," 9.

[114] BStU MfS BV Berlin Leitung 75, "Kreisdienststelle Marzahn," 9.

[115] BStU MfS BV Berlin Leitung 75, "Kreisdienststelle Marzahn," 9.

be 55,000 children and adolescents in Marzahn, a population of youngsters larger than most municipalities in the GDR overall, a veritable city of children.[116] The huge number of children, the Stasi noted, represented "great potential, for example, for recruiting future military officers [*militärischen Berufnachwuchses*]."[117] However, it also represented a serious threat to law and order, especially as all the cute young toddlers who moved to Marzahn in the late 1970s entered their adolescences—their rebellious years—in the latter part of the 1980s.[118] Growing with Marzahn, the Stasi realized, could also mean rebelling against Marzahn and the new social order it represented. By 1985 this had already become a major problem, as the Stasi had begun to need to expend considerable energy and resources on investigating acts of vandalism and other crimes committed by youths—usually teenagers. In 1984 alone, there had been 964 crimes committed in Marzahn by 724 perpetrators, of whom 213 were aged 14–17 and 237 were aged 18–24. The vast majority of these crimes were against either "communal property" or "personal property." One-hundred and thirty-nine were more overtly political crimes, or at least crimes against the social order, such as "rowdiness," "asocial behavior," "vilifying the state," or otherwise obstructing state operations.[119] The Stasi was especially concerned about the tendency of rebellious youths, especially "punks," to concentrate in the youth clubs and youth centers where the other, presumably "good" kids and teenagers were, and to exert their subversive and corrosive influence.[120] Indeed, since Marzahn had been built in such a way that there were no obviously "underground" places for bad kids to hang out—no alleyways, abandoned buildings, stoops in crowded, crumbling neighborhoods, etc.—the places built into the plan for young people to concentrate, such as the schools and *Jugendklubs*, would pull in the "punks" as well as the conformist kids.

Of course, the revolution of 1989, the *Wende*, which led ultimately to the fall of the Wall and the end of East Germany and the Cold War, was felt in Marzahn as it was felt everywhere in the GDR. Indeed, some of the Stasi's concerns about the concentration of high-ranking Party and State officials living in Marzahn—that is, people with inside knowledge, leverage, and influence—seemed to partially be validated in the months leading up to the *Wende.* In the weeks leading up the May 1989 elections—in which the SED's ruling block won nearly 96 percent of the votes, as it always did—protests and calls to boycott the election spread throughout East Germany, and pervaded Marzahn. On April 21, flyers began appearing in the mailboxes of buildings in Marzahn, produced by the previously unknown "Group '89," accusing the SED regime of "paternalism, mismanaged economy [*Mißwirtschaft*], subsidization chaos, travel restrictions, press restrictions and

116 BStU MfS BV Berlin AKG 1019 BV-Leitung 84: Bezirksverwaltung für Staatssicherheit Berlin Kreisdienststelle Marzahn, "Entwicklung des Stadtbezirkes Marzahn," November 7, 1985, 9.

117 BStU MfS BV Berlin AKG 1019 BV-Leitung 84, "Entwicklung," 9.

118 BStU MfS BV Berlin AKG 1019 BV-Leitung 84, "Entwicklung," 9.

119 BStU MfS BV Berlin AKG 1019 BV-Leitung 84, 19, Appendix 6, "Entwicklungen der Straftaten im Stadtbezirk Marzahn im Zeitraum von 1980–1985."

120 BStU MfS BV Berlin AKG 1019 BV-Leitung 84, 19, Appendix 6, "Entwicklungen der Straftaten im Stadtbezirk Marzahn im Zeitraum von 1980–1985."

orders to shoot at the border."[121] The flyers called for East Germans to take the initiative: "Do not wait for a miracle; there won't be an East German Gorbachev any time soon!"[122] It went on: "The population of the GDR has grown up—it no longer needs a clique of functionaries to dictate how it is supposed to live!"[123] Furthermore, someone made use of the fact that, because of the "towers in a park" design of Marzahn, there was an abundance of walls with clear visibility upon which to paint slogans, such as "May 7th—No" and "May 7th—No Votes."[124]

The Stasi's response was swift and effective. By April 25, the district offices of Marzahn, Lichtenberg, and Hohenschönhausen had launched Operation (OV) "Echo." Within one day they had collected all the fliers, analyzed the kind of paper and typewriter ink used, the kind of paint used, and stored the bodily odors found on the fliers as well as on a partial boot print near one of the vandalized walls.[125] More importantly, the fact that there were so many eyes able to see the entrances and exits of the buildings, and the fact that the Stasi had already recruited so many informants throughout Marzahn meant that they could very quickly track down the troublemakers in the district. Within a week, they had a sketch of the suspect seen by multiple witnesses entering and leaving the building lobbies from above, including a detailed physical description. Witnesses also saw the suspect in the act of painting the walls, and so they knew he had a moped.[126] In less than a month they identified the culprit: Otto Schlieker, who lived on the ninth floor of a WBS 70/11 at 88 Heinrich-Rau-Strasse, and who had been an editor at *Neues Deutschland*; he had resigned in 1986, but his wife Christine continued to work there.[127]

In the end, of course, the Stasi's effectiveness in districts like Marzahn could not stem the tide that was sweeping over the country, and Marzahners adapted as the rest of the country did. By February 1989, they had set up a "round table"—a temporary governing council with representatives from all the political parties as well as the activists' groups which had instigated the *Wende*.[128] Round tables were a key feature of the transition between the top-down control of the old system and the eventual merger with the Federal Republic, and often were the only bodies that held any authority during those months. Mayor Cyske was indicted by the district attorney for falsifying the vote tally from the year before, even though this was a common practice and was ordered by his superiors in the Party. He resigned as Mayor. In the first truly free elections of March 18, 1990, Marzahners' political beliefs could finally be discerned: the PDS (Party of Democratic Socialism, the rump party left by the disintegration of the ruling SED) won 35.9 percent of the vote, followed by the SPD's 31.7 percent, the CDU's 17.5 percent, and the Bündnis (Federation) 90's 5 percent.[129] Subsequent elections showed a continued

121 BStU MfS HA XX 10008, 9–14.
122 BStU MfS HA XX 10008, 9.
123 BStU MfS HA XX 10008, 9.
124 BStU MfS HA XX 10008, 28.
125 BStU MfS HA XX 10008, 16.
126 BStU MfS HA XX 10008, 28.
127 BStU MfS HA XX 10008, 67.
128 Bezirksmuseum Marzahn, *20 Jahre Marzahn*, 44–5.
129 Hübner, Nicolaus, and Teresiak, eds., *20 Jahre Marzahn*, 69.

and lingering loyalty to the old regime, with the PDS garnering 35 percent again in 1992 and peaking at 45 percent in 1995.[130]

For the Stasi, settlements like Marzahn and Grünau were new challenges, but also tremendous opportunities. It was a chance to be present at the creation of a new world, and thus to understand that world spatially and socially better than almost anyone else—to literally know it from the ground up. Furthermore, they were aided by the Corbusian design of the settlements, both because the "towers in a park" model allowed for more vantage points and clearer sight lines, but also because the models of the buildings were largely identical, so understanding one meant a kind of automation or reproducibility of clandestine work that allowed the Stasi to become much more efficient.

It is likely not the case that Le Corbusier, in the 1920s, envisioned the kind of efficiency and interpenetration of society and private life that the Stasi was able to achieve a half-century later in perhaps one of the fullest realizations of his architectural vision. But the fact that he set his urban plans over and against "revolution" and "disorder" is also not a coincidence—and in this James Scott is on the right track. The fact that the Stasi was always watching, and able to see even better in a *Plattenbausiedlung* than in older neighborhoods, did not necessarily and should not detract from the fact that for most Marzahners, the experience of moving to Marzahn was one of a new beginning, and a drastic improvement in their lifestyle—a step closer to the promise of utopia. It is for us to be able to hold both thoughts at once, in our considerations of spaces like Marzahn—a place that was at once both utopia and dystopia.

[130] Bezirksmuseum Marzahn, *20 Jahre Marzahn*, 45.

Conclusion

Like many revolutions, the *Wende* of 1989–90 in East Germany turned a society on its head. Those who had been at the top suddenly found themselves at the bottom of their world. These included top Party members, Stasi agents, and border guards; but it also included a whole class of East Germans whose state had brought them up and trained them for a kind of economy that no longer existed—engineers, construction workers, and economic and urban planners, like the tens of thousands who participated in planning and building Marzahn. Some of them tried to retrain themselves. Some of the people I interviewed for this project, for example, retrained as computer technicians, travel agents, or English teachers. For most of them, though, this was beyond their ability. The social inversion also impacted the many heavy industry and factory workers, who had been the favorite sons (and occasionally daughters) of the GDR, and who populated places like Marzahn. Their skills were suited for outdated machinery and technological systems, and there were too many of them—the factories that did survive the transition to capitalism saw their workforces slashed by upwards of 80 percent, as Western management brought technological efficiency, and its eternal side-effect, unemployment, to the former GDR. In short, a large number of people in the GDR were tied to an economic and technological system, and when the GDR dissolved, so did that system, and so did their lives.

They found themselves looking up at people once at the "bottom" of East German society: dissidents, intellectuals—people who had suffered limitations on their careers or opportunities to travel because of their religious beliefs or their class background. Such people included Joachim Gauck, the dissident Lutheran pastor who was placed in charge of managing the millions of files on East German citizens left behind by the Stasi. People who for years had suffered surveillance and persecution because of their family ties to the West were now able to easily avail themselves of those connections and start a new life. Young people who had marginalized themselves by gravitating towards Western trends such as punk rock or hip hop, in many cases drawing the suspicion of the authorities, now found themselves more at home and welcomed in the popular culture that came flooding in from where the Wall had once held firm.

This inversion had its corollary in spatial terms, as well. Inner-city slum districts like Prenzlauer Berg, Pankow, and Friedrichshain in Berlin (and similar areas in smaller cities such as Rostock and Leipzig), often simply called the *Altstadt* or "old city", changed dramatically—these had been places from which to escape, yet they soon became the most desirable real estate in the city.[1] This inversion was as much about property values as it was about social and cultural values; those who remained in the crumbling, drafty, dark, cramped, century-old apartments were often the "left-behind" of socialism—literally and figuratively. Many stayed for the same reason that people stay in inner-city ghettoes in the West; because they were at the bottom of the social, economic, and political hierarchy. They did not work for a state factory, and thus found it hard to join an AWG to get their name on a list for an apartment in Marzahn or Hellersdorf or Neu Hohenschönhausen. Or they were dissidents, and so were watched closely by the Stasi; and the state, through the Stasi, did its best to ensure that such suspicious people were not rewarded in the same way as those who did join the mainstream were, so new, modern apartments in prefabricated housing settlements remained unattainable.

Of course, there were always exceptions. But over the course of the 1980s, it became clear that the older neighborhoods—the ones that had been the birthplaces of the working-class movement, the cradle of the "social question," and the fortresses of anti-fascism and anti-capitalism—had become ghettoes of dissent against the communist system. It was not a coincidence that the churches of such neighborhoods in Leipzig, Berlin, Rostock, and elsewhere, including the Zionskirche and the Gesthemanekirche in Berlin's Prenzlauer Berg, were the wellspring of the "Monday demonstrations" of 1989, which eventually mushroomed, overwhelming the state, and bringing an end to the Wall, and with it, the Cold War. Jurgen Hinze's "catastrophic" apartment was just down the block from the Zion Church (Zionskirche), which was an epicenter for the grass-roots environmental movement in Berlin, providing the spark for many of the 1989 protests. Its basement housed an "environmental library" (*Umweltsbibliothek*) founded by a circle of opposition activists who lived at 7 Fehrbellinerstrasse, right on Teutobergerplatz, the same neighborhood where Luise Schmidt had fought a Sisyphusian struggle against decay, and lived amongst the ghosts of fascism and war.[2] Often, when people got the good news that their apartment had come through, in Marzahn or elsewhere, they packed up and left—and no one moved in after them. Where the elements did not overwhelm the abandoned flats, squatters moved in—artists, punks, or just disaffected young people. This was one of the few truly free spaces in the GDR, even if plaster was peeling and windows broken—after all, if you did not have an address, it was much harder for the Stasi to find you, and to watch you. And of course, all the physical and spatial reasons that such neighborhoods had provided the seedbed of resistance to previous states still held true. Such spaces, like the basement of the Zion Church, were known to the residents much better than to the state, because they had not been built by the state.

[1] See Thomas Dörfler's *Gentrification in Prenzlauer Berg? Milieuwandel eines Berliner Sozialraums seit 1989* (Bielefeld: Transcript, 2010).

[2] See: Barbara Felsmann and Annette Gröschner, eds., *Durchgangszimmer Prenzlauer Berg: eine Berliner Künstlersozialgeschichte der 70er und 80er Jahre in Selbstauskünften* (Berlin: Lukas, 2012); Philip Brady and Ian Wallace, eds., *Prenzlauer Berg: Bohemia in East Berlin?* (Amsterdamn: Rodopi, 1995); and Klaus Grosinski, *Prenzlauer Berg: eine Chronik* (Berlin: Kulturamt Prenzlauer Berg, Prenzlauer Berg Museum für Heimatgeschichte und Stadtkultur, 2008).

They were a link to a German past that both reminded everyone who moved through them that the GDR had not always been and thus might not always be, *and* in being older than the state, they were only known in the minds of the people attached to them—a mental mapping that resisted the state's desire to build everything anew in its own, hyper-rationalized and modernized image.

It was almost as if these neighborhoods had revolution and resistance built into them from the beginning—the GDR was right to let them crumble, and to try to move everyone out to the blank slate of the green fields outside the city, as the Third Reich and earlier regimes before it had wanted to do. It should have been done sooner, at least from the point of view of what was best for the East German state. And had the *Wende* not happened when it did, if it had waited another ten or fifteen years, the Housing Program would have been much, much further developed. Far more of the East German population would have found itself living in places similar to Marzahn, in WBS 70 or QP 71 apartment blocks, or whatever next-generation model might have evolved from those designs. Would there have been, in this hypothetical case, nearly as large a core of disaffected people, living in squalor, reminded every day of the pre-GDR past as well as the failings of the GDR system? Would there have been an *Umweltsbibliothek* in the basement of the church in Marzahn? (There was, in fact, no basement in that church.) Would there have been such motivation to form *Bürgerbewegungen*—the citizens' initiatives like the one at 7 Fehrbellinerstrasse—if the same people had had running, hot water, fully equipped bathrooms, new kitchens, and fabulous views? "You don't need to go to Capri" to see the sunsets, said Renate Bautz, describing the view from her westward-facing WBS 70 high-rise apartment. Could Corbusian vertical living—with plentiful doses of sunshine and verdancy, as prescribed by the Athens Charter—really have placated East Germans? Was Le Corbusier right when he said "architecture or revolution?" What if no one could receive Western TV because of the concrete and rebar in the walls blocking their signal, and the use of central antennae in the buildings? Even if there had been a dissident movement in a Republic dominated by *Plattenbausiedlungen*, would it not have been much easier to track, observe, and eradicate because of the panopticon-like effect of these spaces, as the experience of the Stasi in Marzahn and Grünau suggests? Is this not the real definition of *Durchherrschung*—"thorough domination"—as a product of the interaction of state and society, refracted from a multitude of sources, rather than from just one unilateral source, as Lindenberger and Lüdtke have suggested?

This is, of course, hypothetical history. For a combination of reasons, the GDR ran out of time to convince its population (or at least a large segment thereof) that it was a superior system to the alternative on the other side of the Wall. Almost overnight, it seemed, the polarity between crumbling inner city and newly built housing project was flipped. Unlike a decade earlier, people began to move out of Marzahn—to move to the West, like many East Germans, or to move back to the inner city. The population of Marzahn-Hellersdorf has shrunk, since the *Wende*, from over 400,000 people to 250,000. Other housing projects have experienced similar depopulation. Those who had and kept their apartments in Marzahn had them converted to private dwellings—which had little chance of being sold on the now open and free real estate market. To a communist urban planner, such apartments look desirable, but to a capitalist real estate agent, they are dim prospects, at best, for a sale.

And, the opposite is true for the older neighborhoods, where private equity firms and individual speculators, often taking advantage of overly generous tax abatements from the city, state and federal, governments, quickly moved in to rehab and flip the crumbling rental barracks. The GDR had considered such renovations as well, and carried some out, but for a state concerned with quantity over quality, knocking down walls to combine two or three smaller apartments into one made little sense. For a real estate speculator, doing so often makes perfect sense. As the federal government moved most of its operations to Berlin, making the city a massive center of political and cultural power, tens of thousands of upwardly mobile young professionals moved to the city, and often found themselves attracted to neighborhoods like Prenzlauer Berg, Friedrichshain, and Mitte, where only a decade before the same upwardly mobile young professionals—of socialist vintage—were desperately trying to escape. Many, if not most of these, at first, were from West Germany. Later, young people, who were East Germans, but were just finishing school as the Wall came down, also joined the influx to the "Szene"—the "hip" neighborhoods. These were the very young people who were of the same generation as Ilka Jütte, and indeed Marzahn and places like it lost much of their young population, going from being the youngest and most "child-rich" district to being one of the oldest. In the past two decades, the inner-city "misery" districts, saturated with urban professional couples, have become the most child-rich—in particular Prenzlauer Berg/Pankow, which has by far the largest concentration of children in Berlin, as Marzahn once did. Today, elderly citizens are much more common than small children in Marzahn, whereas the playgrounds and (often still crumbling) sidewalks of Prenzlauer Berg teem with children. Where once people had children just to get out, now, parents search for spaces in Kindergartens, often in vain.

What was, in fact, so attractive about moving back to what had once been nineteenth-century slums? For one, many did indeed have attractive façades—baroque, neoclassical, or rococo themes, which, once fully renovated, looked attractive to Western eyes—they had "curb appeal." Here again was an example of how the socio-spatial dialectic operated to bind together the decades and centuries in Germany—the most violently different economic and political regimes and structures came and went, but if they left behind a spatial legacy, they left behind the possibility of their own return. In general, however, the capitalist real estate market often values—or overvalues—historicity and authenticity, or the illusion thereof, at least, with precisely the kind of uncritical sentimentality that modernists hated and had fought against all century; a fight they eventually convinced some in the West and most in the East to join. The cobblestone streets and neoclassical façades were just much more appealing than architecture as a hyper-rationalized, socio-technological system.

So, property values and rents in the old parts of towns throughout the GDR rose, and the "left-behind" were now those in the satellite, prefabricated settlements, left literally on the outside looking in. Often the original inhabitants of the old neighborhoods, many of them the same activists who had bravely risen up against the state in 1989, could no longer afford to stay there as rents rose after 1990. These people, the "authentic ones" whose authenticity derived partially from their dream of a "third way" and their detachment from both socialism and capitalism, were forced out to less "authentic" districts. To this day, there exists in places like Berlin an undercurrent of resentment from older residents against the new yuppies, who are often called "Swabians" as a kind of quasi-slur meant to signify transient gentrifiers. Most of those who spray-paint threatening slogans like "Swabians Get Out" on walls, or who fight against condo development or real estate speculation in their neighborhoods, are not the original residents either; they were the first generation of Western "authenticity seekers" who displaced the real East Germans, who are by now long scattered to the four winds.

Meanwhile, Marzahn, Hellersdorf, Lichtenberg, and places like them have been the source of even more intensive efforts by the new state to keep them from becoming ghettoes. Often, Western eyes look at the Marzahns and Neu-Hohenschönhausens of the East and think: "Nanterre," or worse: "Pruitt-Igoe" or "Robert Taylor." Here again is another irony, which is that Marzahn is nothing like those Western slums, especially not the ones in the United States. One reason for this difference is the immense amount of subsidization provided to former East German prefabricated settlements to keep them from falling into disrepair and ruin; to keep them at least somewhat attractive places in which to live. Since 1989 funds from the city, the federal government, and even the European Union have been used to repaint all the prefabricated buildings, to give them balconies, and to make sure that the grounds are not neglected.[3] Even with all that, there has still been a significant amount of what Germans call *Rückbau*; a euphemism not easily translatable into English, but which could mean "un-building"—that is, not simply demolishing properties, but reducing them; in some cases, by simply taking off the top three or four stories as a strategy of reducing the amount of vacant apartments. (In other cases, entire buildings have been demolished.)[4] Of course, considering that these buildings were put together almost like giant Lego sets, *Rückbau* is not nearly as difficult as it would have been if these were older, pre-industrial buildings. As it is, they were easily assembled, and can be easily disassembled.

Another irony in the fact that so much money has been sunk into keeping Marzahn and other places like it afloat is that so much money was also sunk into them during the communist era. The Housing Program was a gigantic money pit for the SED regime. It was one of the prime drivers of the regime's indebtedness, both internally and externally. The sheer cost of the operations involved in building Marzahn and other places—laying new utilities, new roads, and then keeping the rents and utilities subsidized—was far more than the state could afford. In

[3] See Platform Marzahn, ed., *Marzahn—ein Stadtteil mit Zukunft in Berlin* (Tagungsdokumentation zu Symposium; Berlin: MAZZ Verlag, 2000).

[4] For more on *Rückbau* see Bezirksamt Marzahn-Hellersdorf, ed., *Im Wandel Beständig: Stadtumbau in Marzahn und Hellersdorf: Projekte, Reflexionen, Streitgespräche* (Berlin: Selbstverlag des Bezirksamtes Marzahn Hellersdorf von Berlin, 2007).

addition, as we have seen, large amounts of the technological infrastructure necessary for projects on this scale had to be bought from non-CMEA countries, meaning the loss of precious "hard" currency; for example, in the purchase of the *entire* concrete panel factory from the Finnish Partek corporation. And it was this indebtedness that played one of *the* major roles in the collapse of the GDR, and of communism more generally. What communist countries needed to do to prove their superiority over capitalism in the eyes of their citizen-consumers, they could not afford to do; and they had to borrow from those very capitalist nations to finance their own development. In the end, the GDR owed at least $12 billion to the West, and over 200 billion deutschmarks in internal debts, almost 40 billion of which were due to the Housing Program.[5] Regardless of the actual economic ramifications of this debt, the knowledge of how in debt the government really was proved to be poisonous for morale among those in the Party and state charged with running the country—it was people like the former editor at *Neues Deutschland* who knew about and used terms like "mismanagement" (*Mißwirtschaft*) to describe their country, and it was this knowledge that moved many to join the protests in 1989; or at any rate not to resist them.

To return to the hypothetical mode of thought, it may have been the case that, had the events of 1989 fizzled out, the SED survived, and the Housing Program been allowed to continue until almost all East Germans lived in Marzahn-like spaces, the regime would have been on much more solid footing. On other hand, it still might not have been, because to have allowed the Housing Program to continue for another decade-and-a-half might very well have increased the GDR's indebtedness beyond the breaking point. Certainly, over the long haul, unless the world economic situation had changed drastically in the favor of communist nations, the maintenance of such infrastructure would have been simply unsustainable.

And yet we should be very wary of tying this narrative off with a neat twist of inevitability and Western, capitalist triumphalism. Ever since industrialization had created the first modern slums, communists had recognized that housing crises were among the very worst effects and causes of inequality and misery under capitalism, and had sought ways to provide adequate and comfortable housing to everyone, rather than lovely housing for a small elite and squalor for the masses. On a broader scale, this was the substance of the famous kitchen debates, between Khrushchev and Nixon. The United States managed to win this debate by providing single-family housing, often in suburbs, to working- and middle-class Americans, beginning before the Great Depression but especially in the several decades of prosperity after the World War Two. Places like Marzahn were, essentially, communism's belated response to 1950s United States suburbia.

Furthermore, it is a highly questionable matter whether the American model is itself sustainable. As I write this, the United States and Western Europe are struggling

[5] For more on the indebtedness of the GDR at the end of its life, and the role of Honecker's policies of "real existing socialism," see among others, Arnd Bauerkämper, *Die Sozialgeschichte der DDR* (Munich: Oldenbourg, 2005), Christoph Boyer and Peter Skyba, "Sozial- und Konsumpolitik als Stabilisierungsstrategie," *Deutschland Archiv* 4, 1999, 577–90, and Steiner, *Plans that Failed.*

to emerge from the Great Recession, which was caused by the insatiable need for Americans, as well as Spaniards and the Irish and the Greeks and the British, etc., to make more housing available to more of their population than could afford it, for both economic and political reasons. George W. Bush, during his presidency, often spoke of an "ownership society," and government-sponsored agencies like Fannie Mae, as well as investment banks from Goldman Sachs to UBS, treated the mortgage industry like a casino, artificially inflating real estate prices while making extremely risky loans. When the bubble burst, it went off like a bomb in the new exurbs—where a middle class owned far more house, and far more debt, than it could afford—as well as in low-income neighborhoods, where single-family homes were owned by precisely the people unable to afford them at all. In an instant, the reality of the Western economy was laid bare—it is an economy that is over reliant on housing, and credit, in which the socio-spatial dialectic is intertwined with an unseen ocean of debt which serves to propagate the illusion of winning that "kitchen debate." In the West, building houses must never stop, as a shark must never stop swimming, lest the economy completely implode; new housing starts are the most important economic indicator, and a mortgage is the great investment of a lifetime. The Western "ownership society" is as much an unsustainable illusion as Corbusian mega-settlements of state socialism; both look solid, but are never far from melting into the air.

Whether 2008 was a depression or just a severe recession, it marked the second time in eighty years that a capitalist real estate bubble has plunged the world's economy into catastrophe. The last time it happened, fascism, global war, and genocide were the result. It is unclear what the result will be this time, though at many points in the recent past it has been hard to feel optimistic about the future of Europe, and certainly the so-called "Washington consensus" of neo-liberal economics, with countries like Greece and Spain caught in downward economic spirals, and political extremism in those countries rising as a result.

In the end, what is perhaps most important about housing and urban space is that, regardless of what economic and political system builds it, it represents "facts on the ground." It is perhaps the most indelible mark of a state and its system and values; much more so than a statue, a monument, a temple, a royal palace, or a Wall. All of those things are, especially in the age of modern technology, relatively easy to disassemble, knock down, blow up, or haul away. Housing, neighborhoods, a *Kiez*, or a *Heimat* are often too widespread, occupy too much geographical space, to be physically removed—even when subjected to a near-apocalyptic bombing campaign. But they are more than just large and voluminous—they are a mnemo-topography; a socio-spatial dialectic. They are where people live, and where they store their memories, and their sense of themselves, through time. Many of those young married couples who moved to Marzahn are now retired, and they still live there. For them, their personal history starts in year zero, their *Stunde Null*, where the story of their lives that they tell to themselves and others is narrated along with a place, a place built by the socialist state of the GDR. Many of them are still at least partially caught in the sway of 'Ostalgia', as they watch their prefabricated, timeless utopia grow greener each year. They miss the GDR—it was their home, even if they mostly rejected the incompetence, pettiness, and power of the Party itself. The power to shape space, especially domestic spaces, is the power to shape life memories in a way that resists almost all forms of change.

Still, when one wanders the leafy, labyrinthine spaces of Marzahn, one gets a sense of a place with no past—and no future. Marzahn, the flagship settlement of the Housing Program, was intended to be the blueprint for the future. It was part of a trajectory of history that was heading to a very clear destination—a society built on rationality, functionalism, and, most importantly, a complete break with the mnemonic traces of the past. It was a place with no memory—an amnesiopolis, a place with no past, only a future. After 1990, it became a place with no past and no *future*—a truly stranded space. In the end, this is what the confluence of modern architecture and the legacy of working-class oppression, state socialism, and the dream of colonizing the "Mark" outside Berlin had led to—this very bittersweet, stranded utopia.

Appendices

The statistics below were compiled through a combination of sources, but are especially indebted to the work of Tobias Nagel, an amateur historian who has created a central database of statistics on all prefabricated housing settlements in East and West Germany, which can be found at <http://www.machmaplazda.com>. Nagel's work is based on a wide range of printed and online sources, which are listed on the site. His data uses dwellings (*Wohneinheiten*), rather than residents; there is no one source that compiles residents per settlement, throughout the GDR. To estimate the number of residents per settlement, I have multiplied the number of dwellings by 2.9. For the settlements where reliable sources record both residents and dwellings (generally the larger ones, such as Marzahn or Grünau) the ratio of residents to dwellings ranges from 2.8 to 3, likely due to the larger apartment sizes and abundance of young families with children in these settlements.

In the case of the largest (> 25,000 residents) settlements, I have rounded to the nearest 500. I have intentionally left out settlements built before 1959, the first year that prefabrication was used widely, albeit on an experimental basis (the P1 in Hoyerswerda, for example). Thus, I have left out some settlements built earlier during the 1950s, most notably Stalinstadt (today Eisenhüttenstadt), and Rostock-Reutershagen, which were not built in a style that would be recognized as modernist or Corbusian. Most of the settlements counted here, both larger and smaller than 25,000 residents, are built on the edges of older municipalities, but not all; some were built specifically as "factory towns," mainly during the 1960s, and some are nestled close to the city center.

Appendix 1. Prefabricated settlements in the GDR with more than 25,000 residents (1989)

Name of settlement	Number of residents
Berlin Marzahn-Hellersdorf	290,000
Berlin Hohenschönhausen	100,000
Rostock Nordwest (incl. Groß-Klein and Lütten-Klein)	98,500
Halle-Neustadt	93,500
Karl-Marx-Stadt (Chemnitz) Fritz Heckert	90,000
Leipzig Grünau	85,000
Hoyerswerda	59,000
Berlin Friedrichsfelde	56,500
Berlin Karl Marx Allee	53,000
Berlin Fennpfuhl	50,000
Schwerin Grosser Dreesch	50,000
Erfurt Nord	45,500
Gera-Lusan	44,000
Halle Silberhöhe	39,000
Dresden Gorbitz	38,000
Erfurt Sudost	37,500
Rostock Dierkow	35,500

(*continued*)

Appendix 1. Continued

Name of settlement	Number of residents
Bitterfeld Wolfen	35,000
Jena-Lobeda	34,500
Lübbenau WK I, II, Neustadt	32,500
Zwickau-Eckersbach	31,500
Cottbus Sachsendorf-Madlow	31,000
Magdeburg Neu Olvenstedt	30,000
Stralsund-Kneiper	29,500
Halle-Südstadt	29,000
Dresden Prohlis	27,000
Potsdam-Drewitz/Am Stern	26,000
Total:	**1,571,000**

Appendix 2. Total residents in East German housing settlements

Total residents, settlements less than 25,000	**3,083,450**
Total East Germans residing in prefabricated housing settlements	**4,649,450 (28% of population in 1989)**

Appendix 3. Post-war housing settlements in West Germany over 25,000 residents

Name	Total residents
München-Neuperlach	55,000
Berlin-Gropiusstadt	46,500
Berlin-Märkisches Viertel	42,500
Berlin-Falkenhagener Feld	34,000
Nürnberg-Langwasser	32,500
Braunschweig-Weststadt	27,500
Bremen-Neue Vahr	25,000
Köln-Chorweiler	25,000
Total	**288,000**

Appendix 4. Prefabricated settlements in East Berlin (less than 25,000 residents)

Name of settlement	Number of residents
Ahrensfelde (Marzahn)	10,000
Albert-Norden-Straße (Hellersdorf)	6,500
Alexanderplatz (Mitte)	11,750
Altglienicke (WK 1 & 2) (Treptow)	18,750
Altglienicke (WK 3 & 4) (Treptow)	23,250
Alt-Köpenick (Köpenick)	4,250
Alt-Lichtenberg (Lichtenberg)	10,000
Baumschulenweg (Treptow)	9,250
Blankenburger Straße (Pankow)	6,250
Borsig-Wohnungen (Reinickendorf)	3,750
Buch (Pankow)	15,500
Buckow (Neukölln)	4,500
Ernst-Thälmann-Park (Prenzlauer Berg)	3,250

(*continued*)

Appendix 4. Continued

Name of settlement	Number of residents
Frankfurter Allee (Lichtenberg)	13,750
Friedrichshagen (Köpenick)	10,250
Friedrichstadt (Mitte)	7,000
Greifswalder Straße (Prenzlauer Berg)	10,500
Heinrich-Heine-Viertel (Mitte)	9,250
Köllnische Vorstadt (Köpenick)	7,500
Königstor (Prenzlauer Berg)	2,500
Köpenick Nord (Köpenick)	5,250
Landsberger Allee (Prenzlauer Berg)	5,250
Leninplatz (Friedrichshain)	3,125
Musiker Viertel (Weissensee)	11,000
Neumannstrasse (Pankow)	7,250
Niederschöneweide (Treptow)	5,250
Oberschöneweide (Köpenick)	5,250
Osthafen (Friedrichshain)	3,500
Ostseestraße (Prenzlauer Berg)	7,000
Plänterwald (Treptow)	9,250
Platz der Vereinten Nationen (Friedrichshain)	3,125
Rummelsburger Bucht (Lichtenberg)	5,000
Salvador-Allende-Viertel (Köpenick)	12,250
Wendenschloß (Köpenick)	5,750
Total	**276,000**
Berlin, settlements greater than 25,000	411,603
Total East Berliners in prefabricated settlements	**687,603**

Bibliography

PRIMARY SOURCES

Archives

Bundesarchiv Berlin-Lichterfeld (BArch-BL)
  Stiftung Archiv Parteien und Massenorganisationen (BArch-SAPMO)
Landesarchiv Berlin (LA-B)
Bundesbeauftragte der Stasi-Unterlagen (BStU)
  Außenstelle Leipzig
  Außenstelle Rostock
  Außenstelle Chemnitz
Bezirksmuseum Marzahn-Hellersdorf

Periodicals

Neues Deutschland
für dich
Neue Berliner Illustrierte
Der Neunte/Marzahn Aktuell
Deutsche Architektur/Architektur der DDR
Kultur im Heim
Jugend und Technik
Kraftverkehr

Films

Spur der Steine
Die Architekten
Die Legende von Paul und Paula
Insel der Schwäne: directed by Herrmann Zschoche, 1983; Berlin: DVD, Icestorm Entertainment GmbH, 2006

Printed Sources

Autorenkollektiv. *Chronik der Kreisparteiorganisation Bauwesen Berlin der SED für die Zeit zwischen dem VIII. und IX. Parteitag der Sozialistischen Einheitspartei Deutschlands*. Berlin, Kreisgeschichtskommission der Kreisleitung Bauwesen Berlin der SED, 1983.

Bezirksleitung der SED, ed. *Die Erbauer des 9. Stadtbezirks und ihre Ziele: materialien der Gewerkschaftsaktivtagung vom 3. Februar 1977*. Berlin, 1977.

Bräuer, Helmut, et al., *Karl-Marx-Stad: Geschichte der Stadt in Wort und Bild*. Berlin: Verlag der Wissenschaft, 1988.

Le Corbusier. *Urbanisme*. Paris: Éditions G. Crés & Co., 1924.

Le Corbusier. *La Ville Radieuse: Soleil, Espace, Verdure*. Boulogne-sur-Seine: Éditions de l'Architecure d'Aujourd'hui, 1935.

Le Corbusier. *The Radiant City: Elements of a Doctrine of Urbanism to Be Used as the Basis of Our Machine-age Civilization*. New York: Orion Press, 1967.

Le Corbusier. *The Athens Charter*. New York: Grossman Publishers, 1973.

Le Corbusier. *The Modulor: A Harmonious Measure to the Human Scale, Universally Applicable to Architecture and Mechanics*. Basel and Boston: Birkhäuser, 2000.

Le Corbusier. *Toward an Architecture*. Los Angeles: Getty Research Institute, 2007.

Czok, Karl and Horst Thieme et al., *Leipzig: Geschichte der Stadt in Wort und Bild*. Berlin: VEB Deutscher Verlag der Wissenschaften, 1978.

Dallmann, Alfred and Hugo Schulze. *50 Jahre Kampf gegen die Mietskaserne*. Berlin: Baugenossenschaft "freie Scholle" G.m.b.H in Berlin-Tegel, 1947.

Eberstadt, Rudolf. "Die Mietskaserne." In Nitsche, ed. *Häuserkämpfe*, 29–34.

Engels, Friedrich. *The Housing Question*. London: Lawrence and Wishart, 1942.

Engels, Friedrich. *Zur Wohnungsfrage*. Berlin: Dietz Verlag, 1962.

Frederick, Eberhard. *10 Jahre Stadtbezirk Berlin-Marzahn*. Berlin, publisher unknown, 1989.

Geelhaar, Helmut. *Das alte Dorf Marzahn—seine Geschichte und seine landwirtschaftliche Entwicklung bis 1945*. Verlag Tribüne, 1989.

Grandke, Anita, Gerhard Misgeld, and Rosemarie Walther, eds. *Unsere Familie: Ein Ratgeber für jung und alt*. Leipzig: Verlag für die Frau, 1973.

Haupt, Hanna, Birgit Heißner, Ingeborg Frackmann, Stefan Römisch, and Manfred Wockenfuß, eds. *Marzahn und seine Bürger: eine Sozialstudie*. Berlin: Bezirksamt Marzahn, 1999.

Helwig, Gisela. *Frau und Familie: Bundesrepublik Deutschland—DDR*. Cologne: Verlag Wissenschaft und Politik, 1987.

Hirte, Werner, and Christina Soll. *Wohnungs ABC*. Leipzig: Verlag für die Frau, 1973.

Junker, Wolfgang. *Das Wohnungsbauprogramm der Deutschen Demokratischen Republik für die Jahre 1976 bis 1990*. Berlin: Dietz, 1973.

Kulturbund der DDR. *Alte Dorfkerne in Berlin: Kaulsdorf, Heinersdorf, Marzahn*. Berlin, publisher unknown, 1983.

Noak, Viktor. *Wohnungsnot und Mieterelend. Ein Erbstück des alten Stadt*. Berlin: Verlag Ernst Wasmuth, 1918.

Peters, Günter. *Chronik der Kreisparteiorganisation Bauwesen Berlin der SED, 1976–1980*. Berlin: Kreisgeschichtskommission der Kreisleitung Bauwesen Berlin der SED, 1985.

Peters, Günter. *Chronik der Kreisparteiorganisation Bauwesen Berlin der SED, 1966–1970*. Berlin: Kreisgeschichtskommission der Kreisleitung Bauwesen Berlin der SED, 1987.

Peters, Günter. *Chronik der Kreisparteiorganisation Bauwesen Berlin der SED, 1981–1985*. Berlin: Kreisgeschichtskommission der Kreisleitung Bauwesen Berlin der SED, 1988.

Peters, Günter. *Hütten, Platten, Wohnquartiere. Berlin-Marzahn: Ein junger Bezirk mit altem Namen*. Berlin: MAZZ Verlagsgesellschaft, 1998.

Pfeil, Johannes. "Die Wandlung des Wuhle-Fließes in den Jahren 1950–1955." In *Berliner Heimat* Jg., 1957.

Pludra, Benno. *Insel der Schwäne*. Berlin: Kinderbuch Verlag, 2007 (orig. published 1982).

Reimann, Brigitte. *Franziska Linkerhand*. Berlin: Aufbau Taschenbuch Verlag, 2005.

Rennhack, Horst. *Marzahn zum 20! Ein Geburtstagsstrauß in Versen*. Self-published manuscript: Berlin, 1999.

Scheffler, Karl. *Berlin: Ein Stadtschicksal*. Berlin: Erich Reiss Verlag, 1910.

Speer, Albert. *Inside the Third Reich: Memoirs*. Trans. Richard and Clara Winston. New York: Macmillan, 1970.

Weber, Hans. *Einzug ins Paradies*. Berlin: Verlag Neues Leben, 1980.

Zschoche, Herrmann, Director. *Insel der Schwäne*. Berlin: 1983. DVD: Icestorm Entertainment GmbH, 2006.

SECONDARY SOURCES

Akademie der Künste, ed. *1945. Krieg—Zerstörung—Aufbau*. Berlin: Henschel, 1995.

Alexander, Anthony. *Britain's New Towns: Garden Cities to Sustainable Communities*. New York: Routledge, 2009.

Arnold, Jörg. *The Allied Air War and Urban Memory: The Legacy of Strategic Bombing in Germany*. New York: Cambridge University Press, 2011.

Atwood, Lynne. "Housing in the Khrushchev Era." In Melanie Ilic, Susan E. Reid, and Lynne Atwood, eds., *Women in the Khrushchev Era*. New York: Palgrave Macmillan, 2004, 177–202.

Augustine, Dolores. *Red Prometheus: Engineering and Dictatorship in East Germany, 1945–1990*. Cambridge, Mass: MIT Press, 2007.

Auslander, Leora. "Beyond Words." *American Historical Review* 110, 4 (2005): 1015–41.

Bachelard, Gaston. *The Poetics of Space*. Trans. Maria Jolas. Boston: Beacon Press, 1994.

Badstübner, Evemarie, ed. *Befremdlich Anders: Leben in der DDR*. Berlin: Dietz, 2000.

Bahnsen, Uwe and Kerstin von Stürmer. *Die Stadt, die sterben sollte. Hamburg im Bombenkrieg, Juli 1943*. Hamburg: Convent Verlag, 2003.

Bald, Alexandra, Ana Lessing, and Esra Rotthoff, eds. *Berlin Haushoch* Berlin: Conrad Citydruck, 2006.

Barth, Holger, ed. *Projekt Sozialistische Stadt*. Berlin: 1998.

Barth, Holger, and Thomas Topfstedt, eds. *Vom Baukünstler zum Komplexprojektanten: Architekten in der DDR: Dokumentation eines IRS Sammlungsbestandes biografischer Daten*. Erkner: Institut für Regionalentwicklung und Strukturplanung (Dokumentenreihe des IRS, No. 3): 2000.

Bärthel, Hilmar. "Wie der Berliner Osten städtischen Charakter bekam. Zur Entwicklung der technischen Infrastruktur in den Bezirken Hellersdorf und Marzahn." *Hellersdorfer Heimathefte* 7, Berlin: MAZZ-Verlagsgesellschaft, 1998.

Bauerkämper, Arnd. *Die Sozialgeschichte der DDR*. Munich: Oldenbourg, 2005.

Berdahl, Daphne. *On the Social Life of Postsocialism: Memory, Consumption, Germany*. Ed. Matti Bunzl. Bloomington, Ind: Indiana University Press, 2010.

Berdahl, Daphne. "Re-Presenting the Socialist Modern: Museums and Memory in the Former GDR" in Pence and Betts, eds., *Socialist Modern*, 345–66.

Bernet, Claus. "The 'Hobrecht Plan' (1862) and Berlin's Urban Structure," *Urban History*, 31, 3 (2004).

Bernhardt, Christoph. *Bauplatz Groß-Berlin. Wohnungsmärkte, Terraingewebe und Kommunalpolitik im Städtewachstum der Hochindustrialisierung (1871–1918)*. New York: W. de Gruyter, 1998.

Bernhardt, Christoph, and Heinz Reif, eds. *Sozialistische Städte zwischen Herrschaft und Selbstbehauptung: Kommunalpolitik, Stadtplanung und Alltag in der DDR*. Stuttgart: Franz Steiner Verlag, 2009.

Bernhardt, Christoph and Thomas Wolfes, eds. *Schönheit und Typenprojektierung: Der DDR-Städtebau im internationalen Kontext*. Erkner: Institut für Regionalentwicklung und Strukturplanung, 2005.

Bessel, Richard and Ralph Jessen, eds. *Die Grenzen der Diktatur: Staat und Gesellschaft in der SBZ/DDR*. Göttingen: Vandenhoeck and Rüprecht, 1996.

Betts, Paul. "The Twilight of the Idols: East German Memory and Material Culture." *Journal of Modern History* 72, 3 (2000): 731–65.

Betts, Paul. *Within Walls: Private Life in the German Democratic Republic*. New York: Oxford University Press, 2010.

Beutelschmidt, Thomas and Julia M. Novak, eds. *Ein Palast und seine Republik. Ort—Architektur—Programm*. Berlin: Verlag Bauwesen, 2001.

Bezirksamt Marzahn von Berlin, ed. *Marzahn—ein Stadtteil mit Zukunft in Berlin: Internationales Symposium: Tagungsdokumentation*. Berlin: MAZZ, 2000.

Bezirksamt Marzahn von Berlin, Arbeitskomitee 20. Jahrestag, ed. *1979–1999: 20 Jahre Bezirk Marzahn von Berlin: So sehe ich mein Marzahn*. Berlin: MAZZ, 1998.

Bezirksamt Marzahn von Berlin, Abt. Jugend, Bildung und Kultur, *20 Jahre Marzahn. Geschichte-Bauen-Leben*. Berlin: Holga Wende, 1999.

Bezirksamt Marzahn–Hellersdorf Abt. Ökologische Stadtentwicklung Natur- und Umweltamt, ed. *Zwischen Barnim und Spree: Das südliche Wuhletal*, 2001.

Bezirksamt Marzahn–Hellersdorf von Berlin, ed. *Berlin-Marzahn-Hellersdorf: Der Friedhofswegweiser: Dieseits und Jenseits: information, Hinweise, Standorte, Historie, Anschriften, Inserate*. Berlin: Mammut-Verlag, 2006.

Bezirksamt Marzahn–Hellersdorf von Berlin, ed. *Im Wandel beständig. Stadtumbau in Marzahn und Hellersdorf. Projekte, Reflexionen, Streitgespräche*. Berlin: Selbstverlag des Bezirkamts Marzahn–Hellersdorf, 2007.

Bittner, Regina. *Kolonien des Eigensinns: Ethnographie einer ostdeutschen Industrieregion*. Frankfurt: Campus Verlag, 1998.

Blackbourn, D. *The Conquest of Nature: Water, Landscape and the Making of Modern Germany*. New York: W.W. Norton, 2006.

Bloss, Peter, et al. *Altenreport Marzahn 1995*. Berlin: Abteilung Sozialwesen des Bezirksamtes Marzahn durch das Sozialwissenschaftliche Forschungszentrum Berlin-Brandenburg e.V. 1995.

Bodek, Richard. "Not-So-Golden-Twenties" *Journal of Social History* 30, 1 (1996): 55–78; 59.

Bohm, Eberhard. "Die Fruhgeschichte des Berliner Raumes (6. Jahrhundert vor Chr. Bis zum 12. Jahrhundert nach Chr.)" in Ribbe, ed., *Geschichte Berlins*.

Bouvier, Beatrix. *Die DDR—Ein Sozialstaat? Sozialpolitik in der Ära Honecker*. Bonn: Dietz, 2002.

Boyer, Christoph and Peter Skyba. "Sozial- und Konsumpolitik als Stabilisierungsstrategie," *Deutschland Archiv* 4 (1999): 577–90.

Philip Brady and Ian Wallace, eds. *Prenzlauer Berg: Bohemia in East Berlin?* Amsterdamn: Rodopi, 1995.

Brandes, Karin, Petra Rosenberg, and Lutz-Rainer Düsing, eds. *Das war für uns das Aus: Deportation der Berliner Sinti und Roma in das Zwangslager Marzahn*. Berlin: Der Präsident des Abgeordnetenhauses von Berlin, Referat Öffentlichkeitsarbeit in Zusammenarbeit mit dem Landesverband Deutscher Sinti und Roma Berlin Brandenburg, 2007.

Bruce, Gary. *The Firm: The Inside Story of the Stasi*. New York: Oxford, 2010.

Brumfield, William ed. *Reshaping Russian Architecture: Western Technology, Utopian Dreams*. Cambridge, UK: Woodrow Wilson International Center for Scholars and Cambridge University Press, 1990.

Buchwald, Kurt. *Firmament der Dinge: Hellersdorfer Himmelsscheibe. Großsiedlung Hellersdorf, Quartier Mageburger Allee*. Berlin: S.T.E.R.N/Berliner Senat, 2004.

Buck, Hannsjörg. *Mit hohem Anspruch gescheitert. Die Wohnungspolitik der DDR*. Münster: Lit, 2004.

Bündnis Kein Vergessen, ed. *Kein Vergessen: 70. Jahrestag der Errichtung des Sinti und Roma Zwangslagers in Berlin-Marzahn*. Berlin: 2006.

Butter, Andreas. *Neues Leben, Neues Bauen. Die Moderne in der Architektur der SBZ/DDR 1945–1951*. Berlin: Schiler, 2006.

Butter, Andreas and Ulrich Hartung. *Ostmoderne: Architektur in Berlin, 1945–1965*. Munich: Jovis/Deutsche Werkbund e.V., 2005.

Emily Calacci. "Ujamaa Urbanism: History, Urban Culture and the Politics of Authenticity in Socialist Dar-es-Salaam, 1967–1980." PhD dissertation, Northwestern University, 2012.

Casey, Edward. *The Fate of Place: A Philosophical History*. Berkeley: University of California Press, 1997.

Cosgrove, Denis. "Landscape and Landschaft" (Lecture delivered at the "Spatial Turn in History" Symposium at the German Historical Institute, Washington, DC, 2004) in *Bulletin of the German Historical Institute, Washington DC*, no. 35 (Fall 2004), 57–71.

Cresswell, Tim. *In Place/Out of Place: Geography, Ideology and Transgression*. Minneapolis: University of Minnesota Press, 1996.

Cresswell, Tim. *Place: A Short Introduction*. Padstow, UK: Blackwell, 2004.

Crew, David, ed. *Consuming Germany in the Cold War*. Oxford: Berg, 2003.

Cronon, William. *Nature's Metropolis: Chicago and the Great West*. New York: WW Norton, 1992.

Crowley, David, and Susan E. Reid, eds. *Socialist Spaces: Sites of Everyday Life in the Eastern Bloc*. Oxford: Berg, 2002.

Cupers, Kenny. *The Social Project: Housing Postwar France*. Minneapolis: University of Minnesota Press, 2014.

Davis, Mike. *City of Quartz: Excavating the Future in Los Angeles*. New York: Vintage, 1992.

DeHaan, Heather. *Stalinist City Planning: Professionals, Performance, and Power*. Toronto, Ontario: University of Toronto Press, 2013.

Demps, Laurenz et al. *Geschichte Berlins. Von den Anfängen bis 1945*. Berlin: Dietz Verlag, 1987.

Demps, Laurenz with Kerstin Bötticher. *Luftangriffe auf Berlin: Die Berichte der Hauplufischutzstelle 1940–45*. Berlin: Ch. Links, 2013.

Dennis, Mike. *The Stasi: Myth and Reality*. London: Pearson, 2003.

Dieffendorf, Jeffrey. *In the Wake of War: The Reconstruction of German Cities after World War II*. New York: Oxford University Press, 1993.

Diewald, Martin. "'Kollektiv,' 'Vitamin B,' oder "Nische'? Persönliche Netzwerke in der DDR." In Huinik, et al., eds., *Kollektiv und Eigensinn*, 223–60.

Diewald, Martin, Johannes Huinink, Hekie Solga and Annemette Sorensen. "Umbrüche und Kontinuitäten—Lebensverläufe und die Veränderung von Lebensbedingungen seit 1989." In Huinik, et al., eds., *Kollektiv und Eigensinn*, 307–48.

Dobbrick, Katrin, ed. *Die Fischerinsel—Zeugnisse und Spuren: Dokumentation zur Ausstellung des KREATIVHAUS e.V.* Berlin: KREATIVHAUS, e.V., 2004.

Domröse, Ulrich and Jack Gelfort, eds. *Peripherie als Ort: Das Hellersdorfer Projekt*. Stuttgart: Arnoldsche, 1999.

Dörfler, Thomas. *Gentrification in Prenzlauer Berg? Milieuwandel eines Berliner Sozialraums seit 1989*. Bielefeld: Transcript, 2010.

Dörhöfer, Kerstin, ed. *Wohnkultur und Plattenanbau: Beispiele aus Berlin und Budapest*. Berlin: Reimer Verlag, 1994.

Dörhöfer, Kerstin, and Ulla Terlinden, eds. *Verbaute Räume: Auswirkungen von Architektur und Stadtplanung auf das Leben von Frauen*. Cologne: Pahl-Rugenstein Verlag, 1985.

Dowling, Timothy Charles. "Stalinstadt/Eisenhüttenstadt: A Model for (Socialist) Life in the German Democratic Republic, 1950–1968." PhD dissertation, Tulane University, 1999.

Durth, Werner; Jörn Düwel and Niels Gutschow. *Aufbau: Städte, Themen, Dokumente—Architektur und Städtebau der DDR, Band 2*. Frankfurt: Campus Verlag, 1998.

Durth, Werner; Jörn Düwel and Niels Gutschow. *Ostkreuz: Personen, Pläne, Perspektiven—Architektur und Städtebau der DDR, Band 1.* Frankfurt: Campus Verlag, 1998.

Edition Berliner Unterwelten, ed. *Mythos Germania: Schatten und Spuren der Reichshauptstadt.* (Begleitsbuch der Ausstellung des Berliner Unterwelten E.V.) Berlin: Lehmanns Media, 2008.

Eley, Geoff. "The Unease of History: Settling Accounts with the East German Past." *History Workshop Journal* 57 (2004): 175–201.

Engelman, Roger, et al. *Das MfS Lexicon: Begriffen, Personen und Strukturen der Staatssicherheit der DDR.* Berlin: Ch. Links, 2012.

Engler, Wolfgang. *Die Ostdeutschen: Kunde von einem verlorenen Land.* Berlin: Aufbau Taschenbuch, 2005.

Ensikat, David. *Kleines Land, große Mauer: Die DDR für alle, die (nicht) dabei waren.* Munich: Piper, 2007.

Eppelmann, Rainer, Bernd Faulenbach and Ulrich Mählert, eds. *Bilanz und Perspektiven der DDR-Forschung.* Paderborn: Ferdinand Schöningh, 2003.

Epstein, Catherine. "East Germany and its History since 1989" (review article). *The Journal of Modern History* 75, 3 (2003): 634–61.

Ettrich, Frank. *Die andere Moderne: Soziologische Nachrufe auf den Staatssozialismus.* Berlin: Berliner Debatte, 2005.

Evans, Jennifer. *Life Among the Ruins: Cityscape and Sexuality in Cold War Berlin.* New York: Palgrave Macmillan, 2011.

Felber, Bärbel, ed. *1979–1999: 20 Jahre Marzahn.* Berlin: Pressestelle Bezirksamt Marzahn, 1999.

Felsmann, Barbara and Annette Gröschner, eds. *Durchgangszimmer Prenzlauer Berg: eine Berliner Künstlersozialgeschichte der 70er und 80er Jahre in Selbstauskünften.* Berlin: Lukas, 2012.

Flagge, Ingeborg, ed. *Geschichte des Wohnens, Bd.5, 1945 bis heute: Aufbau, Neubau, Umbau.* Stuttgart: Deutsche Verlags-Anstalt, 1996.

Foucault, Michel. *Discipline and Punish: The Birth of the Prison.* Trans. Alan Sheridan. New York: Vintage Books, 1995.

Frampton, Kenneth. *Le Corbusier.* London: Thames and Hudson, 2001.

Friedrich, Jörg. *The Fire: The Bombing of Germany, 1940–1945.* Trans. Alison Brown. New York: Columbia University Press, 2006.

Frisby, David. *Cityscapes of Modernity: Critical Explorations.* Cambridge: Polity Press, 2001.

Frisby, David, and Iain Boyd Whyte. *Metropolis Berlin: 1880–1940.* Berkeley, CA: University of California Press, 2012.

Fulbrook, Mary. *Anatomy of a Dictatorship: Inside the GDR, 1949–1989.* Oxford, UK: Oxford University Press, 1995.

Fulbrook, Mary. *The People's State: East German Society from Hitler to Honecker.* New Haven and London: Yale University Press, 2005.

Fulbrook, Mary, ed. *Power and Society in the GDR, 1961–1979: The "Normalisation of Rule"?* New York: Berghahn, 2009.

Fulbrook, Mary. "Ein 'ganz normales Leben'? Neue Forschungen zur Sozialgeschichte der DDR." In Timmermann, ed., *Das war die DDR*, 115–34.

Fulbrook, Mary. "Generationen und Kohorten in der DDR: Protagonisten und Widersacher des DDR-Systems aus der Perspektive biographischer Daten." In Schüle, Ahbe, and Gries, eds., *DDR aus generationgeschichtler Perspektiv*, 113–30.

Fulbrook, Mary. "Retheorising 'state' and 'society' in the German Democratic Republic." In Major and Osmond, eds., *The Workers' and Peasants' State*, 280–98.

Gandy, Matthew. *Concrete and Clay: Reworking Nature in New York City*. Cambridge, Mass: MIT Press, 2003.

Garrett, Stephen. *Ethics and Airpower in World War II: The British Bombing of German Cities*. New York: St. Martin's Press, 1993.

Gärtner, Karl-Heinz. *Marzahner Straßennamen—Ortsteil Biesdorf*. Berlin: Heimatsmuseum Marzahn, 1994.

Geist, Friedrich and Klaus Kürvers. *Das Berliner Mietshaus*. Vols 1–3. Munich: Prestel, 1980.

Gerasimova, Katerina. "Public Privacy in the Soviet Communal Apartment." In Crowley and Reid, eds., *Socialist Spaces*, 207–30.

Gerchuk, Iurii. "The Aesthetics of Everyday Life in the Khruschev Thaw in the USSR (1954–1964)." In Crowley and Reid, eds., *Style and Socialism*, 81–100.

Gieske, Jens. *Die hauptamtlichen Mitarbeiter der Staatssicherheit. Personalstruktur und Lebenswelt 1950–1989/90*. Berlin: Ch. Links, 2000.

Gieske, Jens, ed. *Staatssicherheit und Gesellschaft: Studien zum Herrschaftsalltag der DDR*. Göttingen: Vandenhoeck and Ruprecht, 2007.

Gieske, Jens. *The History of the Stasi: East Germany's Secret Police, 1945–1990*. Trans. David Burnett. New York: Berghahn, 2014.

Gieske, Jens. "The Stasi and East German Society: Some Remarks on Current Research." *Bulletin of the German Historical Institute*. Supplement 9, 2014, "Stasi at Home and Abroad: Domestic Order and Foreign Intelligence," edited by Uwe Spiekermann, 59–72.

Gieske, Jens. "Staatssicherheit und Gesellschaft—Plädoyer für einen Brückenschlag." Gieseke ed., *Staatssicherheit und Gesellschaft*, 7–22.

Glatzer, Ruth. *Berlin wird Kaiserstadt. Panorama einer Metropole 1871–1890*. Berlin: Siedler Verlag, 1993.

Grabowski, Regine. "Wohnungspolitik" in Manz, Sachse and Winkler, eds., *Sozialpolitik in der DDR*, 227–42.

Grosinski, Klaus. *Prenzlauer Berg: eine Chronik*. Berlin: Kulturamt Prenzlauer Berg, Prenzlauer Berg Museum für Heimatgeschichte und Stadtkultur, 2008.

Gruner, Petra. "Betonköpfe, oder: Schöner wohnen im Plattenbau." In Ludwig, ed., *Tempolinsen und P2 …*, 81–6.

Gruner, Petra. "P2 macht das Rennen: Wohnungsbau als sozio-kulturelles Programm." In Ludwig, ed., *Tempolinsen und P2 . . .*, 87–102.

Gumbert, Heather. *Envisioning Socialism: Television and Cultural Change in the German Democratic Republic*. Ann Arbor: University of Michigan Press, 2014.

Haben, Michael. "'Die waren so unter sich:' Über Kneipen, Vereine und Politik in Berlin Kreuzberg" in Karl-Heinz Fiebig et. al., eds., *Kreuzberger Mischung: Die innerstädtische Verflechtung von Architektur, Kultur und Gewerbe*. Berlin: Äesthetik und Kommunikation, 1984.

Haendcke-Hoppe-Arndt, Maria. *Die Hauptabteilung XVIII: Volkswirtschaft (MfS-Handbuch)*. Berlin: BStU, 1997.

Hain, Simone. "Berlin-Marzahn: Vollkommen subjektive Betrachtungen vor Ort." In Hans G. Helms, ed., *Die Stadt als Gabentisch: Beobachtungen der aktuellen Städtebauentwicklung*, Leipzig, 1992.

Hain, Simone, ed. *Warum zum Beispiel die Stalinallee? Beiträge zu einer Transformationsgeschichte des modernen Planens und Bauens*. Erkner: Institut für Regionalentwicklung und Strukturplanung, 1999.

Hain, Simone. "Marzahn, das sozialistische Projekt zwischen rational choice und Diktatur." In Quiesser and Tirri, *Allee der Kosmonauten*, 9–13.

Hain, Simone. "Between *Arkonaplatz* and the *Nikolaiviertel.* The City as Social Form Versus the City as Mise-en-Scène. Conflicts Raised by the Return to the City," in Scheer, Kleihues, and Kahlfeldt, eds., *City of Architecture of the City*, 337–48.

Hannemann, Christine. *Die Platte: Industrialisierte Wohnungsbau in der DDR.* Berlin: Schiler, 2005.

Harris, Steven. *Communism on Tomorrow Street: Mass Housing and Everyday Life After Stalin.* Washington, DC: Woodrow Wilson Center Press/Baltimore: Johns Hopkins University Press, 2013.

Harsch, Donna. *Revenge of the Domestic: Women, the Family, and Communism in the German Democratic Republic.* Princeton: Princeton University Press, 2006.

Harvey, David. *Consciousness and the Urban Experience: Studies in the History and Theory of Capitalist Urbanization.* Baltimore, MD: The Johns Hopkins University Press, 1985.

Harvey, David. *The Condition of Postmodernity: An Enquiry into the Origins of Cultural Change.* Cambridge, Mass: Blackwell, 1990.

Heimatsverein Marzahn–Hellersdorf, eds. *Hundert Jahre Siedlungsgebiete—Geschichte und Zukunft: Tag der Regional- und Heimatgeschichte Marzahn–Hellersdorf 2002, Tagungsmaterialien.* Berlin: Lokal Verlag, 2003.

Heldmann, Philip. *Herrschaft, Wirtschaft, Anoraks: Konsumpolitik in der DDR der Sechzigerjahre.* Göttingen: Vandenhoeck & Ruprecht, 2004.

Helmer, Stephen. *Hitler's Berlin: The Speer Plans for Reshaping the Central City.* Ann Arbor, MI: UMI Research Press, 1985.

Hentschel, G, and K. Hentschel. *Berlin–Marzahn.* Berlin: Bezirksamt Marzahn von Berlin, 1991.

Herlyn, Ulfert, Adelheid von Saldern, and Wulf Tessin, eds. *Neubausiedlungen der 20er und 60er Jahre: Ein historisch-soziologischer Vergleich.* Frankfurt am Main: Campus Verlag, 1987.

Hermann, Karl. *Lebensverläufe: Innenansichten aus der DDR.* Berlin: Roehricht Morgenbuch, 1991.

Heym, Stefan. *The Architects.* Evanston: Northwestern University Press, 2006.

Hofmann, Jürgen. *Ende oder Anfang: Die Jahre 1945–46 im Marzahn und Biesdorf.* Berlin: Bezirksamt Marzahn von Berlin, Abt. Jugend, Familie und Kultur, Kulturamt/heimatmuseum, 1995.

Höhne, Günter. *Produktkult (ur): Das DDR-Designbuch.* Cologne: KOMET Verlag, 2008.

Holfelder, Moritz. *Palast der Republik: Aufstieg und Fall eines symbolischen Gebäudes.* Berlin: Ch. Links Verlag, 2008.

Hopf, Susanne and Natalja Meier. *Plattenbau Privat: 60 Interieurs.* Berlin: Nicolai, 2007.

Hoscislawski, Thomas. *Bauen zwischen Macht und Ohnmacht:Architektur und Städtebau in der DDR.* Berlin: Verlag für Bauwesen, 1991.

Hubacher, Simon. "Berlin-Marzahn: Die verhinderte Stadt." In *Stadt der Architektur, Architektur der Stadt,* Exhibition Catalogue. Berlin, 2000.

Hübner, Christa, Herbert Nicolaus, and Manfred Teresiak. *20 Jahre Marzahn—Chronik eines Berliner Bezirkes.* Berlin: Heimatsmuseum Marzahn, 1998.

Hübner, Peter, and Christa Hübner. *Sozialismus als soziale Frage: Sozialpolitik in der DDR und Polen, 1968–1976.* Cologne, Weimar, and Vienna: Böhlau, 2008.

Huchthausen, Liselot. *Alltag in der DDR (1945–1973).* Kückenshagen: Scheunen-Verlag, 1998.

Hudson, Hugh Jr. *Blueprints and Blood: The Stalinization of Soviet Architecture, 1917–1937.* Princeton: Princeton University Press, 1994.

Huinik, Johannes. "Individuum und Gesellschaft in der DDR—Theoretische Ausgangspunkte einer Rekonstruktion der DDR-Gesellschaft in den Lebensverläufen ihrer Bürger." In Huinik, et al., eds., *Kollektiv und Eigensinn*, 25–44.

Huinik, Johannes, et al., eds. *Kolletiv und Eigensinn: Lebensverläufe in der DDR und danach*. Berlin: Akademie Verlag, 1995.

Huinik, Johannes, and Michael Wagner. "Partnerschaft, Ehe und die Familie in der DDR." In Huinik, et al., eds., *Kollektiv und Eigensinn*, 145–88.

Illich, Ivan. *H20 and the Waters of Forgetfulness*. London: Marion Boyars, 1986.

Jackisch, Barry. "The Nature of Berlin: Green Space and Visions of a New German Capital, 1900–45," *Central European History* 47 (2014), 307–33.

Jarausch, Konrad, ed. *Dictatorship as Experience: Towards a Socio-Cultural History of the GDR*. New York: Berghahn Books, 1999.

Jarausch, Konrad. "Between Myth and Reality: The Stasi Legacy in German History." In *Bulletin of the German Historical Institute*. Supplement 9, 2014, "Stasi at Home and Abroad: Domestic Order and Foreign Intelligence, edited by Uwe Spiekermann, 73–86.

Jarausch, Konrad. "Beyond Uniformity: The Challenge of Historicizing the GDR." In Jarausch, ed., *Dictatorship as Experience*, 3–14.

Jarausch, Konrad. "Care and Coercion: The GDR as Welfare Dictatorship." In Jarausch, ed., *Dictatorship as Experience*, 47–73.

Jarausch, Konrad. "Living with Broken Memories: Some Narratological Comments." In Kleßmann, ed., *Divided Past*, 171–98.

Jarausch, Konrad and Christoph Kleßmann. "Vorwort zu den Sammelbänden Herrschaftsstrukturen und Erfahrungsdimensionen der DDR-Geschichte." In Lindenberger, ed., *Herrschaft und Eigen-Sinn*, 11–12.

Jarausch, Konrad, and Michael Geyer. *Shattered Past: Reconstructing German Histories*. Princeton and Oxford: Princeton University Press, 2003.

Jessen, Ralph and Richard Bessel, eds. *Die Grenzen der Diktatur: Staat und Gesellschaft in der DDR*. Göttingen: Vandenhoeck & Ruprecht, 1996.

Jessen, Ralph and Richard Bessel. "Einleitung: Die Grenzen der Diktatur." In Jessen and Bessel, eds., *Die Grenzen der Diktatur*, 7–24.

Jessen, Ralph and Hedwig Richter, eds. *Voting for Hitler and Stalin: Elections under 20th Century Dictatorships*. New York: Campus Verlag, 2011.

Kadow, Sabine, and Harald Kintscher, eds. *Links und Rechts der Wuhle: Biesdorf, Hellersdorf, Kaulsdorf, Mahlsdorf, Marzahn: Heimatkalender 2002*. Berlin: Lokal Verlag, 2002.

Kadow, Sabine, and Harald Kintscher, eds. *Links und Rechts der Wuhle: Biesdorf, Hellersdorf, Kaulsdorf, Mahlsdorf, Marzahn: Heimatkalender 2003*. Berlin: Lokal Verlag, 2003.

Kadow, Sabine, and Harald Kintscher, eds. *Links und Rechts der Wuhle: Biesdorf, Hellersdorf, Kaulsdorf, Mahlsdorf, Marzahn: Heimatkalender 2004*. Berlin: Lokal Verlag, 2004.

Kadow, Sabine, and Harald Kintscher, eds. *Links und Rechts der Wuhle: Biesdorf, Hellersdorf, Kaulsdorf, Mahlsdorf, Marzahn: Heimatkalender 2005*. Berlin: Lokal Verlag, 2005.

Kahl, Alice. *Erlebnis Plattenbau: eine Langzeitstudie*. Opland: Leske & Budrich, 2003.

Karlsch, Rainer and Ray Stokes. *The Chemistry Must Be Right*. Schkopau: Buna Sow Leuna Olefinerbund GmbH, 2001.

Kegel, Jens. *Anspruch und Ohnmacht: DDR-Alltag in den 70er Jahren*. Erfurt: Sutton Verlag, 2008.

Kerblay, Basile. "Socialist Families." In Burguière, et al., eds., *A History of the Family*, 442–76.

Kirchhöfer, Dieter, et al., eds. *Kindheit in der DDR: Die gegenwärtige Vergangenheit*. Frankfurt am Main: Peter Lang, 2003.

Kocka, Hartmut Kaelble and Hartmut Zwahr, eds. *Sozialgeschichte der DDR*. Stuttgart: Klett-Cotta, 1994.

Kolenc, Jonas, and Monica Blotevogel. *Fremdenführer Marzahn*. Berlin: Kinderring Berlin e.V., 2004.

Kopp, Anatole. "Foreign Architects in the Soviet Union during the First Two Five-Year Plans," in William Brumfield, ed., *Reshaping Russian Architecture: Western Technology, Utopian Dreams*. Cambridge: Woodrow Wilson International Center for Scholars and Cambridge University Press, 1990.

Kott, Sandrine. *Communism Day to Day: State Enterprises in East German Society*. Ann Arbor, Mich: University of Michigan Press, 2014.

Kott, Sandrine, and Emmanuel Droit, eds. *Die ostdeutsche Gesellschaft: Eine transnationale Perspektive*. Berlin: Ch. Links Verlag, 2006.

Krone, Michael. *Straßen der DDR: Bilder einer Reise von Tangermünde nach Berlin unmittelbar nach dem Mauerfall*. Zwickau: Schneider, 2008.

Kuhn, Gerd, and Andreas Ludwig, eds. *Alltag und soziales Gedächtnis. Die DDR Objektkultur und ihre Musealisierung*. Ergebnisse Verlag, 2001.

Kwint, Marius, Christopher Breward, and Jeremy Aynsley, eds. *Material Memories: Design and Evocation*. Oxford: Berg, 1999.

Ladd, Brian. *Urban Planning and Civic Order in Germany, 1860–1914*. Cambridge, Mass: Harvard University Press, 1990.

Ladd, Brian. "Socialist Planning and the Rediscovery of the Old City in the German Democratic Republic." *Journal of Urban History* 27, 5 (2001): 584–603.

Lamm, Manfred. "Zur Entwicklung des industriellen Bauens in Berlin-Ost." In Peters and Heimatverein Marzahn-Hellersdorf e.V. eds., *Geschichte und Zukunft des industriellen Bauens*, 122–38.

Larsson, Lars. *Die Neugestaltung der Reichshauptstadt: Albert Speers Generalbebauungsplan für Berlin*. Stockholm: Almqvist and Wiksell: 1977.

Lauber, Andreas. *Wohnkultur in der DDR. Dokumentation ihrer materiellen Sachkultur. Eine Untersuchung zu Gestaltung, Produktion und Bedingungen des Erwerbs von Wohnungseinrichtungen in der DDR*. Eisenhüttenstadt: Das Dokumentationszentrum Alltagskultur der DDR in Eisenhüttenstadt, 2003. (Unpublished manuscript available through the Dokumentationszentrum Alltagskultur der DDR.)

Le Normand, Brigitte. *Designing Tito's Capital: Urban Planning, Modernism and Socialism in Belgrade*. Pittsburgh: University of Pittsburgh Press, 2014.

Lebow, Katherine. *Unfinished Utopia: Nowa Huta, Stalinism and Polish Society, 1949–56*. Ithaca, NY: Cornell University Press, 2013.

Lefebvre, Henri. *The Production of Space*. Trans. Donald Nicholson-Smith. Padstow, UK: Blackwell, 1991.

Leinauer, Irma. "Das Wohngebiet Karl-Marz-Allee: Industrielles Bauen zwischen Strausberger Platz und Alexanderplatz." In Butter and Hartung, eds., *Ostmoderne*, 114–23.

Lindenberger, Thomas, ed. *Herrschaft und Eigen-Sinn in der Diktatur: Studien zur Gesellschaftsgeschichte der DDR*. Cologne: Böhlau, 1999.

Lindenberger, Thomas. "Everyday History: New Approaches to the History of the Post-War Germanies." In Kleßmann, ed., *The Divided Past*, 11–42.

Lindenberger, Thomas. "Die Diktatur der Grenzen. Zur Einleitung." In Lindenberger, ed., *Herrschaft und Eigensinn*, 13–44.

Lindenberger, Thomas. "SED-Herrschaft als soziale Praxis, Herrschaft und 'Eigen-Sinn:' Problemstellung und Begriffe." In Giesek, ed., *Staatssicherheit und Gesellschaft*, 23–47.

Lindenberger, Thomas. "In den Grenzen der Diktatur: Die DDR als Gegenstand von 'Gesellschaftgeschichten.'" In Eppelmann, Faulenbach, and Mählert, eds., *Bilanz und Perspektiven der DDR-Forschung*, 239–45.

Lindenberger, Thomas, Belinda Davis, and Michael Wildt. *Alltag, Erfahrung, Eigensinn: Historisch anthropologische Erkundungen*. New York: Campus, 2008.

Lindenberger, Thomas. "Normality, Utopia, Memory, and Beyond: Reassembling East German Society." *German Historical Institute London Bulletin* 33, 1 (2011): 67–91.

Lokale Agenda 21 Berlin-Marzahn. *Ungeschminkt: Die Marzahner Umwelt. Vol 1., "Umweltgeschichte, Wasser, Naturschutz und Landschaftsplanung."* Berlin: Bezirksamt Marzahn Abt. Stadtgestaltung und Umweltschutz, Amt für Umweltschutz, 1998.

Lowe, Keith. *Inferno: The Devastation of Hamburg, 1943*. New York: Penguin Books, 2007.

Lüdtke, Alf, ed. *Herrschaft als sozialer Praxis. Historische und sozio-anthropologische Studien*. Göttingen: Vandenhoeck and Ruprecht, 1991.

Lüdtke, Alf, ed. *The History of Everyday Life: Reconstructing Historical Experiences and Ways of Life*. Trans. William Templer. Princeton, NJ: Princeton University Press, 1995.

Lüdtke, Alf. "Ouvriers, Eigensinn et politique dans l'Allemagne du XXe siècle." *Actes de la recherche en sciences sociales* 113 (1996), 91–101.

Lüdtke, Alf. "La République Démocratique Allemande comme histoire. Réflexions historiographiques." *Annales* HSS 53 (1998), 3–39.

Lüdtke, Alf. "Die DDR als Geschichte. Zur Geschichtsschreibung über die DDR." *Aus Politik und Zeitgeschichte* 36 (1998): 3–16.

Lüdtke, Alf and Peter Becker, eds. *Akten. Eingaben. Schaufenster. Die DDR und ihre Texte: Erkundungen zu Herrschaft und Alltag*. Berlin: Akademie Verlag, 1997.

Ludwig, Andreas, ed. *Tempolinsen und P2... Alltagskultur der DDR*. Berlin: BenBra Verlag, 1996.

Ludwig, Andreas, ed. "Kurze Geschichte Eisenhüttenstadts." In Stadtverwaltung Eisenhüttenstadt, ed., *Eisenhüttenstadt: Architektur—Skulptur, Stadtbilder*. Eisenhüttenstadt: Fürstenberger Druck and Verlag GmbH, 1998.

Ludwig, Andreas, ed. *Fortschritt, Norm und Eigensinn: Erkundungen im Alltag der DDR*. Berlin: Ch. Links, 1999.

Ludwig, Andreas and Katja Böhme eds. *Alles aus Plaste. Versprechen und Gebrauch in der DDR*. Cologne: Böhlau, 2012.

Mandel, Ruth. *Cosmopolitan Anxieties: Turkish Challenges to Citizenship and Belonging in Germany*. Durham, NC: Duke University Press, 2008.

Manz, Günter, Ekkehard Sachse and Gunnar Winkler, eds. *Sozialpolitik in der DDR: Ziele und Wirklichkeit*. Berlin: Trafo, 2001.

Marcoux, Jean-Sèbastien. "The Refurbishment of Memory." In Miller, ed., *Home Possessions*. 69–86.

Massey, Doreen. *Space, Place and Gender*. Minneapolis, MN: University of Minnesota Press, 1994.

Massey, Doreen. *For Space*. Thousand Oaks, CA: SAGE, 2005.

McClellan, Josie. *Love in the Time of Communism: Intimacy and Sexuality in the GDR* New York: Cambridge University Press, 2011.

Merkel, Ina, ed. *Wunderwirtschaft: DDR-Konsumkultur in den 60er Jahren*. Cologne: Böhlau, 1996.

Merkel, Ina. *Utopie und Bedürfnis. Die Geschichte der Konsumkultur in der DDR*. Cologne: Böhlau, 2000.

Merkel, Ina, Franziska Becker, and Simone Tippach-Schneider (and in conjunction with the Dokumentationszentrum Alltagskultur der DDR, Eisenhüttenstadt), eds., *Das Kollektiv bin Ich: Utopie und Alltag in der DDR*. Cologne: Böhlau, 2000.

Messenger, Charles. *"Bomber" Harris and the Strategic Bombing Offensive.* London: Arms and Armour Press, 1984.

Mittman, Elizabeth. "Between Home and Hoyerswerda: Arrival and Departure in the Works of Brigitte Reimann." *Amsterdamer Beiträge zur neueren Germanistik* 38/39 (1995): 259–79.

Mittman, Elizabeth. "Venus in Hoyerswerda? Weiblichkeit als Herausforderung in den Texten von Brigitte Reimann." In Bircken and Hampel eds., *Als habe ich zwei Leben: Beiträge zu einer wissenschaftlichen Konferenz in Neubrandenburg über Leben und Werk der Schriftstellerin Brigitte Reimann.* Neubrandenburg: Federlese, 1998, 113–20.

Mittman, Elizabeth. "'Ich habe kein Ortsgedächtnis': Ort und Identität bei Brigitte Reimann." In Margrid Bircken and Heide Hampel, eds., *Reisen Hals über Kopf: Reisen in der Literatur von Frauen.* Neubrandenburg: Federchen Verlag, 2002, 89–110.

Molnar, Virag Eszter. *Building the State: Architecture, Politics and State Formation in Postwar Central Europe.* New York: Routledge, 2013.

Mumford, Eric. *The CIAM Discourse on Urbanism, 1928–1960.* Cambridge: MIT Press, 2000.

Niethammer, Lutz, ed. *Wohnen im Wandel: Beiträge zur Geschichte des Alltags in der bürgerlichen Gesellschaft.* Wuppertal: Hammer, 1979.

Niethammer, Lutz and Franz Brüggemeier. "Wie wohnten Arbeiter im Kaiserreich?" *Archiv für Sozialgeschichte,* 16 (1976): 61–134.

Nitsche, Rainer, ed. *Häuserkämpfe 1872/1920/1945/1982.* Berlin: TRANSIT, 1981.

Oberle, Clara. "City in Transit: Ruins, Railways, and the Search for Order in Postwar Berlin." PhD dissertation, Princeton University, 2006.

Olsen, Jon Berndt. *Tailoring Truth: Politicizing the Past and Negotiating Memory in East Germany, 1945–1990.* New York: Berghahn Books, 2015.

Osang, Alexander. "Die letzte Hausgemeinschaft." In Domröse and Gelfot eds., *Peripherie als Ort,* 45–64.

Palmowski, Jan. *Inventing a Socialist Nation: Heimat and the Politics of Everyday Life in the GDR, 1945–1990.* New York: Cambridge University Press, 2009.

Palutzki, Joachim. *Architektur in der DDR.* Berlin: Riemer, 2000.

Parkin, David. "Mementoes as Transitional Objects in Human Displacement." *Journal of Material Culture* 4, 3 (1999): 303–20.

Pence, Katherine. "A World in Miniature: The Leipzig Trade Fairs in the 1950s and East German Consumer Citizenship." In David Crew, ed., *Consuming Germany in the Cold War.* New York: Berg, 2003, 21–50.

Pence, Katherine. "Schaufenster des sozialistischen Konsums: Texte der ostdeutschen 'consumer culture'." In Lüdtke and Becker eds., *Akten. Eingaben. Schaufenster,* 91–118.

Pence, Katherine, and Paul Betts, eds. *Socialist Modern: East German Everyday Culture and Politics.* Ann Arbor: University of Michigan Press, 2007.

Peters, Günter. *Historische Stadtplanungen für den Berliner Nordosten.* Berlin: Bezirksamt Marzahn von Berlin, Abt. Jugend, Bildung, und Kultur, Kulturamt/Heimatmuseum, 1997.

Peters, Günter. *Hütten, Platten, Wohnquartiere: Berlin-Marzahn: Ein junger Stadtbezirk mit altem Namen.* Berlin: MAZZ, 1998.

Peters, Günter, ed. *Geschichte und Zukunft des industriellen Bauens: Tag der Regional- und Heimatgeschichte Marzahn-Hellersdorf 2001: Tagungsmateriellen.* Berlin: NORA, 2002.

Peters, Oleg and Waldemar Seifert. *Von der Platte bis zum Schloss: Die* Spur der Steine *des Günter Peters.* Berlin: Forschungsstelle Baugeschichte Berlin, 2003.

Phillips, David and Anthony Yeh, eds. *New Towns in East and South-East Asia*. New York: Oxford University Press, 1987.

Podewin, Norbert. *Marx und Engels Grüssen...Aus Friedrichshain*. Berlin: Dietz, 2010.

Poling, Kristin. "On the Inner Frontier: Opening German City Borders in the Long Nineteenth Century." PhD dissertation, Harvard University, 2011.

Poling, Kristin. "Shantytowns and Pioneers Beyond the City Wall: Berlin's Urban Frontier in the Nineteenth Century." *Central European History* 47 (2014): 245–74.

Port, Andrew. *Conflict and Stability in the German Democratic Republic*. New York: Cambridge University Press, 2007.

Poutrus, Patrice. *Die Erfindung des Goldbroilers: Über den Zusammenhang zwischen Herrschaftssicherung und Konsumentwicklung in der DDR*. Cologne: Böhlau, 2002.

Pugh, Emily. *Architecture, Politics and Identity in Divided Berlin*. Pittsburgh: University of Pittsburgh Press, 2014.

QuartiersAgentur Marzahn NordWest, ed. *500,000 Euro in Bürgerhand: Quartiersfonds in Marzahn NordWest*. Berlin: UrbanPlanGmbH, 2004.

Quiesser, Ylva, and Lidia Tirri. *Allee der Kosmonauten: Einblicke und Ausblicke aus der Platte*. Berlin: Verlag Kulturring in Berlin e.V., 2004.

Quiesser, Ylva, and Lidia Tirri. *Leben hinter der Zuckerbäckerfassade: Erstbewohner der Karl-Marx-Allee*. Berlin: form + zweck Verlag, 2004.

Quiesser, Ylva, and Lidia Tirri. *Ein Tag in Marzahn NordWest: Menschen im Quartier*. Berlin: QuartiersAgentur Marzahn NordWest and Kulturring in Berlin e.V., 2006.

Rat des Stadtbezirks Berlin–Marzahn. *Geschichte der Urbanisierung in Deutschland*. Frankfurt: Suhrkamp, 1985.

Rat des Stadtbezirks Berlin–Marzahn, ed. *Marzahner Leben: Bilder aus der Entwicklung des Stadtbezirks Berlin–Marzahn*. Berlin, 1989.

Reich, Julia. "Chefarchitekt des Industriellen Bauens: Richard Paulick in Hoyerswerda." In Thöner and Peter Müller, eds. *Bauhaus Tradition und DDR Moderne: Der Architekt Richard Paulick*. Munich: Deutscher Kunstverlag, 2006.

Ribbe, Wolfgang, ed. *Geschichte Berlins*. Munich: C.H. Beck, 1987.

Richie, Alexandra. *Faust's Metropolis: A History of Berlin*. New York: Carroll & Graf, 1988.

Richter, Hedwig. "Mass Obedience: Practices and Functions of Elections in the German Democratic Republic." In Jessen and Richter, eds., *Voting for Hitler and Stalin*, 103–25.

Ritter, Gerhard and Klaus Tenfelde. *Arbeiter im Deutschen Kaiserreich 1871 bis 1914* Bonn: Verlag J.H.W. Dietz, 1992.

Rohnstock, Katrin, ed. *(Keine) Platten Geschichten*. Berlin: Rohnstock Biografien, 2004.

Rosenhaft, Eve. *Beating the Fascists? The German Communists and Political Violence, 1929–1933*. New York: Cambridge University Press, 1983.

Rowell, Jay. *Le totalitarisme au concret: Les politiques du logement en RDA*. Paris: Economica, 2006.

Rubin, Eli. "The Form of Socialism without Ornament: Consumption, Ideology, and the Fall and Rise of Modernist Design in the German Democratic Republic." *Journal of Design History* 19, 2 (2006): 155–68.

Rubin, Eli. *Synthetic Socialism: Plastics and Dictatorship in the German Democratic Republic*. Chapel Hill, NC: University of North Carolina Press, 2008.

Rubin, Eli. "The Trabant: Consumption, Eigen-Sinn, and a System of Movement." *History Workshop Journal* 68, 1 (Fall 2009): 27–44.

Rubin, Eli. "Berlin–Marzahn: Socialism and Material Culture in the Plattenbau." *Bulletin of the German Historical Institute* Supplement 7, 2011: East German Material Culture and the Power of Memory, 29–45.

Rubin, Eli. "Concrete Utopia: Everyday Life and Socialism in Berlin-Marzahn." *Bulletin of the German Historical Institute.* Supplement 7, 2011: East German Material Culture and the Power of Memory, 29–45.

Rubin, Eli. "Understanding a Car in the Context of a System: Trabants, Marzahn and East German Socialism." In *The Socialist Car: Automobility in the Eastern Bloc*, ed. Lewis Siegelbaum. Ithaca, NY: Cornell University Press, 2011, 124–42.

Rubin, Eli. "From the Grünen Wiesen to Urban Space: Berlin, Expansion, and the *longue durée*: Introduction," *Central European History* 47 (2014, Special Issue): 221–44.

Rubin, Eli. "Amnesiopolis: From *Mietskaserne* to *Wohnungsbauserie 70* in East Berlin's Northeast," *Central European History* 47 (2014, Special Issue): 334–75.

Sabrow, Martin, ed. *Erinnerungsorte der DDR.* Munich: C.H. Beck, 2009.

Sammartino, Annemarie. *The Impossible Border: Germany and the East, 1914–1922.* Ithaca, NY: Cornell University Press, 2010.

Sebald, W. G. *On the Natural History of Destruction.* Trans. Anthea Bell. New York: Random House, 2003.

Schäche, Wolfgang. *Von Berlin nach Germania: Über die Zerstörungen der "Reichshauptstadt" durch Albert Speers Neugestaltungsplanungen.* Berlin: Transit, 1998.

Scheer, Thorsten, Josef Paul Kleihues, and Paul Kahlfeldt, eds. *City of Architecture of the City: Berlin 1900–2000.* Berlin: Nicolai, 2000.

Schildt, Axel. "Urban Reconstruction and Urban Development in Germany after 1945." In Lenger, ed., *Towards an Urban Nation*, 127–41.

Schmieding, Leonard. "Boom Boxes and Backward Caps: Hip Hop Culture in the GDR." In *Bulletin of the German Historical Institute.* Supplement 7, 2011, 67–86.

Schmieding, Leonard. *"Das ist unsere Party:' HipHop in der DDR.* Stuttgart: Franz Steiner Verlag, 2014.

Schmole, Angela. *Hauptabteilung VIII. Beobachtung, Ermittlung, Durchsuchung, Festnahme. (MfS-Handbuch).* Berlin: BStU, 2011.

Schneider, Rolf. "Passagen: Notate." In Domröse and Gelfot eds., *Peripherie als Ort*, 93–108.

Schnitter, Daniela. *Berlin-Marzahn: Von den Anfängen bis zur Gegenwart.* Berlin: Bezirksamt Marzahn von Berlin, 1994.

Schnitter, Daniela. "Der Bezirk Marzahn—Skizzen zur geschichtliche Entwicklung," hosted by the official Heimatverein (local historical society) of Marzahn: <https://www.yumpu.com/de/document/view/22227078/der-bezirk-marzahn-skizzen-zur-geschichtlichen-entwicklung->.

Schreiter, Katrin. "Displaying Germany's Cold War: The Political Aesthetics of East and West German Interior Design, 1949–1989." PhD dissertation, University of Pennsylvania, 2012.

Scott, James. *Seeing Like a State: How Certain Schemes to Improve the Human Condition Have Failed.* New Haven, Conn: Yale University Press, 1998.

Siegelbaum, Lewis. *Cars for Comrades: The Life of the Soviet Automobile.* Ithaca, NY: Cornell University Press, 2008.

Smith, Mark. *Property of Communists: The Urban Housing Program from Stalin to Khruschev.* DeKalb, Ill: Northern Illinois University Press, 2010.

Soja, Edward. *Seeking Spatial Justice: The Reassertion of Space in Critical Social Theory.* Minneapolis: University of Minnesota Press, 2010.

Soja, Edward. *Postmodern Geographies: the Reassertion of Space in Critical Social Theory.* New York: Verso, 2011.

Sommer, Stefan. *Lekikon des DDR-Alltags: Von "Altstoffsammlung" bis "Zirkel schreibender Arbeiter."* Berlin: Schwarzkopf & Schwarzkopf, 1999.

Stadt und Land Wohnbauten-Gesellschaft mbH, Abt. Öffentlichkeitsarbeit, ed. *Zwischen Krötenteich und Mietergarten: Hellersdorfer Kieze und ihr Leben*. Berlin, 2006.

Starke, Holger, ed. *Geschichte der Stadt Dresden: Band 3: Von der Reichsgründung bis zur Gegenwart*. Stuttgart: Theiss Verlag, 2006.

Steiner, André. *Von Plan zu Plan: Eine Wirtschaftsgeschichte der DDR*. Munich: Deutsche Verlags-Anstalt, 2004.

Steiner, André. *The Plans that Failed: An Economic History of the GDR*. Trans. Ewald Osers. New York: Berghahn, 2010.

Stewart, Charles and Peter Fritzsche, eds. *Imagining the Twentieth Century: Exploring the Odd Passages and Side Doors of Our Collective Memory*. Urbana, Ill: University of Illinois Press, 1997.

Stitziel, Judd. *Fashioning Socialism: Clothing, Politics and Consumer Culture in East Germany*. New York: Berg, 2005.

Stokes, Ray. "In Search of the Socialist Artefact: Technology and Ideology in East Germany, 1945–1962." In: *German History* 15, 2 (1997): 221–39.

Stokes, Ray. *Constructing Socialism: Technology and Change in East Germany, 1945–1990*. Baltimore: The Johns Hopkins University Press, 2000.

Süß, Dietmar. *Tod aus der Luft: Kriegsgesellschaft und Luftkrieg in Deutschland und England*. Munich: Siedler, 2011.

Swett, Pamela. *Neighbors and Enemies: The Culture of Radicalism in Berlin, 1929–1933*. New York: Cambridge University Press, 2004.

Tesch, Joachim. *Der Wohnungsbau in der DDR 1971–1990: Ergebnisse und Defizite eines Programms in kontroversen Sichten*. Berlin: Gesellschaftswissenschaftliches Forum e.V. & "Helle Panke," 2001.

Teuteberg, Hans Jürgen and Clemens Wischermann. *Wohnalltag in Deutschland 1850–1914: Bilder—Daten—Dokumente*. Münster: F. Coppenrath Verlag, 1985.

Thöner, Wolfgang and Peter Müller, eds. *Bauhaus Tradition und DDR Moderne: Der Architekt Richard Paulick*. Munich: Deutscher Kunstverlag, 2006.

Thöner, Wolfgang. "From an 'Alien, Hostile Phenomenon' to the 'Poetry of the Future': On the Bauhaus Reception in East Germany, 1945–1970." *Bulletin of the German Historical Institute*, Bulletin Supplement 2 (2005): 115–38.

Till, Karen. *The New Berlin: Memory, Politics, Place*. Minneapolis: University of Minnesota Press, 2005.

Topfstedt, Thomas. "Vom Baukünstler zum Komplexprojektanten: Architekten in der DDR." In Barth and Topfstedt, eds., *Vom Baukünstler zum Komplexprojektanten*, 7–23.

Tscheschner, Dorothea. "Sixteen Principles of Urban Design and the Athens Charter." In Scheer, Kleihues, and Kahlfeldt, eds., *City of Architecture, Architecture of the City*, 259–70.

Tuan, Yi-Fu. *Space and Place: The Perspective of Experience*. Minneapolis: University of Minnesota Press, 1977.

Urban, Florian. *Neohistorical East Berlin: Architecture and Urban Design in the German Democratic Republic, 1970–1990*. Burlington, VT: Ashgate, 2009.

Urban, Florian. *Tower and Slab: Histories of Global Mass Housing*. New York: Routledge, 2012.

Veenis, Milena. "Consumption in East Germany: The Seduction and Betrayal of Things." *Journal of Material Culture* 4, 1 (1999): 79–112.

Veenis, Milena. *Material Fantasies: Expectations of the Western Consumer World Among East Germans*. Amsterdam: Amsterdam University Press, 2012.

Venkatesh, Sudhir. *American Project: The Rise and Fall of a Modern Ghetto*. Cambridge, MA: Harvard University Press, 2002.

Venkatesh, Sudhir. *Gang Leader for a Day: A Rogue Sociologist Takes to the Streets*. New York: Penguin, 2008.

Verein Kids & Co, ed. *Marzahn-Südspitze: Leben im ersten Wohngebiet der Berliner Großsiedlung*. Berlin: Bezirksamt Marzahn–Hellersdorf Abt. Ökologische Stadtentwicklung, 2002.

Vieth, Harald. *Bemerkenswerte Bäume in Berlin und Potsdam*. Hamburg: Selbstverlag Harald Vieth, 2005.

von Braun, Christina, et al. *Heimat Moderne*. Berlin: Jovis, 2006.

von Saldern, Adelheid. "The Workers' Movement and Patters on Urban Housing Estates and in Rural Settlements in Germany and Austria During the 1920s." *Social History* 15, 3 (1990): 333–54.

von Saldern, Adelheid. *Häuserleben: zur Geschichte städtischen Arbeiter Kaiserreich bis heute*. Bonn: Dietz, 1995.

von Saldern, Adelheid. *Inszenierte Einigkeit: Herrschaftsrepräsentationen in DDR-Städten*. Stuttgart: Franz Steiner, 2003.

Wagner-Kyora, Georg. "Spione der Arbeit—Zur Methodik der Alltagsgeschichte im IM Berichten aus Industriebetrieben." In Gieseke, ed., *Staatssicherheit und Gesellschaft*, 209–52.

Ward, Janet. *Post-Wall Berlin: Borders, Space and Identity*. New York: Palgrave Macmillan, 2010.

Weinreb, Alice. "Matters of Taste: The Politics of Food and Hunger in Divided Germany." PhD. dissertation, University of Michigan, 2009.

Weitz, Eric. *Creating German Communism, 1890–1990: From Popular Protests to Socialist State*. Princeton, NJ: Princeton University Press, 1996.

Weitz, Eric. *Creating German Communism, 1890–1990*. Princeton, NJ: Princeton University Press, 1997.

Wietog, Jutta. "Wohnungsstandard der Unterschichten in Berlin." In Werner Conze and Ulrich Engelhardt, eds., *Arbeiterexistenz im 19. Jahrhundert: Lebensstandard und Lebensgestaltung deutscher Arbeiter und Handwerker*. Stuttgart: Klett-Cota, 1981, 114–37.

Wilczek, Bernd, ed. *Berlin—Hauptstadt der DDR, 1949–1989. Utopie und Realität*. Baden-Baden: Elster Verlag, 1995.

Wengst, Udo, and Hermann Wentker, eds. *Das doppelte Deutschland: 40 Jahre Systemkonkurrenz*. Berlin: Ch. Links, 2008.

Wierling, Dorothee. *Geboren im Jahr Eins: der Jahrgang 1949 in der DDR—Versuch einer Kollektivbiographie*. Berlin: Ch. Links, 2002.

Wiesner, Albrecht. "Gestalten oder Verwalten? Überlegungen zum Herrschaftsanspruch und Selbstverständnis sozialistischer Kommunalpoitik im Letzten Jahrzehnt der DDR." In Bernhardt and Reif, eds., *Sozialistische Städte*, 69–94.

Wiesner, Albrecht. "Steinerne Verheißungen einer sozialistischen Zukunft? Der Bau Halle-Neustadts aus gesellschaftsgeschichtlicher Perspektive." In Bernhardt and Wolfes, eds., *Schönheit und Typenprojektierung*, 229–58.

Wilke, Manfred. *Der SED-Staat: Geschichte und Nachwirkungen*. (Gesammelte Schriften zu seinem 65. Geburtstag zusammengestellt und herausgegeben von Hans-Joachim Veen). Cologne, Weimar, Vienna: Böhlau, 2006.

Wischermann. *Wohnen in Hamburg vor dem Ersten Weltkrieg*. Münster: F. Coppenrath Verlag, 1983.

Wittkowski, Gregory. "The German Democratic Republic: State Power and Everyday Life." *History Compass* 5, 3 (2007): 935–42.

Wohnungsbaugenossenschaft "Hellersdorfer Kiez," ed. *Wohnungsbaugenossenschaft "Hellersdorfer Kiez:" Festschrift zur 50-Jahrfeier*. Berlin: MAZZ Verlag, 2004.

Wolle, Stefan and Hans-Hermann Hertle. *Damals in der DDR: Der Alltag im Arbeiter- und Bauernstaat*. Munich: C. Bertelsmann, 2004.

Zacharie, Larrie Benton, ed. *Arbeiterwohnungsbaugenossenschaft*. Saarbrücken: Verpublishing, 2012.

Zarecor, Kimberly Elman. *Manufacturing a Socialist Modernity: Housing in Czechoslovakia, 1945–1960*. Pittsburgh: University of Pittsburgh Press, 2011.

Zatlin, Jonathan. *The Currency of Socialism*. New York: Cambridge University Press, 2008.

Zech, Hermann. *Marzahner Straßennamen—Ortsteil Marzahn*. Berlin: Heimatsmuseum Marzahn, 1994.

Zohlen, Gerwin. "Die Beatmete: Gedanken zur Tradition der Großsiedlungen." In Domröse and Gelfot eds., *Peripherie als Ort*, 137–55.

Index

Printed in the USA/Agawam, MA
August 9, 2022

796867.001